SECRET
AVENGERS

LET'S HAVE A PROBLEM

SECRET AVENGERS

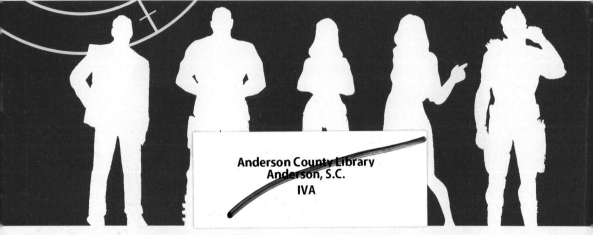

WRITER:
ALES KOT

ARTIST:
MICHAEL WALSH

COLORIST:
MATTHEW WILSON

LETTERER:
VC'S CLAYTON COWLES

COVER ART:
TRADD MOORE & **MATTHEW WILSON**

ASSISTANT EDITOR:
JON MOISAN

EDITOR:
WIL MOSS

EXECUTIVE EDITOR:
TOM BREVOORT

COLLECTION EDITOR: **JENNIFER GRÜNWALD**   ASSISTANT EDITOR: **SARAH BRUNSTAD**
ASSOCIATE MANAGING EDITOR: **ALEX STARBUCK**   EDITOR, SPECIAL PROJECTS: **MARK D. BEAZLEY**
SENIOR EDITOR, SPECIAL PROJECTS: **JEFF YOUNGQUIST**   SVP PRINT, SALES & MARKETING: **DAVID GABRIEL**
BOOK DESIGNER: **RODOLFO MURAGUCHI**

EDITOR IN CHIEF: **AXEL ALONSO**   CHIEF CREATIVE OFFICER: **JOE QUESADA**
PUBLISHER: **DAN BUCKLEY**   EXECUTIVE PRODUCER: **ALAN FINE**

RUN THE MISSION. DON'T GET SEEN. SAVE THE WORLD.

The Avengers and S.H.I.E.L.D. have recently formed an alliance, working together to tackle the world's many problems. But there are some problems too murky in which to publicly involve the Avengers.

To deal with such problems, S.H.I.E.L.D. Director Maria Hill has assembled a black-ops squad known as the **Secret Avengers** — Black Widow, Spider-Woman, and S.H.I.E.L.D. agents Nick Fury and Phil Coulson.

And then there's Hawkeye. Hill didn't ask Hawkeye to join her new team because she already knows he's problems. Hill doesn't want problems. She has enough of those.

Case in point: Hill recently hired M.O.D.O.K., an ex-terrorist and science savant turned S.H.I.E.L.D. informant and developer. None of the Avengers, Secret or otherwise, are aware of this.

The following is what happened a few days before the new team was supposed to meet up for the first time.

SECRET AVENGERS VOL. 1: LET'S HAVE A PROBLEM. Contains material originally published in magazine form as SECRET AVENGERS #1-5 and ORIGINAL SIN: SECRET AVENGERS INFINITE COMIC #1-2. First printing 2014. ISBN# 978-0-7851-9052-3. Published by MARVEL WORLDWIDE, INC., a subsidiary of MARVEL ENTERTAINMENT, LLC. OFFICE OF PUBLICATION: 135 West 50th Street, New York, NY 10020. Copyright © 2014 Marvel Characters, Inc. All rights reserved. All characters featured in this issue and the distinctive names and likenesses thereof, and all related indicia are trademarks of Marvel Characters, Inc. No similarity between any of the names, characters, persons, and/or institutions in this magazine with those of any living or dead person or institution is intended, and any such similarity which may exist is purely coincidental. **Printed in the U.S.A.** ALAN FINE, EVP - Office of the President, Marvel Worldwide, Inc. and EVP & CMO Marvel Characters B.V.; DAN BUCKLEY, Publisher & President - Print, Animation & Digital Divisions; JOE QUESADA, Chief Creative Officer; TOM BREVOORT, SVP of Publishing; DAVID BOGART, SVP of Operations & Procurement, Publishing; C.B. CEBULSKI, SVP of Creator & Content Development; DAVID GABRIEL, SVP Print, Sales & Marketing; JIM O'KEEFE, VP of Operations & Logistics; DAN CARR, Executive Director of Publishing Technology; SUSAN CRESPI, Editorial Operations Manager; ALEX MORALES, Publishing Operations Manager; STAN LEE, Chairman Emeritus. For information regarding advertising in Marvel Comics or on Marvel.com, please contact Niza Disla, Director of Marvel Partnerships, at ndisla@marvel.com. For Marvel subscription inquiries, please call 800-217-9158. **Manufactured between 8/29/2014 and 10/6/2014 by R.R. DONNELLEY, INC., SALEM, VA, USA.**

10 9 8 7 6 5 4 3 2 1

1

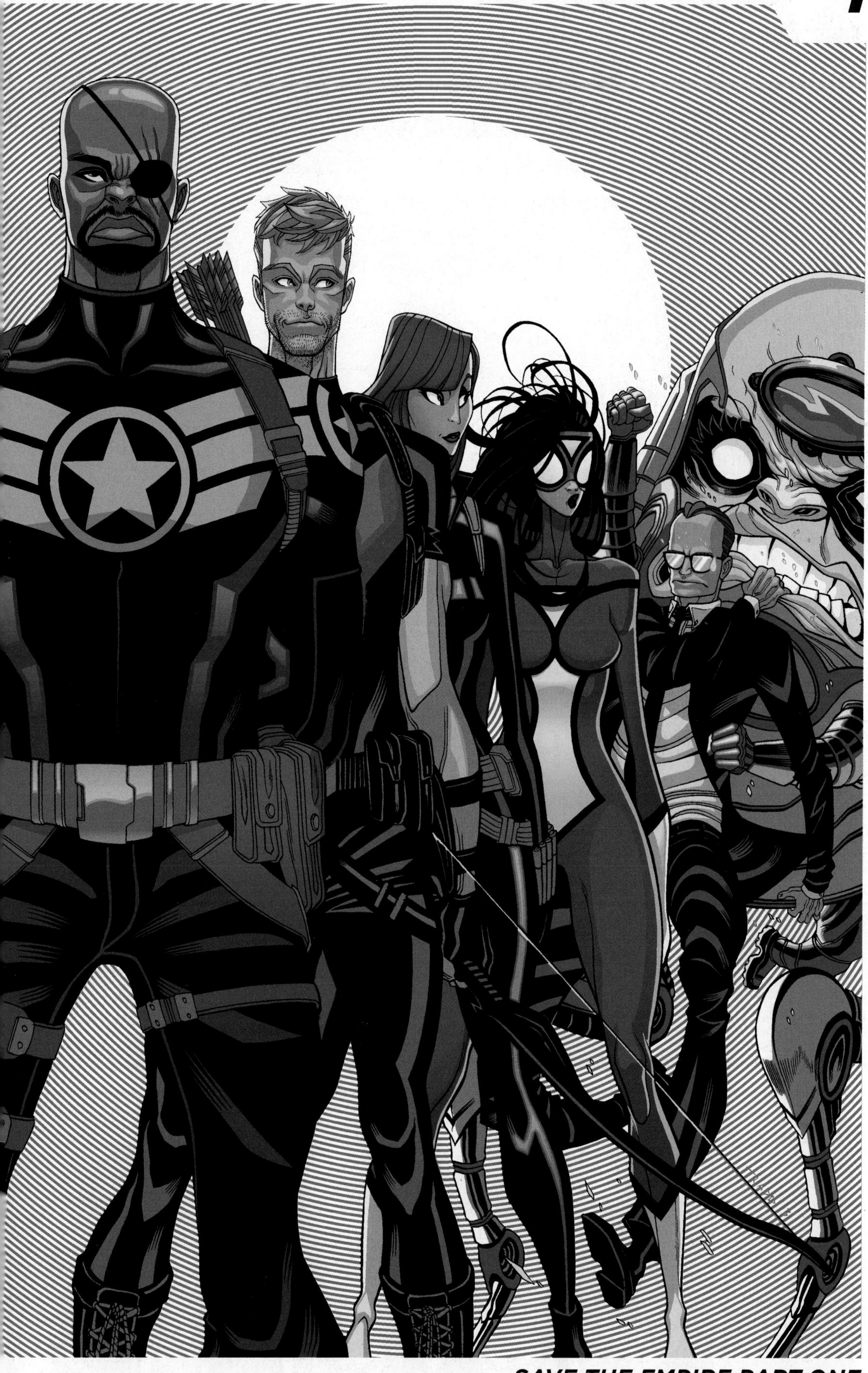

SAVE THE EMPIRE PART ONE

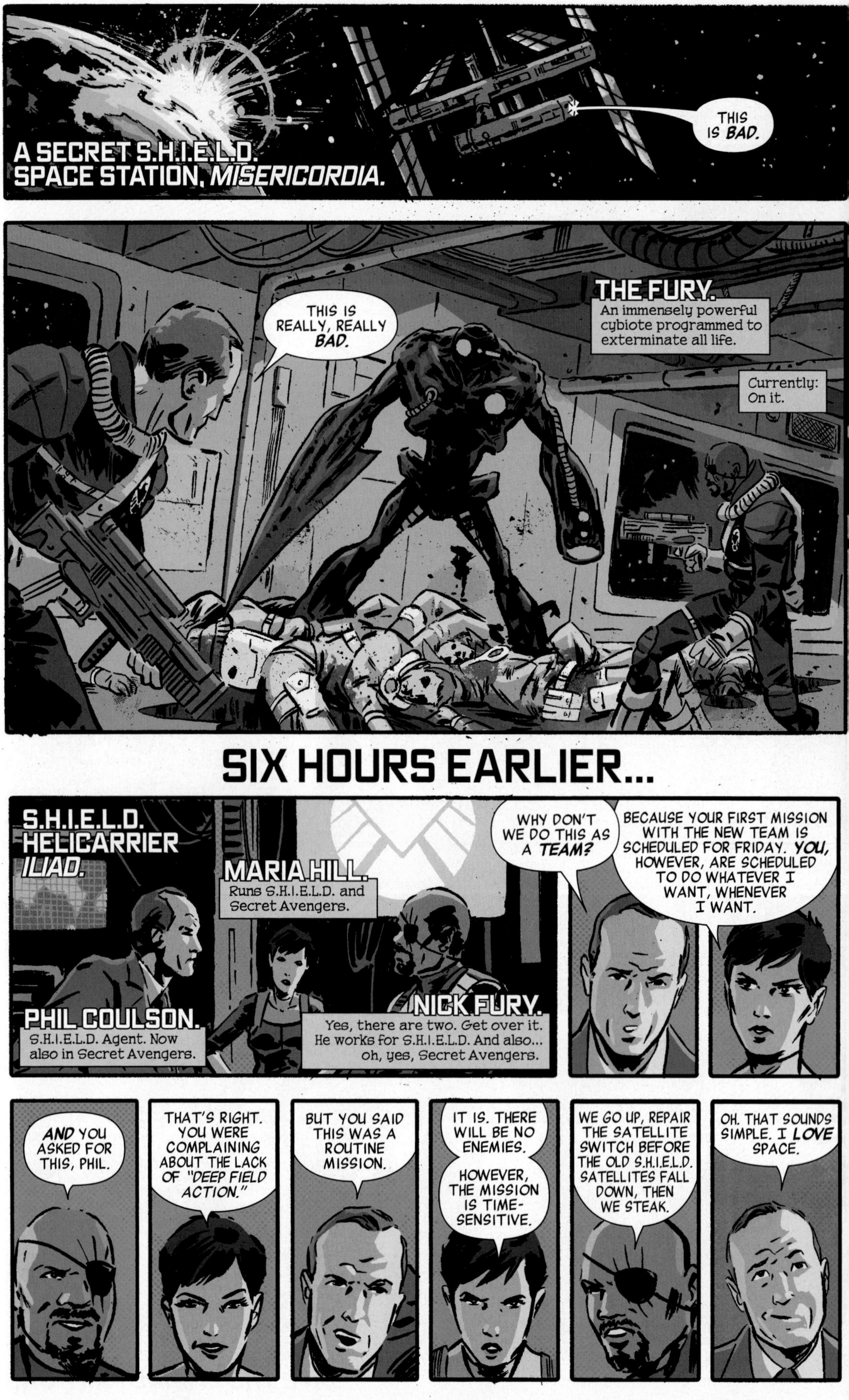

A SECRET S.H.I.E.L.D. SPACE STATION, MISERICORDIA.
THIS IS BAD.
THIS IS REALLY, REALLY BAD.
THE FURY.
An immensely powerful cybiote programmed to exterminate all life.
Currently: On it.
SIX HOURS EARLIER...
S.H.I.E.L.D. HELICARRIER ILIAD.
MARIA HILL.
Runs S.H.I.E.L.D. and Secret Avengers.
PHIL COULSON.
S.H.I.E.L.D. Agent. Now also in Secret Avengers.
NICK FURY.
Yes, there are two. Get over it. He works for S.H.I.E.L.D. And also... oh, yes, Secret Avengers.
WHY DON'T WE DO THIS AS A TEAM?
BECAUSE YOUR FIRST MISSION WITH THE NEW TEAM IS SCHEDULED FOR FRIDAY. YOU, HOWEVER, ARE SCHEDULED TO DO WHATEVER I WANT, WHENEVER I WANT.
AND YOU ASKED FOR THIS, PHIL.
THAT'S RIGHT. YOU WERE COMPLAINING ABOUT THE LACK OF "DEEP FIELD ACTION."
BUT YOU SAID THIS WAS A ROUTINE MISSION.
IT IS. THERE WILL BE NO ENEMIES.
HOWEVER, THE MISSION IS TIME-SENSITIVE.
WE GO UP, REPAIR THE SATELLITE SWITCH BEFORE THE OLD S.H.I.E.L.D. SATELLITES FALL DOWN, THEN WE STEAK.
OH. THAT SOUNDS SIMPLE. I LOVE SPACE.

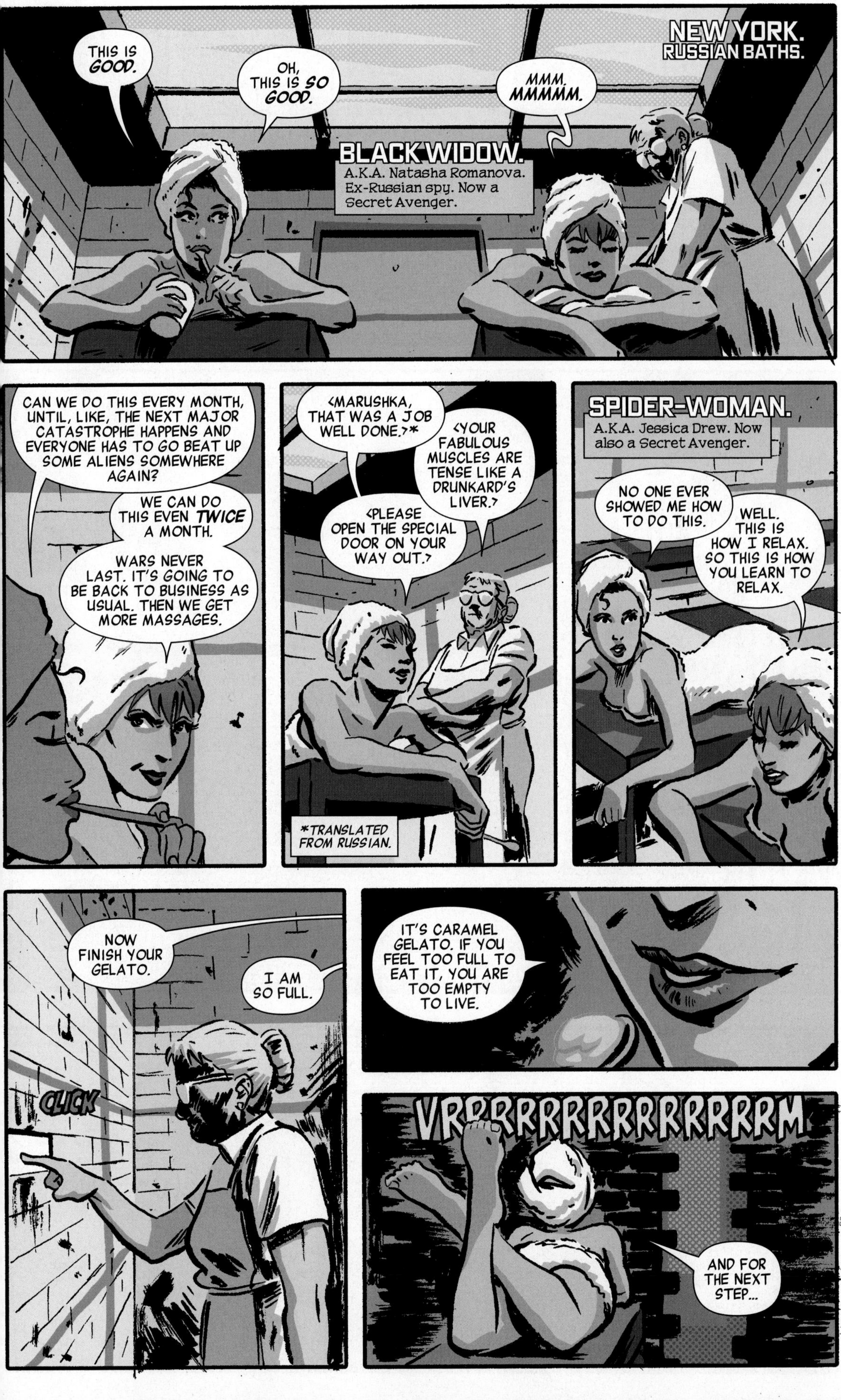
NEW YORK. RUSSIAN BATHS.
THIS IS GOOD.
OH, THIS IS SO GOOD.
MMM. MMMMM.
BLACK WIDOW.
A.K.A. Natasha Romanova. Ex-Russian spy. Now a Secret Avenger.
CAN WE DO THIS EVERY MONTH, UNTIL, LIKE, THE NEXT MAJOR CATASTROPHE HAPPENS AND EVERYONE HAS TO GO BEAT UP SOME ALIENS SOMEWHERE AGAIN?
WE CAN DO THIS EVEN TWICE A MONTH.
WARS NEVER LAST. IT'S GOING TO BE BACK TO BUSINESS AS USUAL. THEN WE GET MORE MASSAGES.
<MARUSHKA, THAT WAS A JOB WELL DONE.>*
<YOUR FABULOUS MUSCLES ARE TENSE LIKE A DRUNKARD'S LIVER.>
<PLEASE OPEN THE SPECIAL DOOR ON YOUR WAY OUT.>
*TRANSLATED FROM RUSSIAN.
SPIDER-WOMAN.
A.K.A. Jessica Drew. Now also a Secret Avenger.
NO ONE EVER SHOWED ME HOW TO DO THIS.
WELL. THIS IS HOW I RELAX. SO THIS IS HOW YOU LEARN TO RELAX.
NOW FINISH YOUR GELATO.
I AM SO FULL.
CLICK
IT'S CARAMEL GELATO. IF YOU FEEL TOO FULL TO EAT IT, YOU ARE TOO EMPTY TO LIVE.
VRRRRRRRRRRRRRRRM
AND FOR THE NEXT STEP...

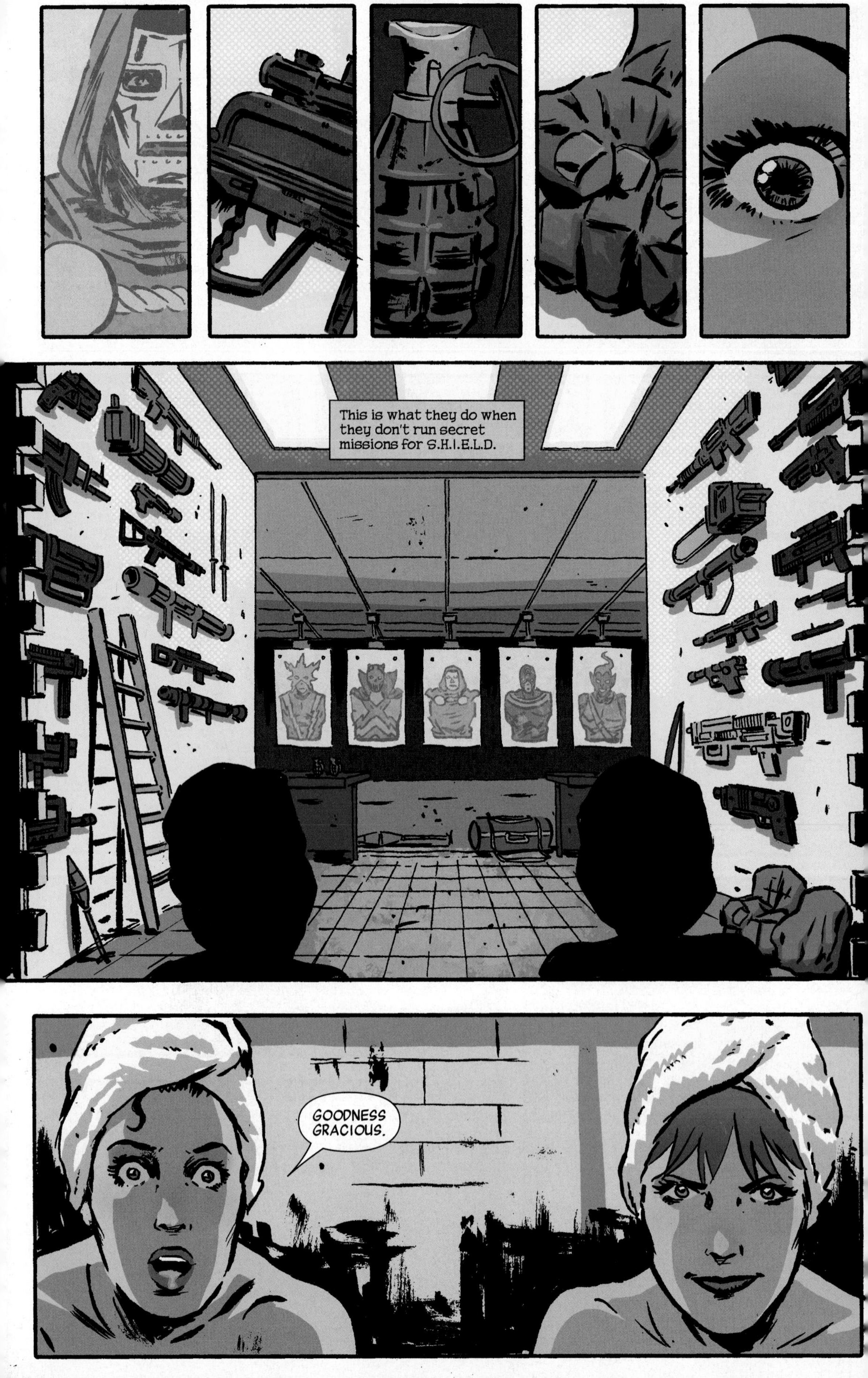
This is what they do when they don't run secret missions for S.H.I.E.L.D.
GOODNESS GRACIOUS.

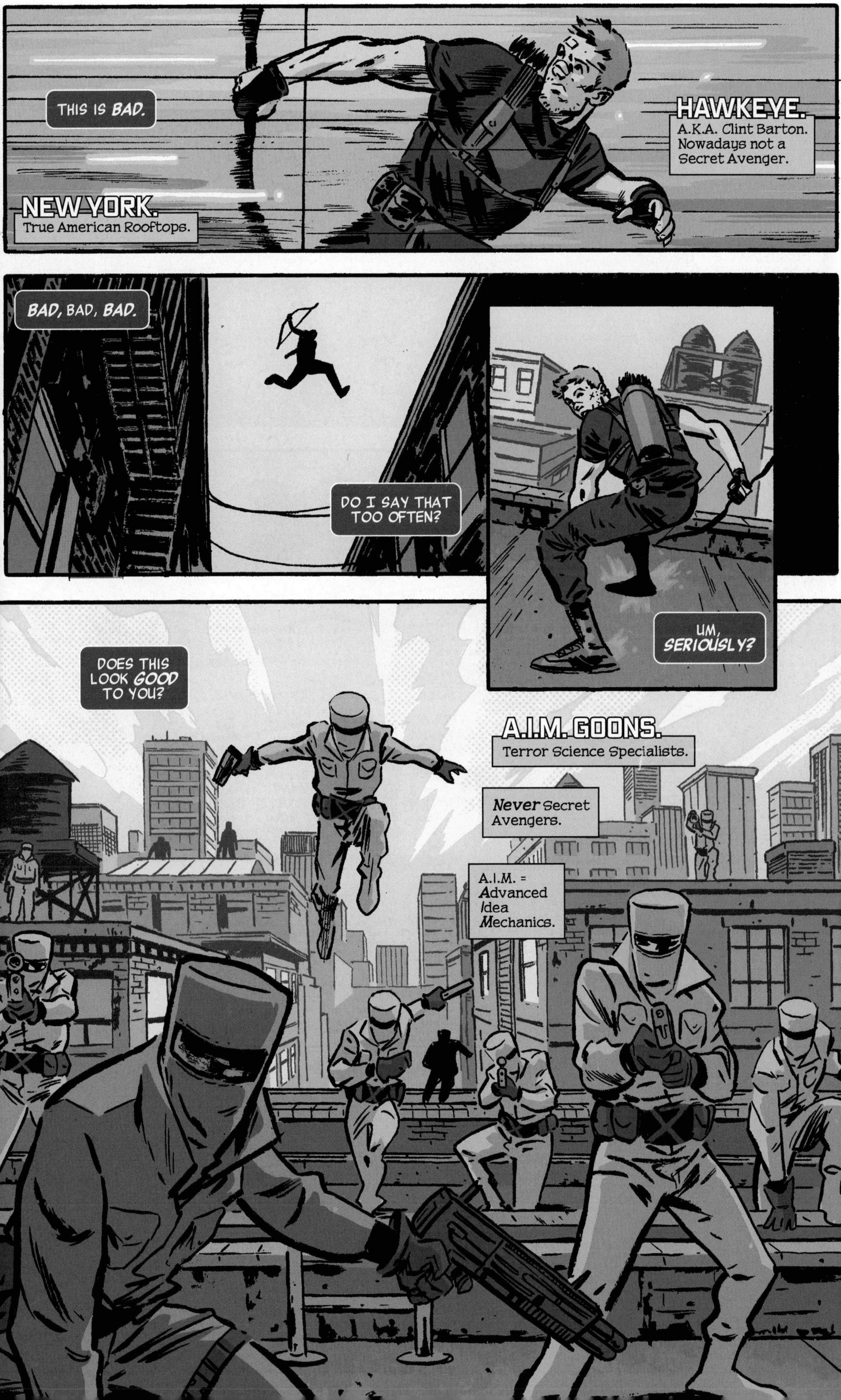
THIS IS BAD.
HAWKEYE.
A.K.A. Clint Barton. Nowadays not a Secret Avenger.
NEW YORK.
True American Rooftops.
BAD, BAD, BAD.
DO I SAY THAT TOO OFTEN?
UM, SERIOUSLY?
DOES THIS LOOK GOOD TO YOU?
A.I.M. GOONS.
Terror Science Specialists.
Never Secret Avengers.
A.I.M. = Advanced Idea Mechanics.

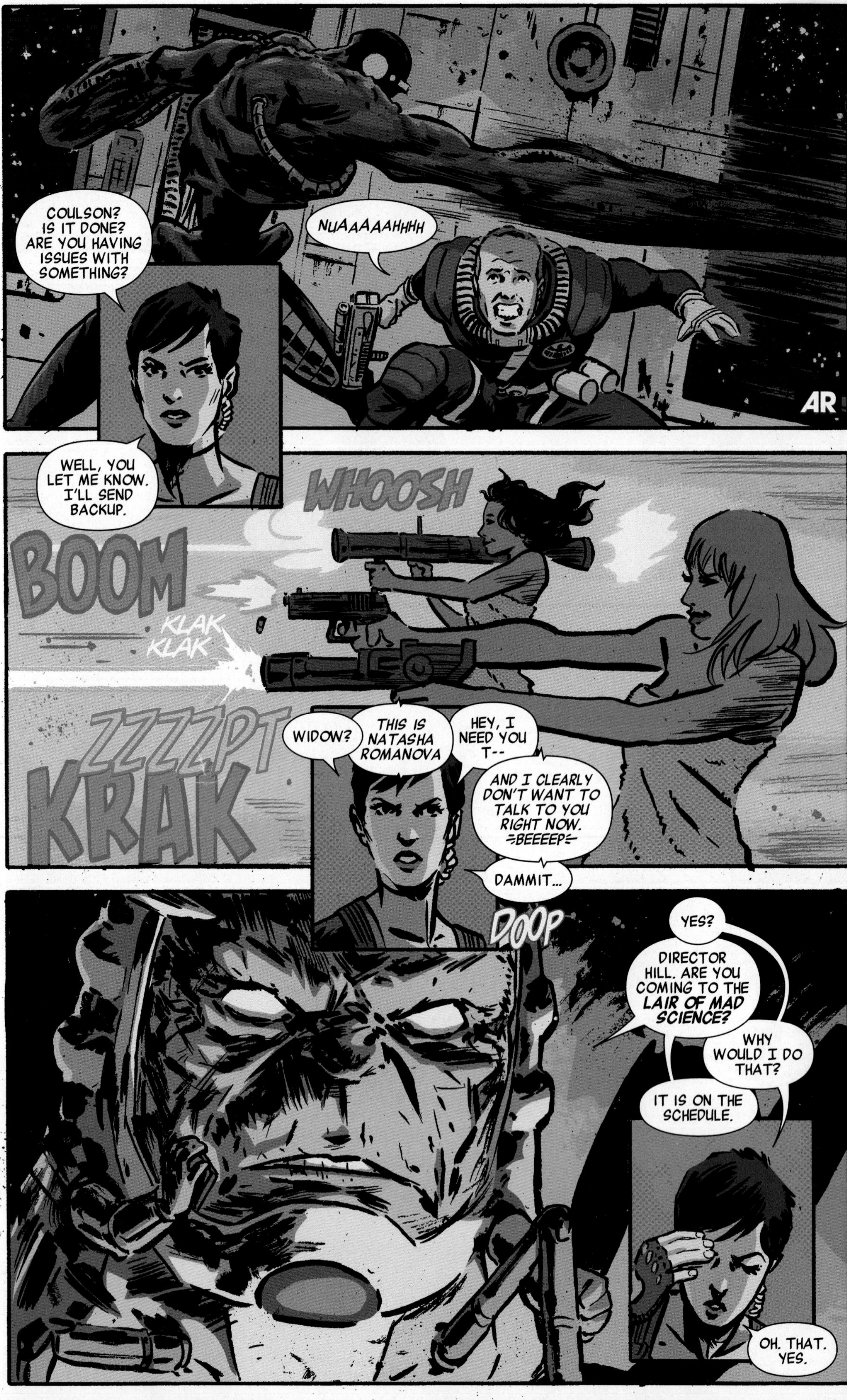
COULSON? IS IT DONE? ARE YOU HAVING ISSUES WITH SOMETHING?
NUAAAAAHHHH
AR
WELL, YOU LET ME KNOW. I'LL SEND BACKUP.
WHOOSH
BOOM
KLAK KLAK
ZZZZPT
KRAK
WIDOW?
THIS IS NATASHA ROMANOVA
HEY, I NEED YOU T--
AND I CLEARLY DON'T WANT TO TALK TO YOU RIGHT NOW. BEEEEP
DAMMIT...
DOOP
YES?
DIRECTOR HILL. ARE YOU COMING TO THE LAIR OF MAD SCIENCE?
WHY WOULD I DO THAT?
IT IS ON THE SCHEDULE.
OH. THAT. YES.

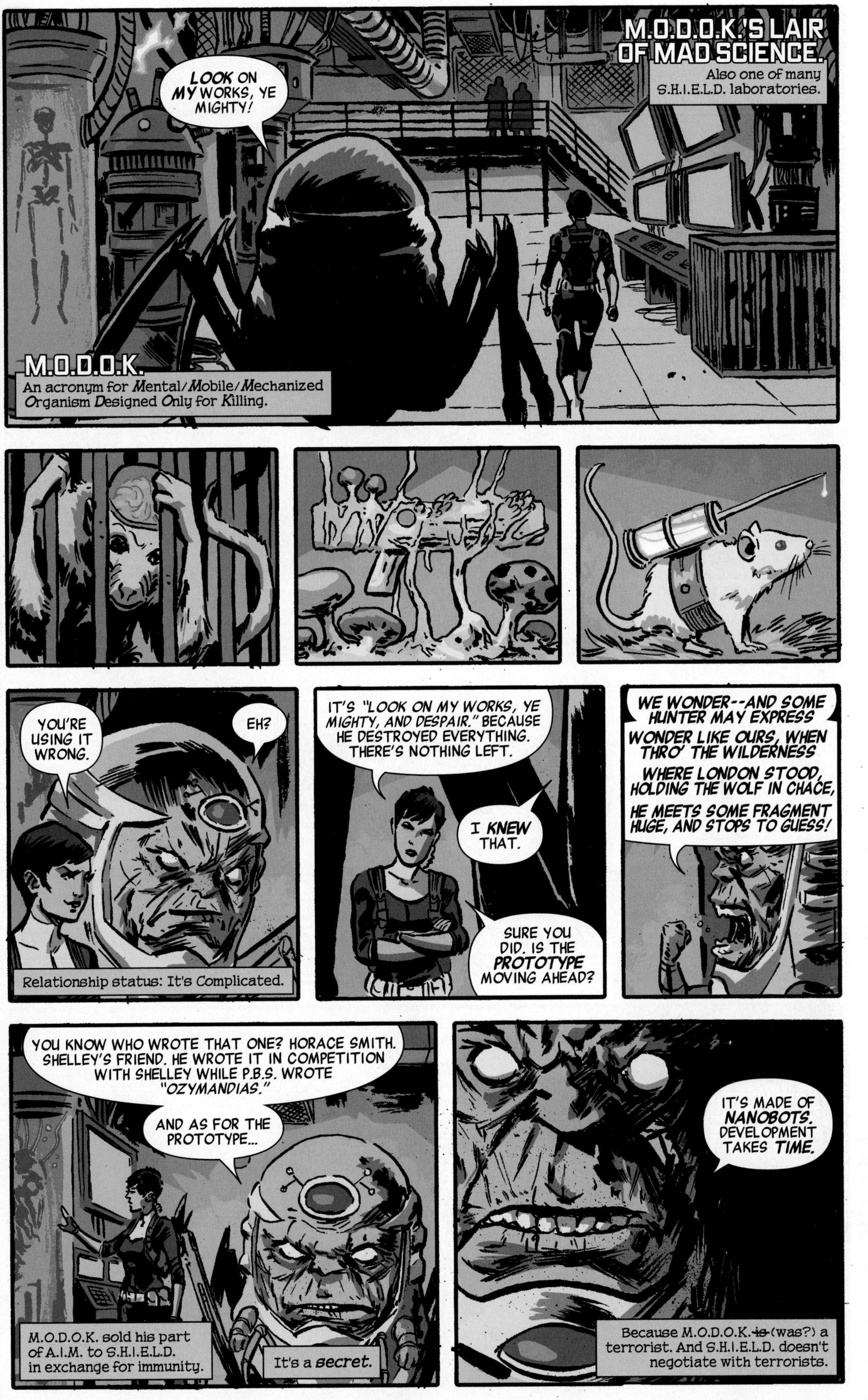
M.O.D.O.K.'S LAIR OF MAD SCIENCE.
Also one of many S.H.I.E.L.D. laboratories.
LOOK ON MY WORKS, YE MIGHTY!
M.O.D.O.K.
An acronym for Mental/Mobile/Mechanized Organism Designed Only for Killing.
YOU'RE USING IT WRONG.
EH?
Relationship status: It's Complicated.
IT'S "LOOK ON MY WORKS, YE MIGHTY, AND DESPAIR." BECAUSE HE DESTROYED EVERYTHING. THERE'S NOTHING LEFT.
I KNEW THAT.
SURE YOU DID. IS THE PROTOTYPE MOVING AHEAD?
WE WONDER--AND SOME HUNTER MAY EXPRESS
WONDER LIKE OURS, WHEN THRO' THE WILDERNESS
WHERE LONDON STOOD, HOLDING THE WOLF IN CHACE,
HE MEETS SOME FRAGMENT HUGE, AND STOPS TO GUESS!
YOU KNOW WHO WROTE THAT ONE? HORACE SMITH. SHELLEY'S FRIEND. HE WROTE IT IN COMPETITION WITH SHELLEY WHILE P.B.S. WROTE "OZYMANDIAS."
AND AS FOR THE PROTOTYPE...
M.O.D.O.K. sold his part of A.I.M. to S.H.I.E.L.D. in exchange for immunity.
It's a secret.
IT'S MADE OF NANOBOTS. DEVELOPMENT TAKES TIME.
Because M.O.D.O.K. ~~is~~ (was?) a terrorist. And S.H.I.E.L.D. doesn't negotiate with terrorists.

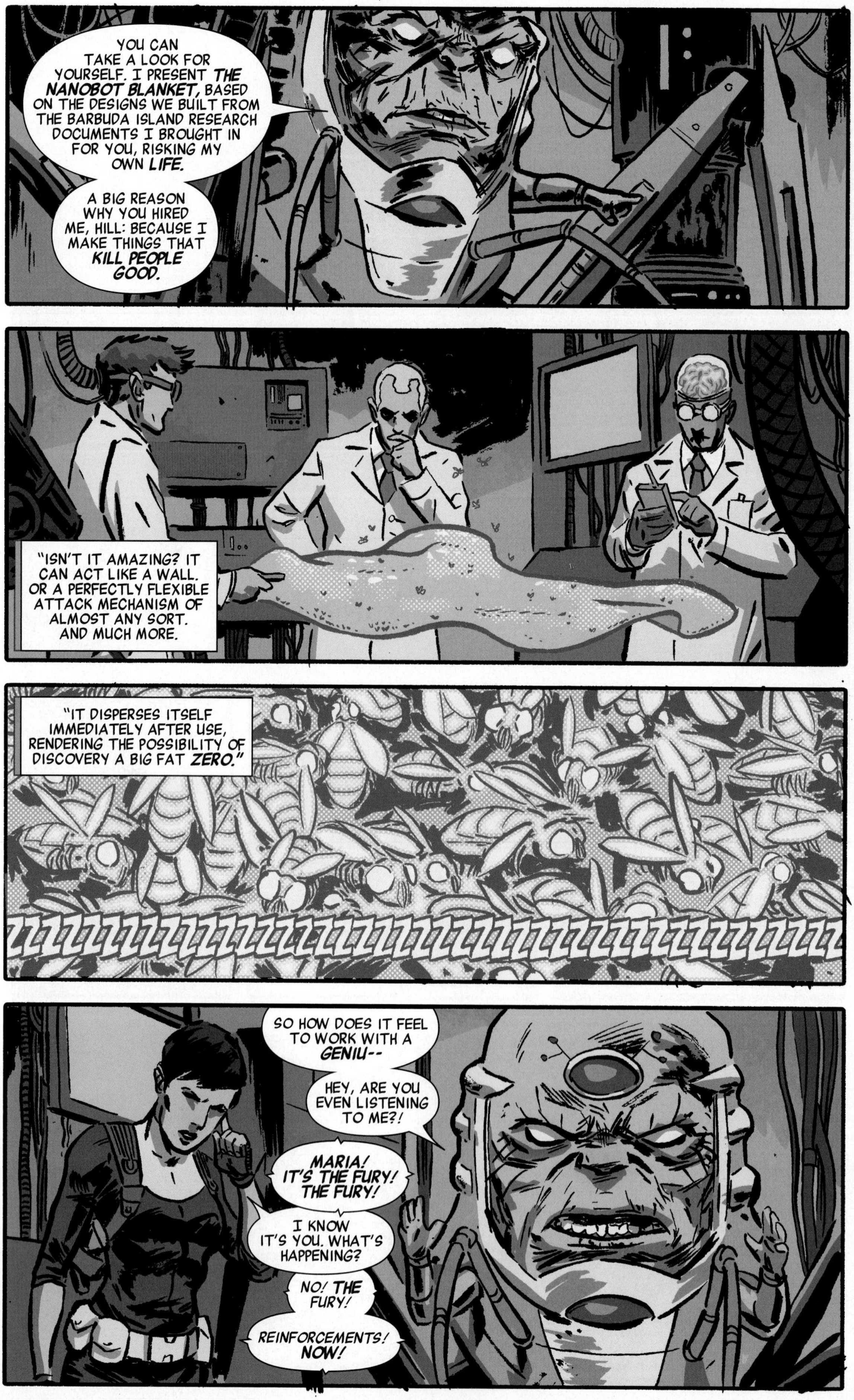
YOU CAN TAKE A LOOK FOR YOURSELF. I PRESENT THE NANOBOT BLANKET, BASED ON THE DESIGNS WE BUILT FROM THE BARBUDA ISLAND RESEARCH DOCUMENTS I BROUGHT IN FOR YOU, RISKING MY OWN LIFE.
A BIG REASON WHY YOU HIRED ME, HILL: BECAUSE I MAKE THINGS THAT KILL PEOPLE GOOD.
"ISN'T IT AMAZING? IT CAN ACT LIKE A WALL. OR A PERFECTLY FLEXIBLE ATTACK MECHANISM OF ALMOST ANY SORT. AND MUCH MORE.
"IT DISPERSES ITSELF IMMEDIATELY AFTER USE, RENDERING THE POSSIBILITY OF DISCOVERY A BIG FAT ZERO."
ZZZZZZZZZZZZZZZZZZZZZZZZZZZZZZZZZZZZZZZZZZZZZZZZZZZ
SO HOW DOES IT FEEL TO WORK WITH A GENIU--
HEY, ARE YOU EVEN LISTENING TO ME?!
MARIA! IT'S THE FURY! THE FURY!
I KNOW IT'S YOU. WHAT'S HAPPENING?
NO! THE FURY!
REINFORCEMENTS! NOW!

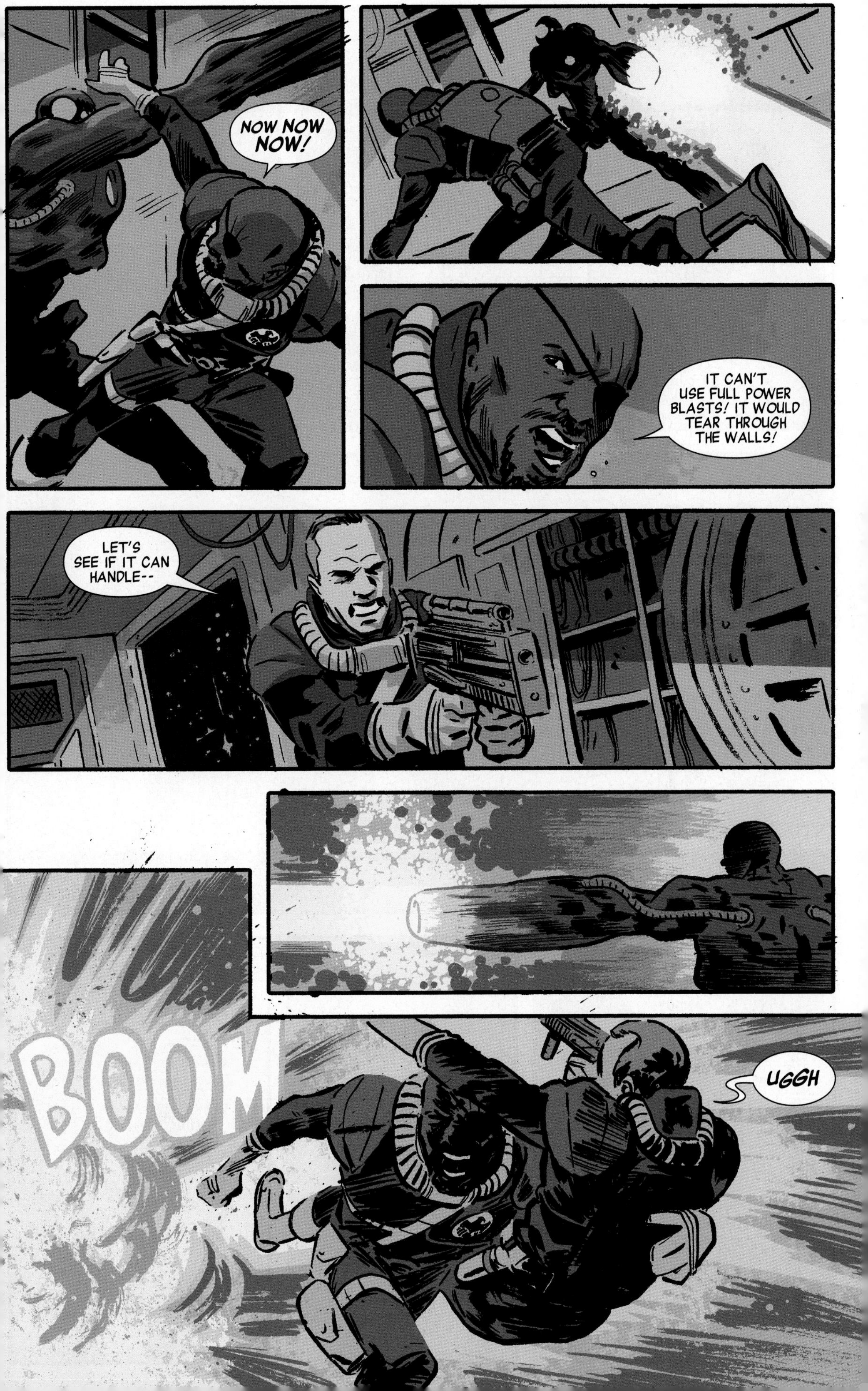
NOW NOW NOW!
IT CAN'T USE FULL POWER BLASTS! IT WOULD TEAR THROUGH THE WALLS!
LET'S SEE IF IT CAN HANDLE--
BOOM
UGGH

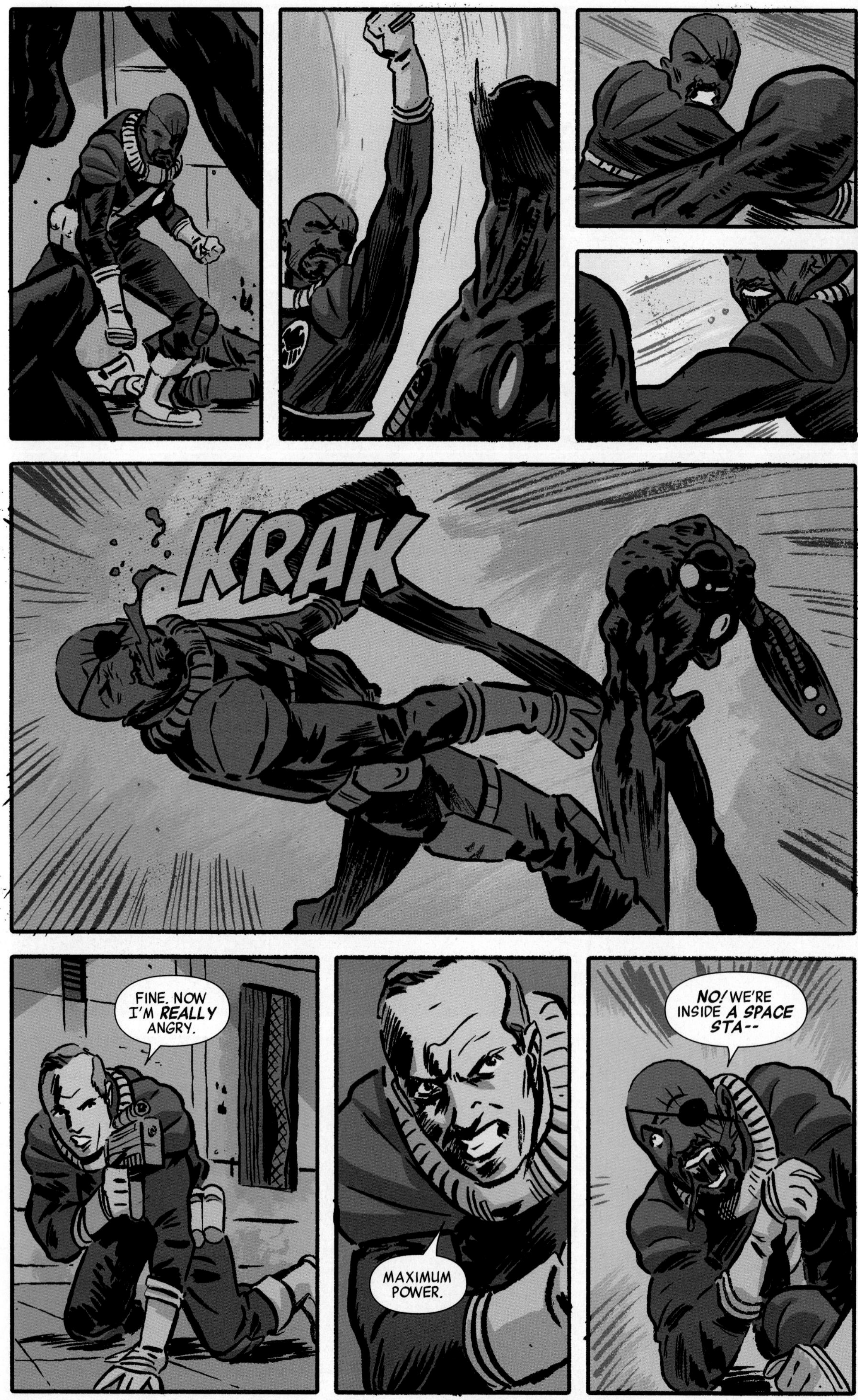
KRAK
FINE. NOW I'M REALLY ANGRY.
MAXIMUM POWER.
NO! WE'RE INSIDE A SPACE STA--

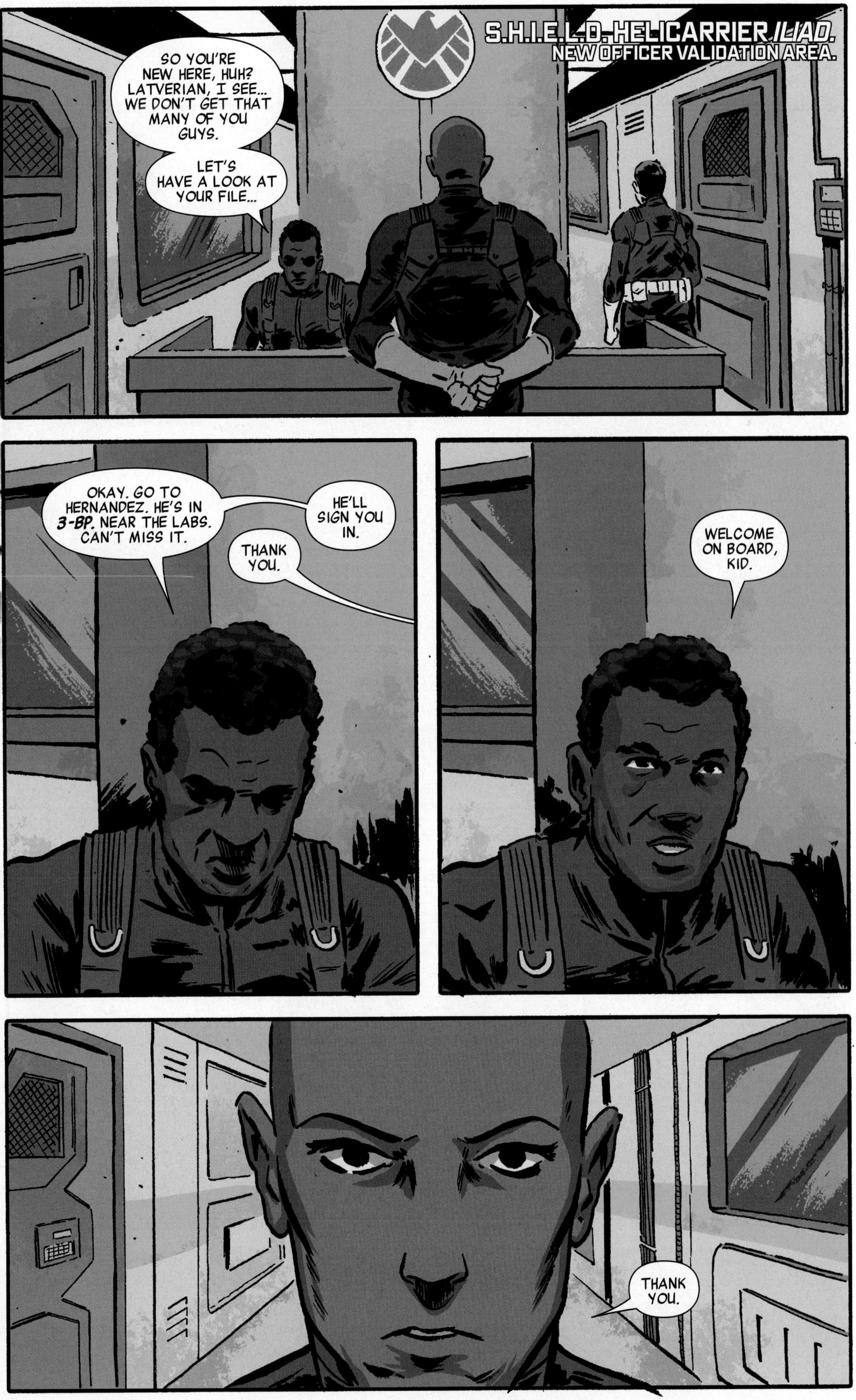
S.H.I.E.L.D. HELICARRIER ILIAD.
NEW OFFICER VALIDATION AREA.
SO YOU'RE NEW HERE, HUH? LATVERIAN, I SEE... WE DON'T GET THAT MANY OF YOU GUYS.
LET'S HAVE A LOOK AT YOUR FILE...
OKAY. GO TO HERNANDEZ. HE'S IN 3-BP. NEAR THE LABS. CAN'T MISS IT.
HE'LL SIGN YOU IN.
THANK YOU.
WELCOME ON BOARD, KID.
THANK YOU.

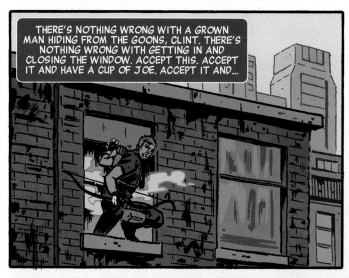

THERE'S NOTHING WRONG WITH A GROWN MAN HIDING FROM THE GOONS, CLINT. THERE'S NOTHING WRONG WITH GETTING IN AND CLOSING THE WINDOW. ACCEPT THIS. ACCEPT IT AND HAVE A CUP OF JOE. ACCEPT IT AND...

...OH.

OH.

I WON'T SAY THIS LOOKS BAD, BECAUSE I AM NOT JUDGING YOU BASED ON YOUR APPEARANCES, GUYS.

THIS IS JUST... AWKWARD.

MY NAME IS CLINT. I REALLY DON'T WANT TO FIGHT.

CAN I BORROW A LOCKER?

TWO MINUTES LATER.

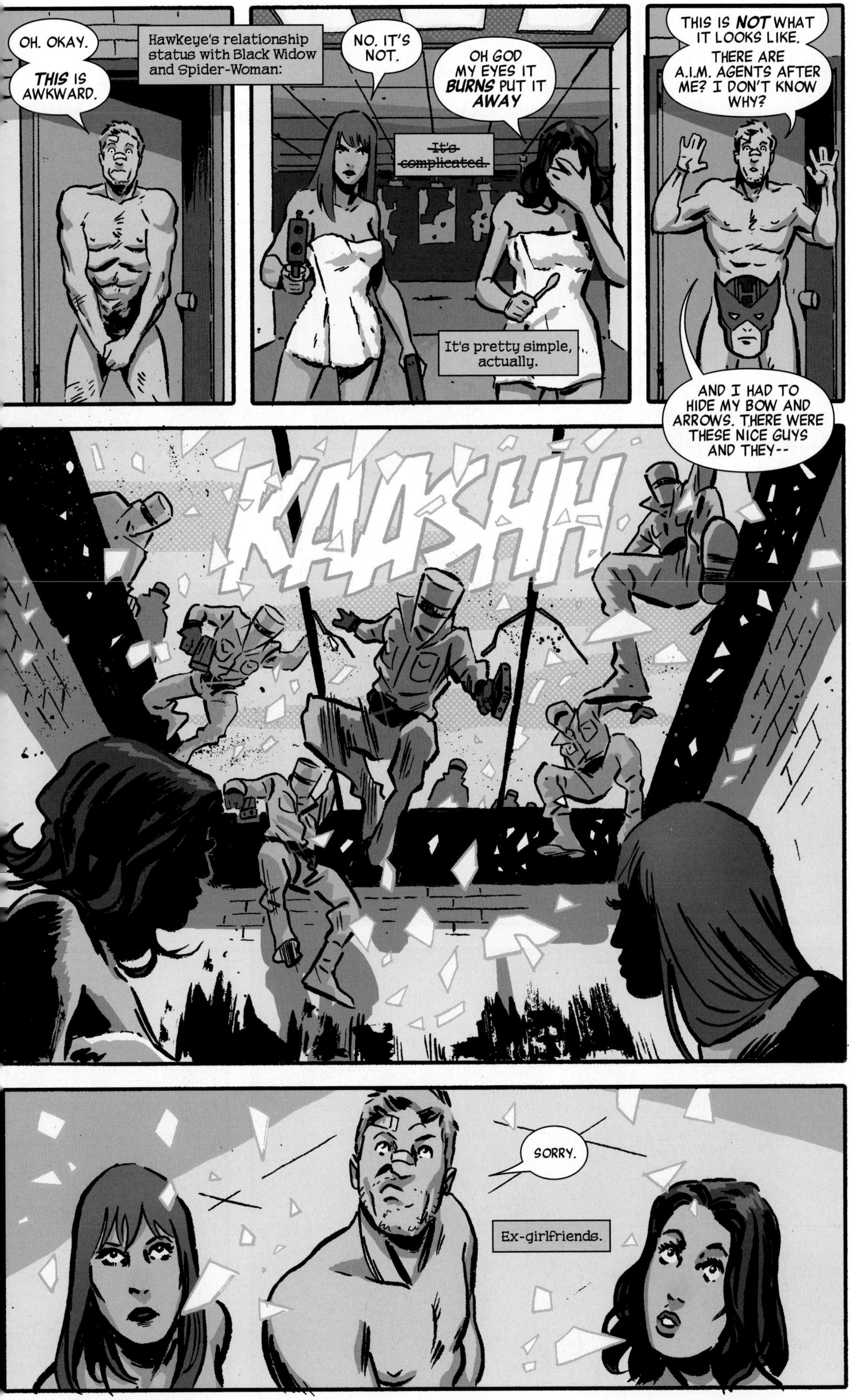

OH. OKAY.
THIS IS AWKWARD.
Hawkeye's relationship status with Black Widow and Spider-Woman:
NO. IT'S NOT.
OH GOD MY EYES IT BURNS PUT IT AWAY
~~It's complicated.~~
It's pretty simple, actually.
THIS IS NOT WHAT IT LOOKS LIKE.
THERE ARE A.I.M. AGENTS AFTER ME? I DON'T KNOW WHY?
AND I HAD TO HIDE MY BOW AND ARROWS. THERE WERE THESE NICE GUYS AND THEY--
KAASHH
SORRY.
Ex-girlfriends.

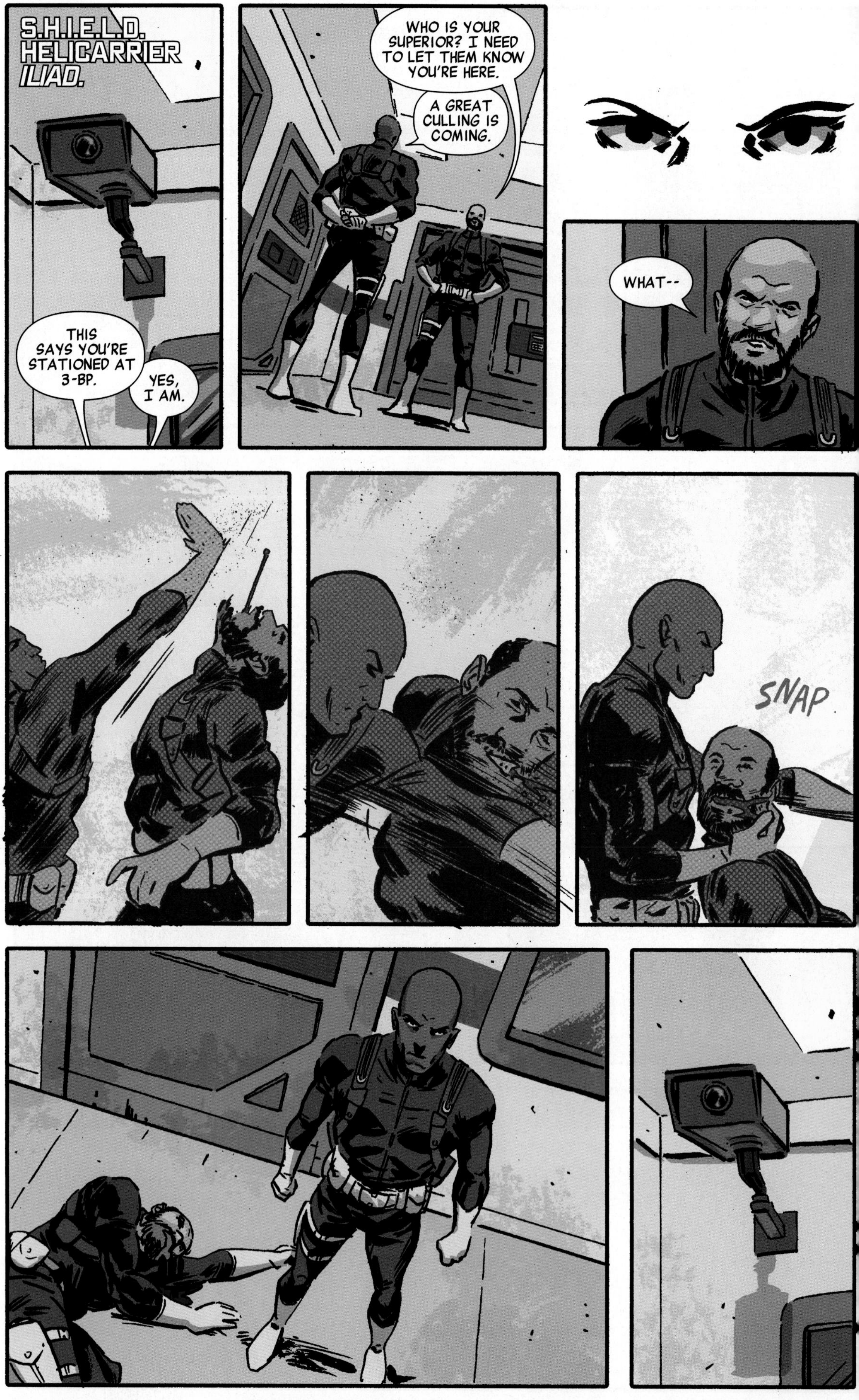
S.H.I.E.L.D. HELICARRIER ILIAD.
THIS SAYS YOU'RE STATIONED AT 3-BP.
YES, I AM.
WHO IS YOUR SUPERIOR? I NEED TO LET THEM KNOW YOU'RE HERE.
A GREAT CULLING IS COMING.
WHAT--
SNAP

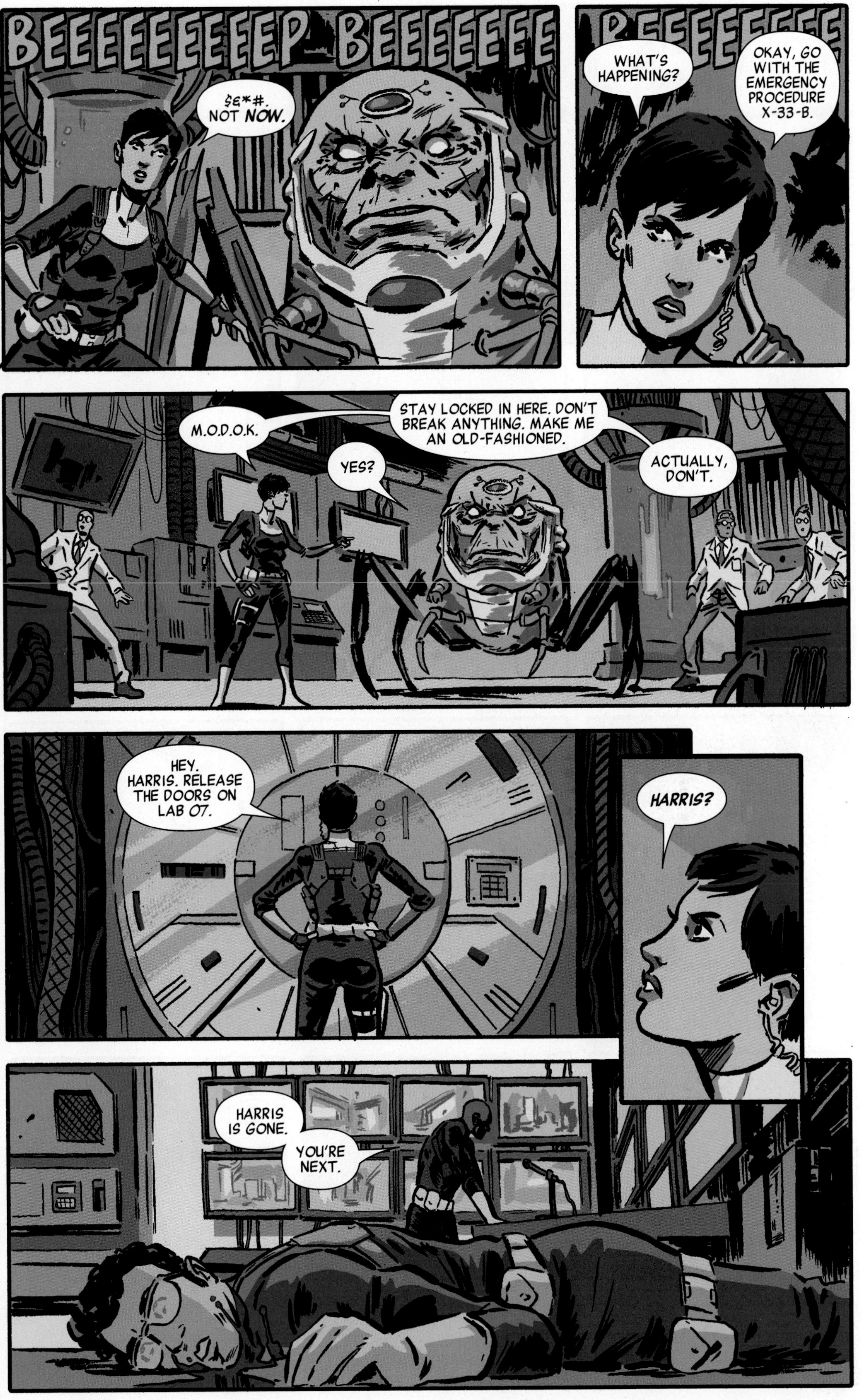
BEEEEEEEEEP BEEEEEEEE
$&*#. NOT NOW.
BEEEEEEEE
WHAT'S HAPPENING?
OKAY, GO WITH THE EMERGENCY PROCEDURE X-33-B.
M.O.D.O.K.
YES?
STAY LOCKED IN HERE. DON'T BREAK ANYTHING. MAKE ME AN OLD-FASHIONED.
ACTUALLY, DON'T.
HEY. HARRIS. RELEASE THE DOORS ON LAB 07.
HARRIS?
HARRIS IS GONE.
YOU'RE NEXT.

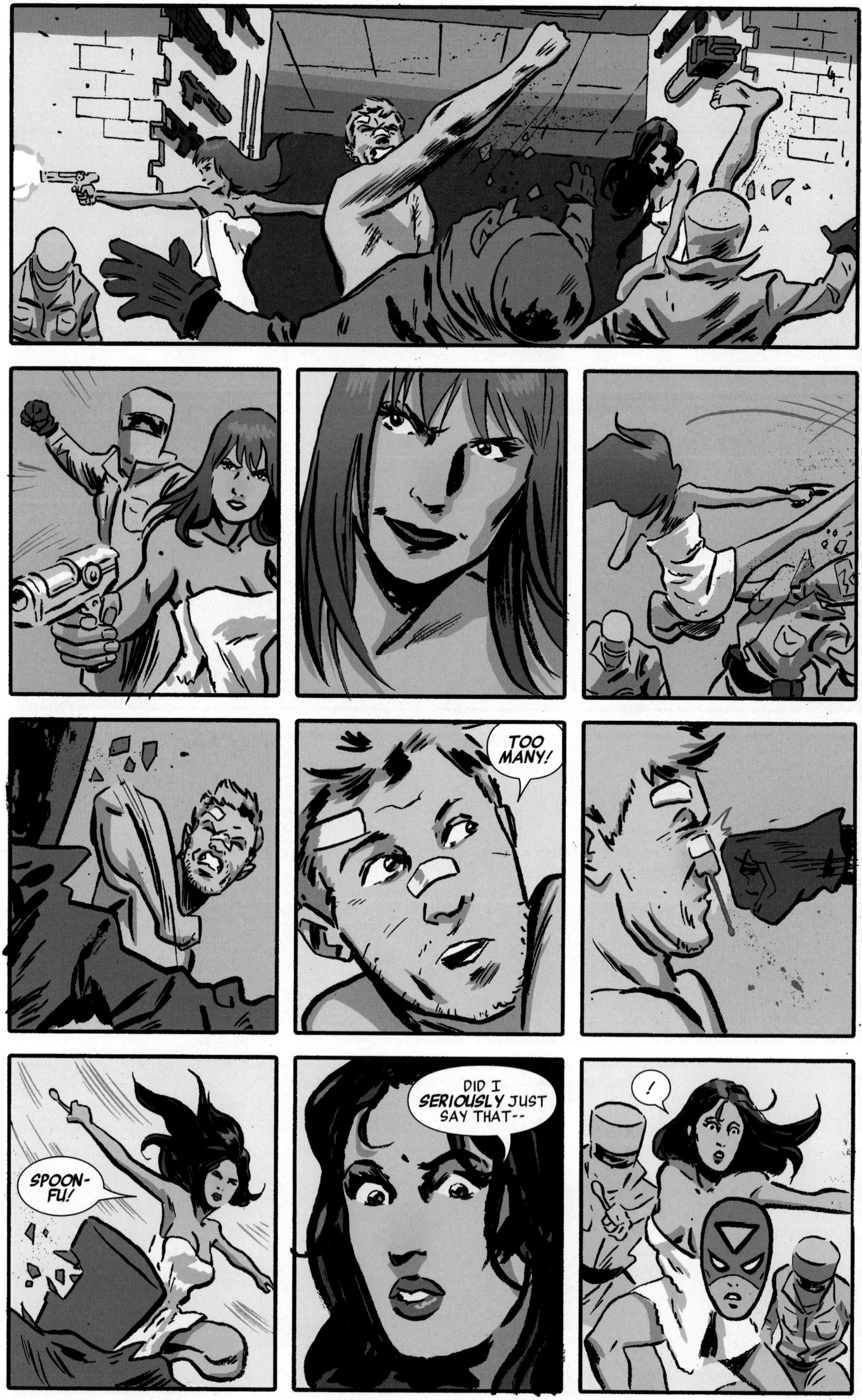
TOO MANY!
SPOON-FU!
DID I SERIOUSLY JUST SAY THAT--
!

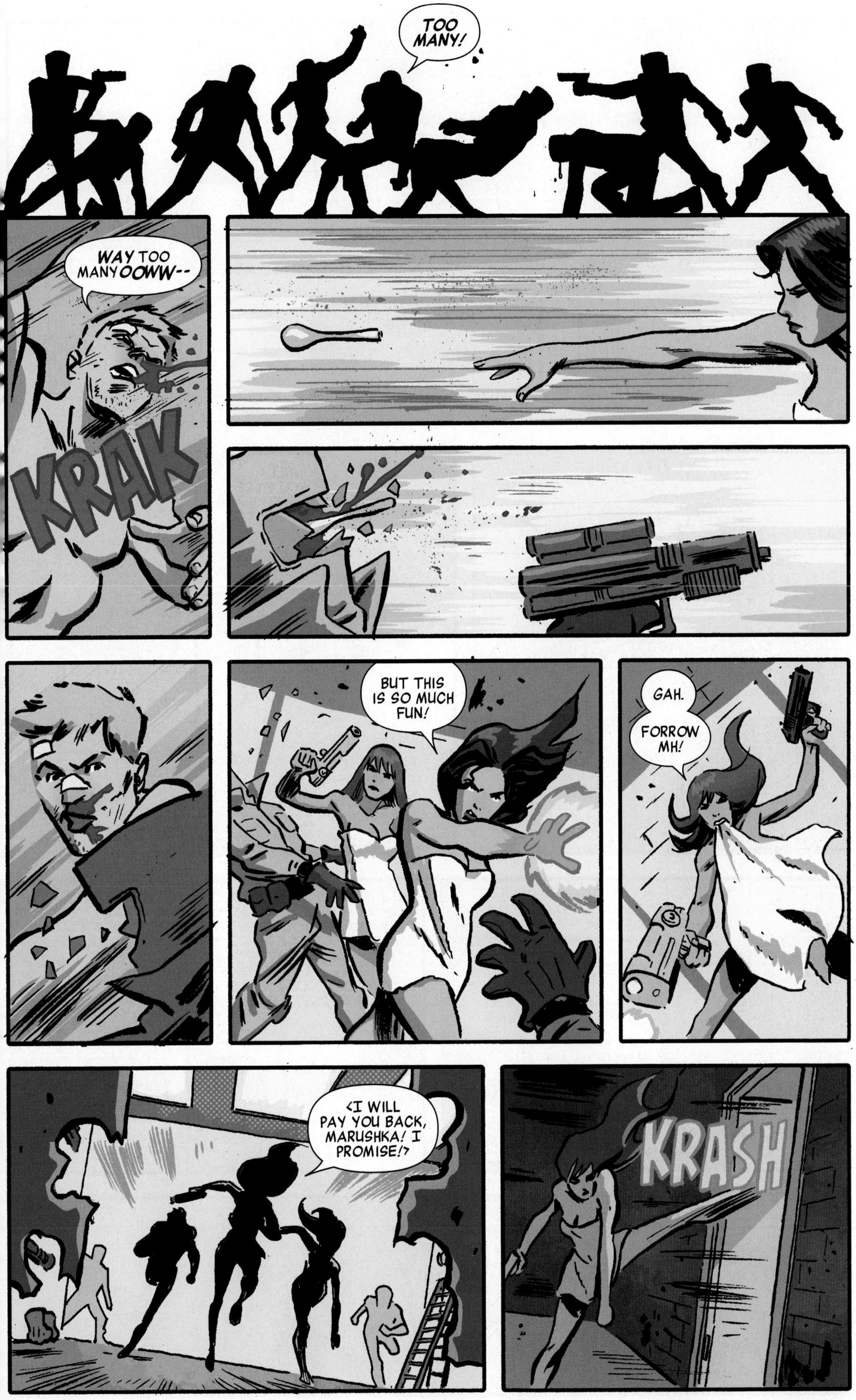
TOO MANY!
WAY TOO MANY OOWW--
KRAK
BUT THIS IS SO MUCH FUN!
GAH.
FORROW MH!
<I WILL PAY YOU BACK, MARUSHKA! I PROMISE!>
KRASH

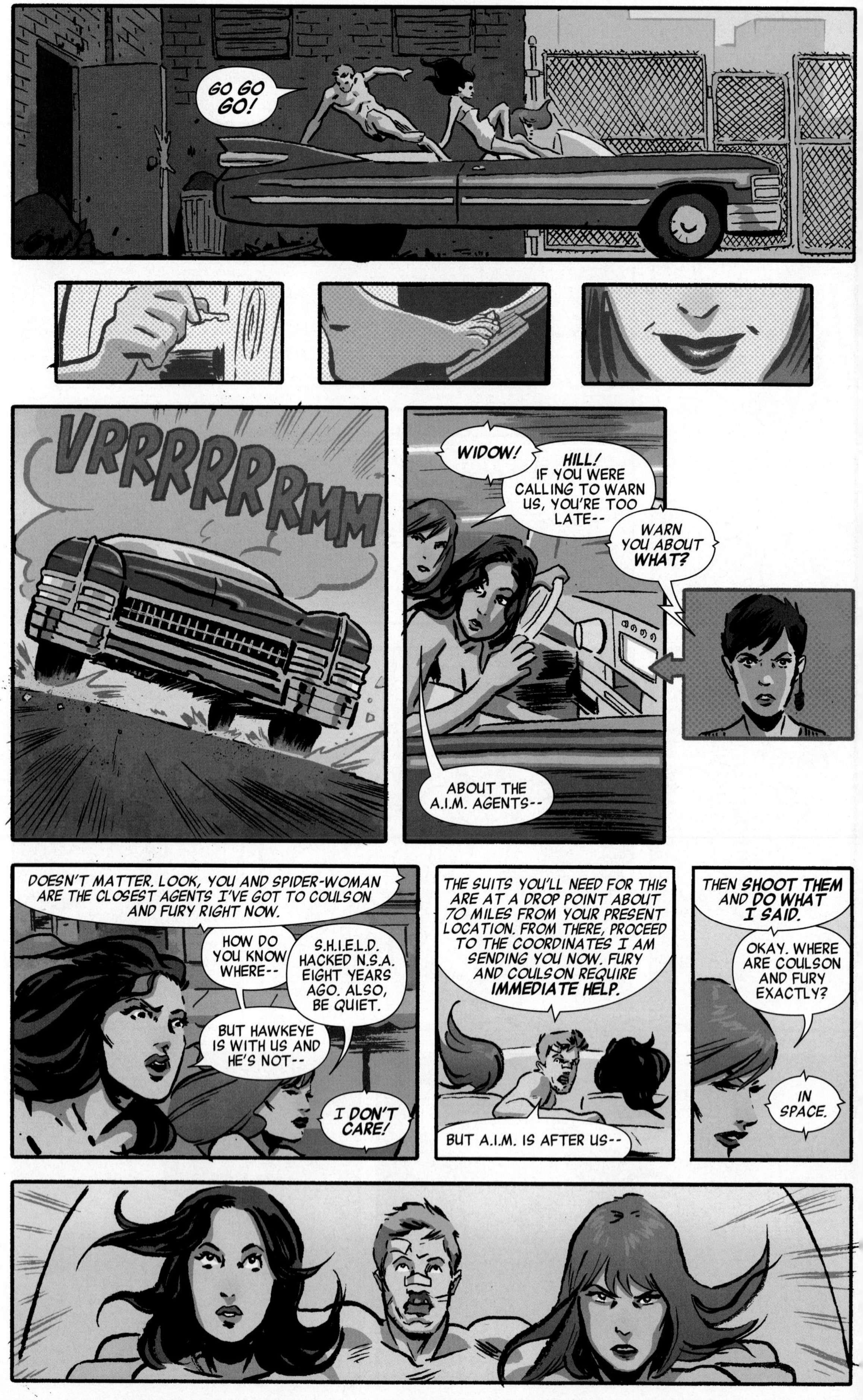

GO GO GO!
VRRRRRRMM
WIDOW!
HILL! IF YOU WERE CALLING TO WARN US, YOU'RE TOO LATE--
WARN YOU ABOUT WHAT?
ABOUT THE A.I.M. AGENTS--
DOESN'T MATTER. LOOK, YOU AND SPIDER-WOMAN ARE THE CLOSEST AGENTS I'VE GOT TO COULSON AND FURY RIGHT NOW.
HOW DO YOU KNOW WHERE--
S.H.I.E.L.D. HACKED N.S.A. EIGHT YEARS AGO. ALSO, BE QUIET.
BUT HAWKEYE IS WITH US AND HE'S NOT--
I DON'T CARE!
THE SUITS YOU'LL NEED FOR THIS ARE AT A DROP POINT ABOUT 70 MILES FROM YOUR PRESENT LOCATION. FROM THERE, PROCEED TO THE COORDINATES I AM SENDING YOU NOW. FURY AND COULSON REQUIRE IMMEDIATE HELP.
BUT A.I.M. IS AFTER US--
THEN SHOOT THEM AND DO WHAT I SAID.
OKAY. WHERE ARE COULSON AND FURY EXACTLY?
IN SPACE.

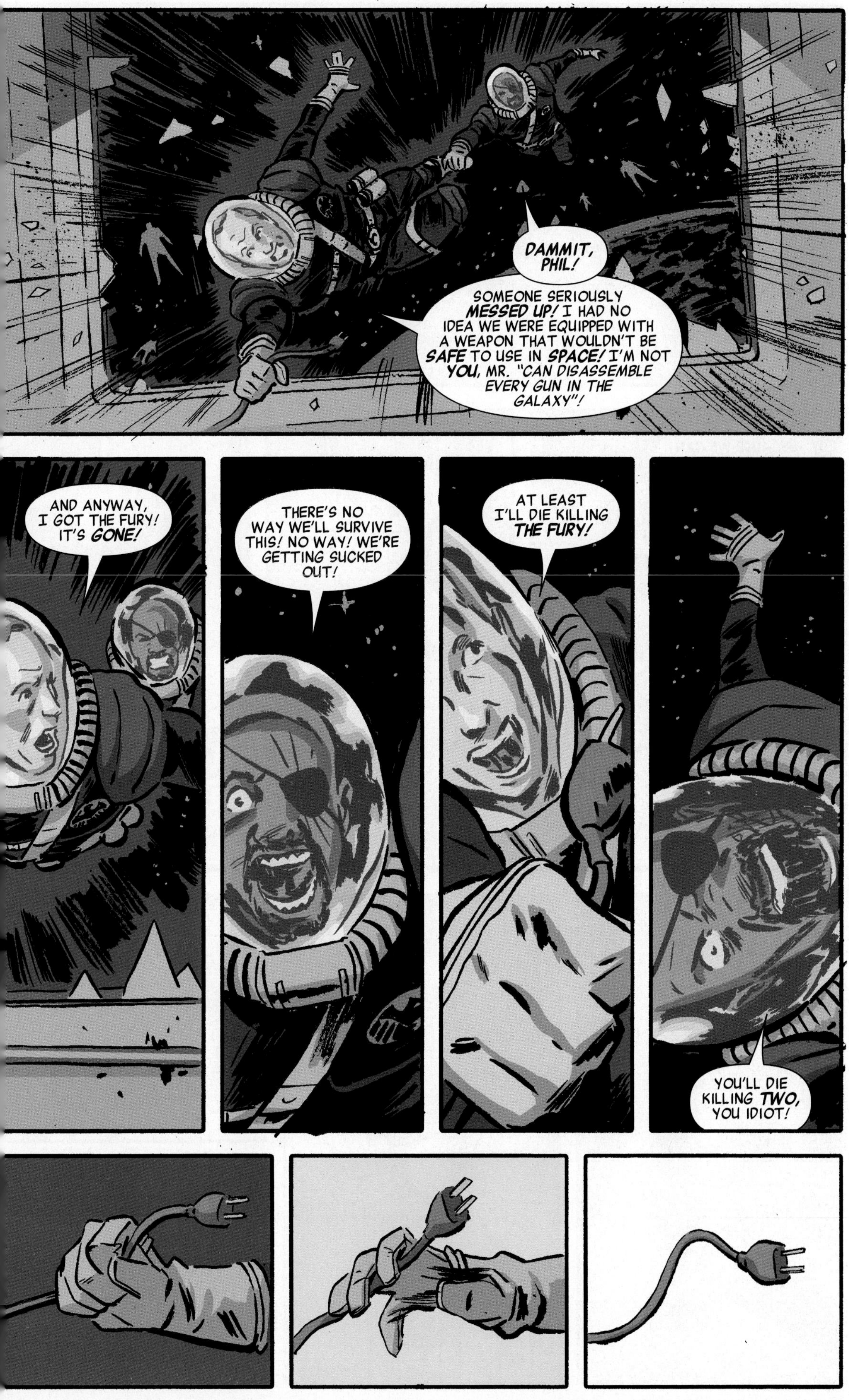
DAMMIT, PHIL!
SOMEONE SERIOUSLY MESSED UP! I HAD NO IDEA WE WERE EQUIPPED WITH A WEAPON THAT WOULDN'T BE SAFE TO USE IN SPACE! I'M NOT YOU, MR. "CAN DISASSEMBLE EVERY GUN IN THE GALAXY"!
AND ANYWAY, I GOT THE FURY! IT'S GONE!
THERE'S NO WAY WE'LL SURVIVE THIS! NO WAY! WE'RE GETTING SUCKED OUT!
AT LEAST I'LL DIE KILLING THE FURY!
YOU'LL DIE KILLING TWO, YOU IDIOT!

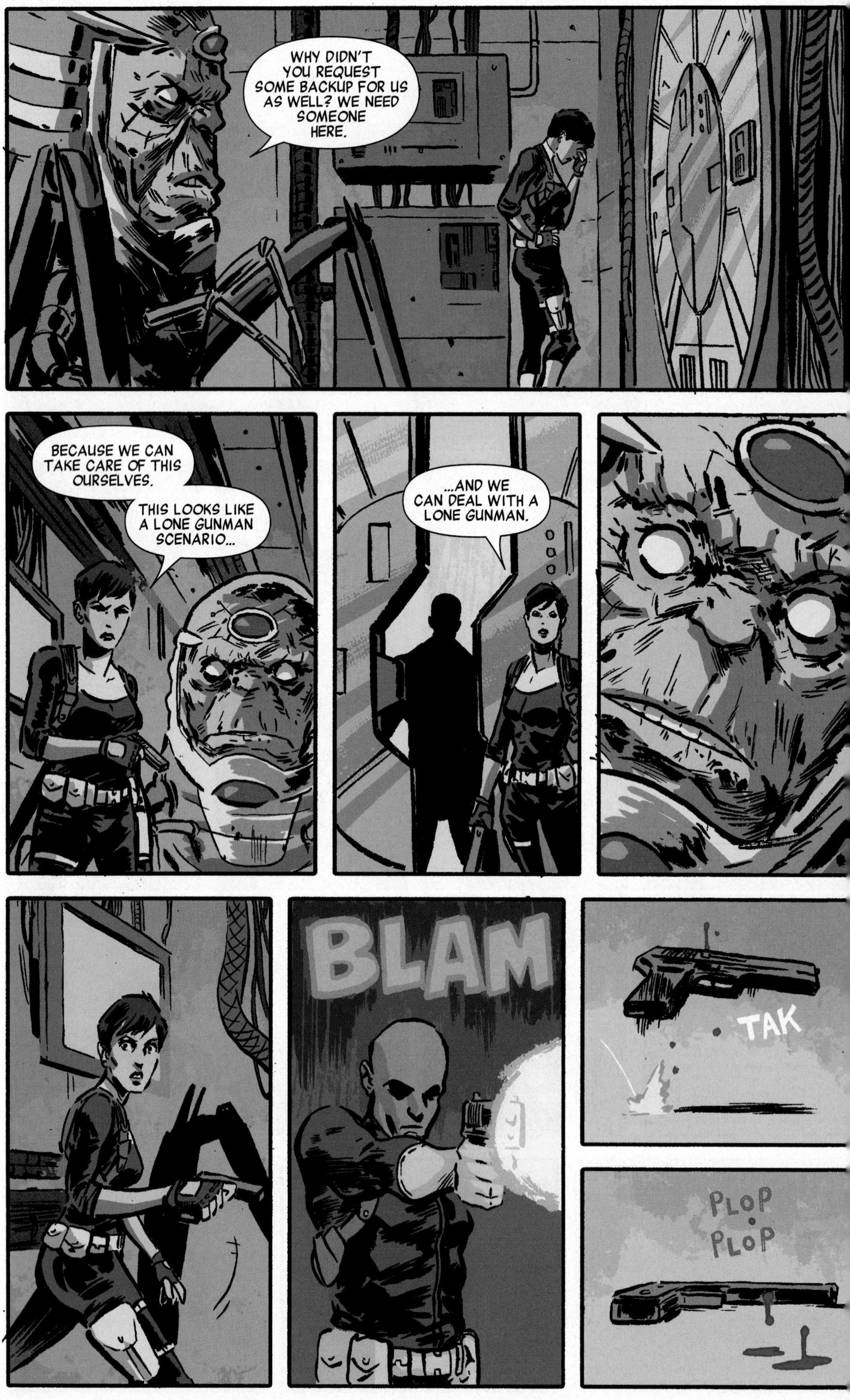
WHY DIDN'T YOU REQUEST SOME BACKUP FOR US AS WELL? WE NEED SOMEONE HERE.
BECAUSE WE CAN TAKE CARE OF THIS OURSELVES.
THIS LOOKS LIKE A LONE GUNMAN SCENARIO...
...AND WE CAN DEAL WITH A LONE GUNMAN.
BLAM
TAK
PLOP
PLOP

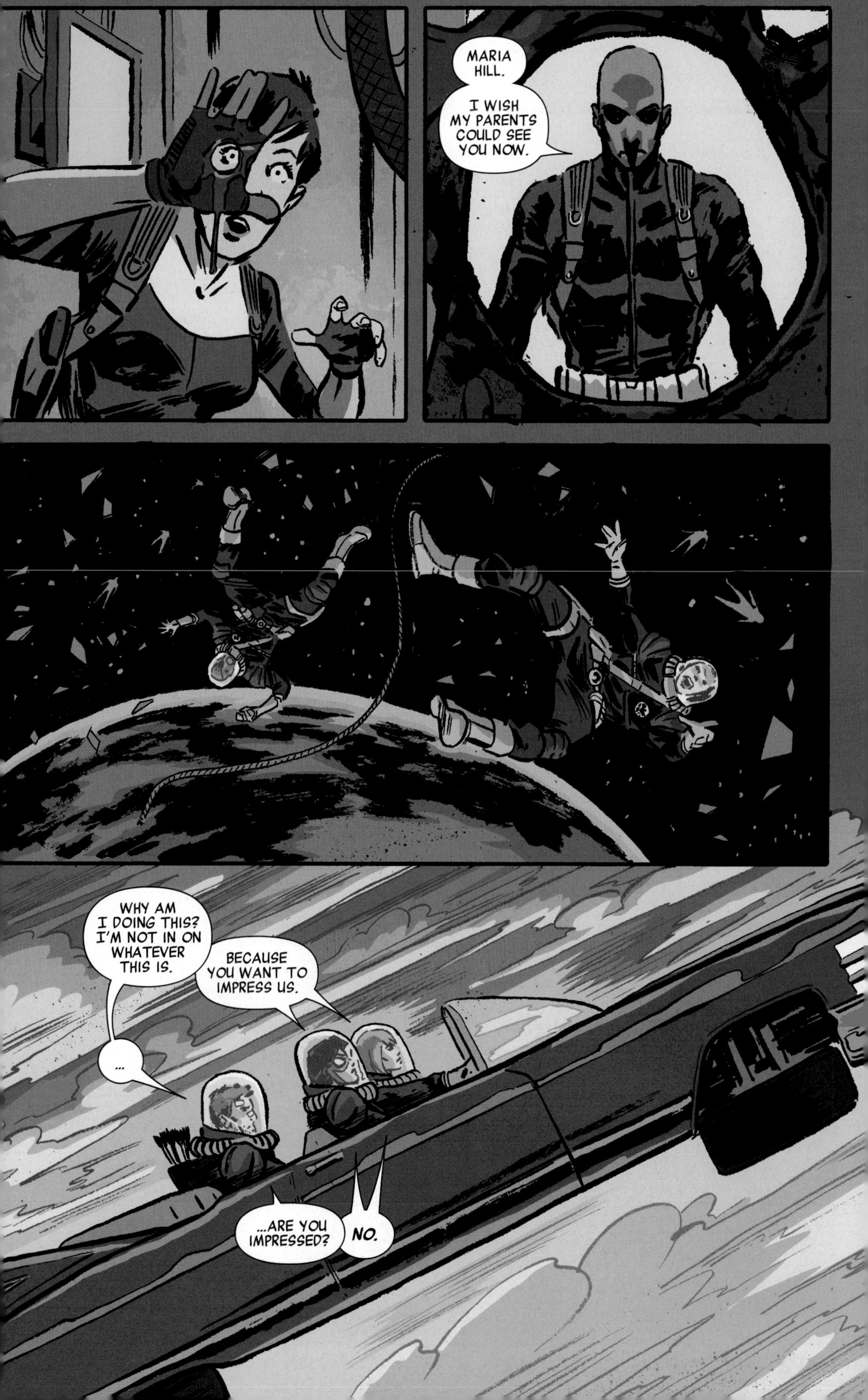
MARIA HILL.
I WISH MY PARENTS COULD SEE YOU NOW.
WHY AM I DOING THIS? I'M NOT IN ON WHATEVER THIS IS.
BECAUSE YOU WANT TO IMPRESS US.
...
...ARE YOU IMPRESSED?
NO.

2

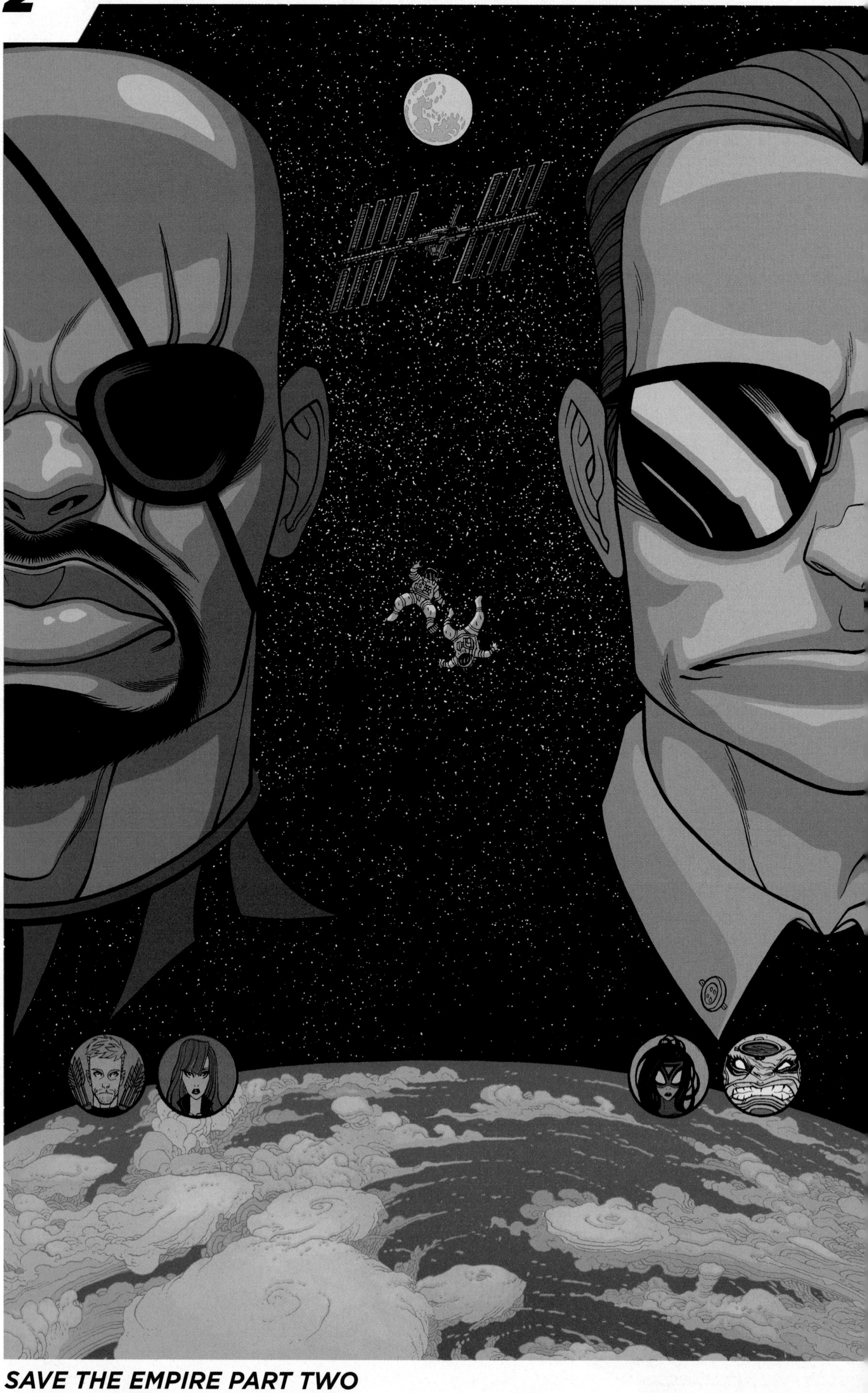

SAVE THE EMPIRE PART TWO

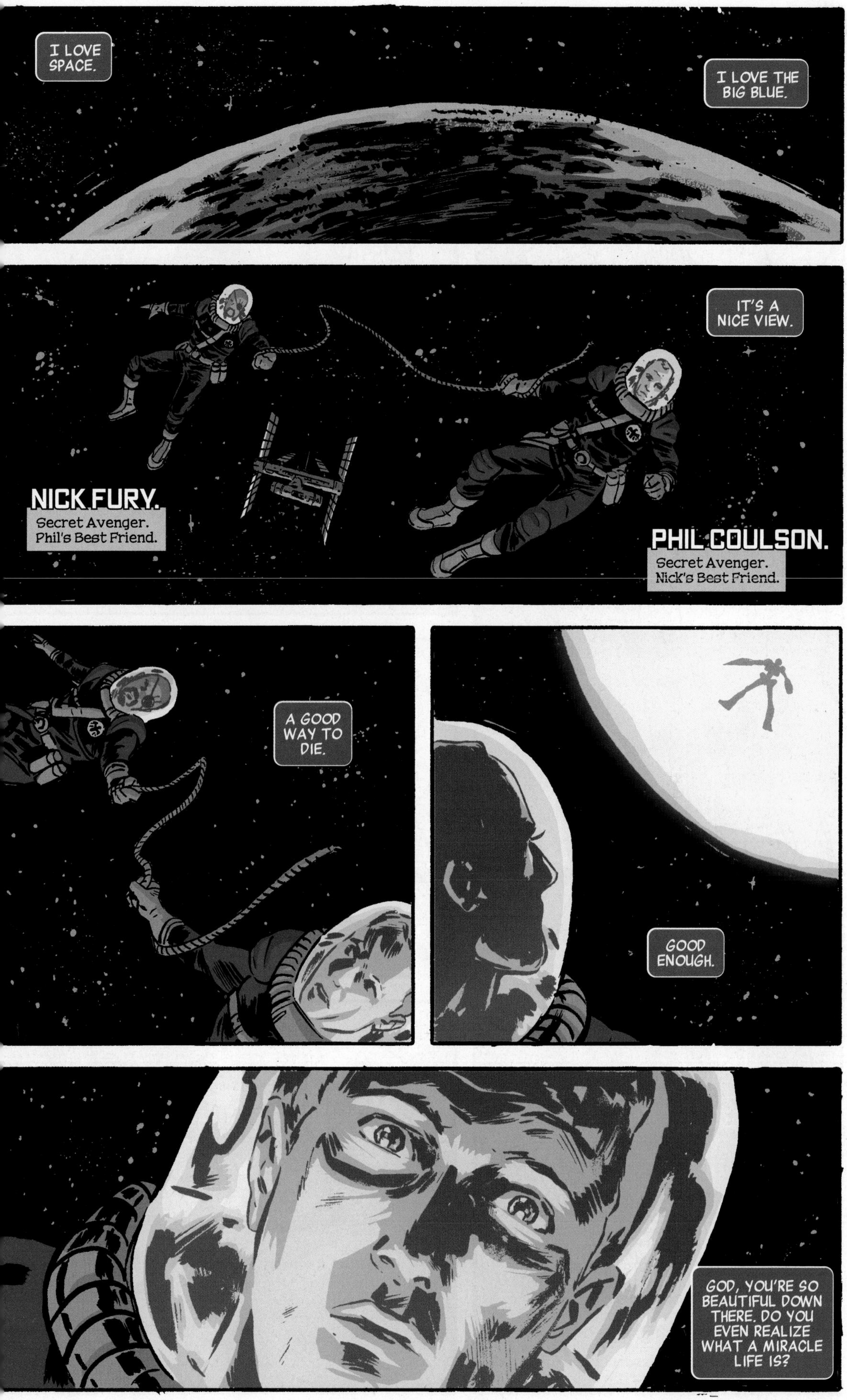
I LOVE SPACE.
I LOVE THE BIG BLUE.
IT'S A NICE VIEW.
NICK FURY.
Secret Avenger. Phil's Best Friend.
PHIL COULSON.
Secret Avenger. Nick's Best Friend.
A GOOD WAY TO DIE.
GOOD ENOUGH.
GOD, YOU'RE SO BEAUTIFUL DOWN THERE. DO YOU EVEN REALIZE WHAT A MIRACLE LIFE IS?

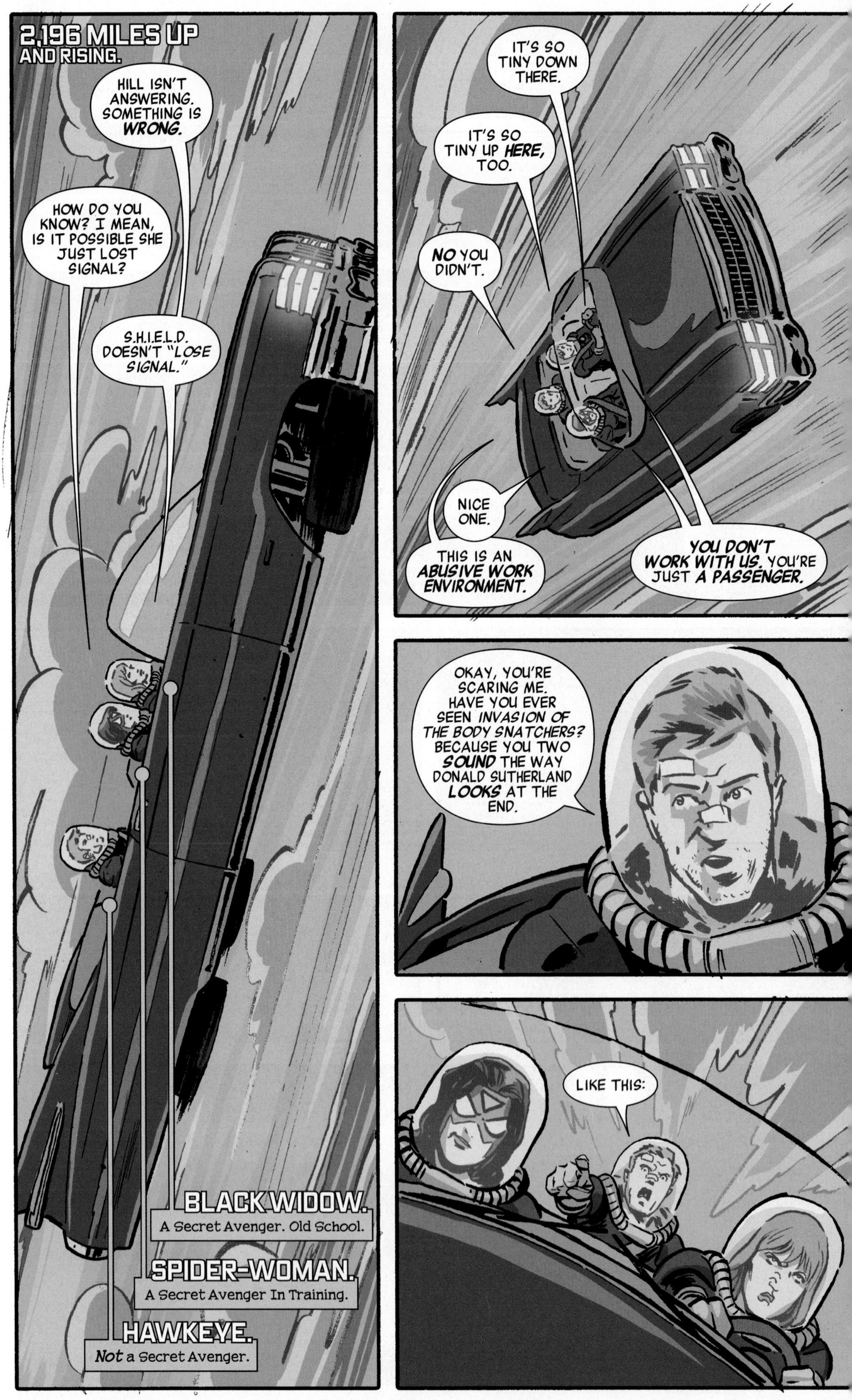

2,196 MILES UP AND RISING.
HILL ISN'T ANSWERING. SOMETHING IS WRONG.
HOW DO YOU KNOW? I MEAN, IS IT POSSIBLE SHE JUST LOST SIGNAL?
S.H.I.E.L.D. DOESN'T "LOSE SIGNAL."
BLACK WIDOW. A Secret Avenger. Old School.
SPIDER-WOMAN. A Secret Avenger In Training.
HAWKEYE. Not a Secret Avenger.
IT'S SO TINY DOWN THERE.
IT'S SO TINY UP HERE, TOO.
NO YOU DIDN'T.
NICE ONE.
THIS IS AN ABUSIVE WORK ENVIRONMENT.
YOU DON'T WORK WITH US. YOU'RE JUST A PASSENGER.
OKAY, YOU'RE SCARING ME. HAVE YOU EVER SEEN INVASION OF THE BODY SNATCHERS? BECAUSE YOU TWO SOUND THE WAY DONALD SUTHERLAND LOOKS AT THE END.
LIKE THIS:

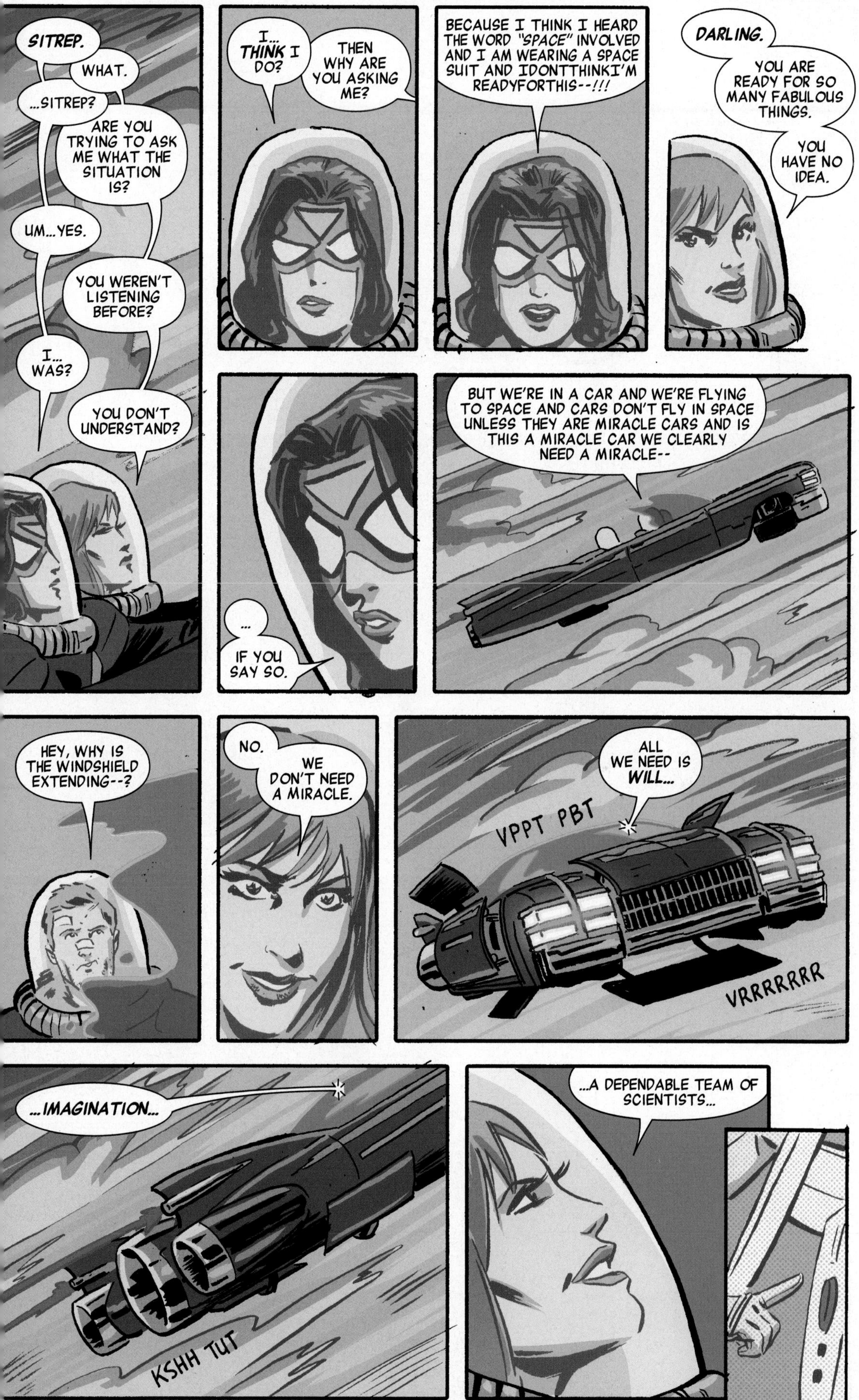
SITREP.
WHAT.
...SITREP?
ARE YOU TRYING TO ASK ME WHAT THE SITUATION IS?
UM...YES.
YOU WEREN'T LISTENING BEFORE?
I... WAS?
YOU DON'T UNDERSTAND?
I... THINK I DO?
THEN WHY ARE YOU ASKING ME?
BECAUSE I THINK I HEARD THE WORD "SPACE" INVOLVED AND I AM WEARING A SPACE SUIT AND IDONTTHINKI'M READYFORTHIS--!!!
DARLING.
YOU ARE READY FOR SO MANY FABULOUS THINGS.
YOU HAVE NO IDEA.
...
IF YOU SAY SO.
BUT WE'RE IN A CAR AND WE'RE FLYING TO SPACE AND CARS DON'T FLY IN SPACE UNLESS THEY ARE MIRACLE CARS AND IS THIS A MIRACLE CAR WE CLEARLY NEED A MIRACLE--
HEY, WHY IS THE WINDSHIELD EXTENDING--?
NO.
WE DON'T NEED A MIRACLE.
ALL WE NEED IS WILL...
VPPT PBT
VRRRRRRR
...IMAGINATION...
KSHH TUT
...A DEPENDABLE TEAM OF SCIENTISTS...

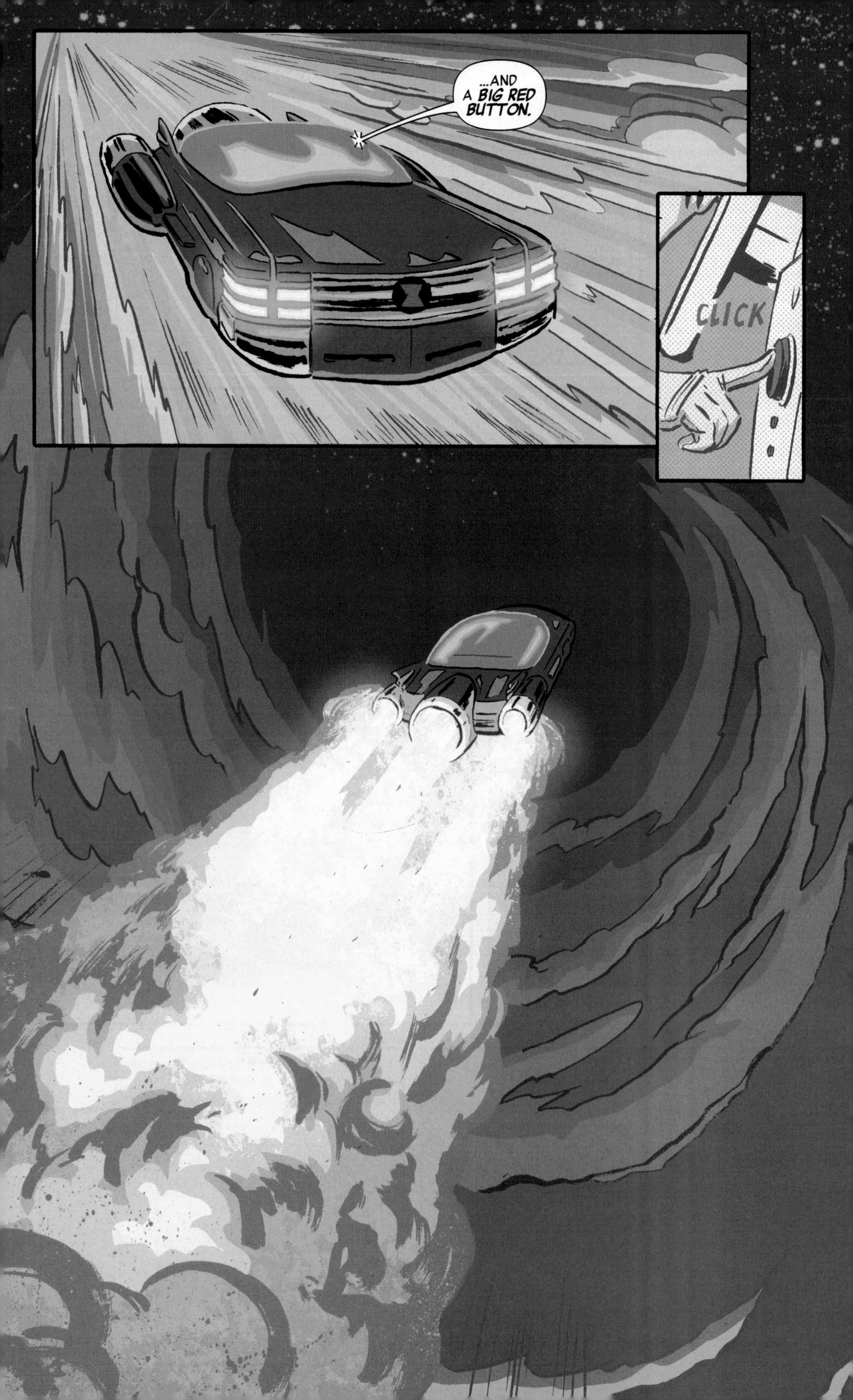
...AND A BIG RED BUTTON.
CLICK

LAB 07.

...AND THAT IS HOW THEY DIED.

MARIA HILL.

Runs Secret Avengers. And S.H.I.E.L.D.

AN UNKNOWN ASSAILANT.

Here to kill Maria Hill.

EMERGENCY LOCK

| 1 | 2 | 3 |
| 4 | 5 | 6 |

I'M SORRY.

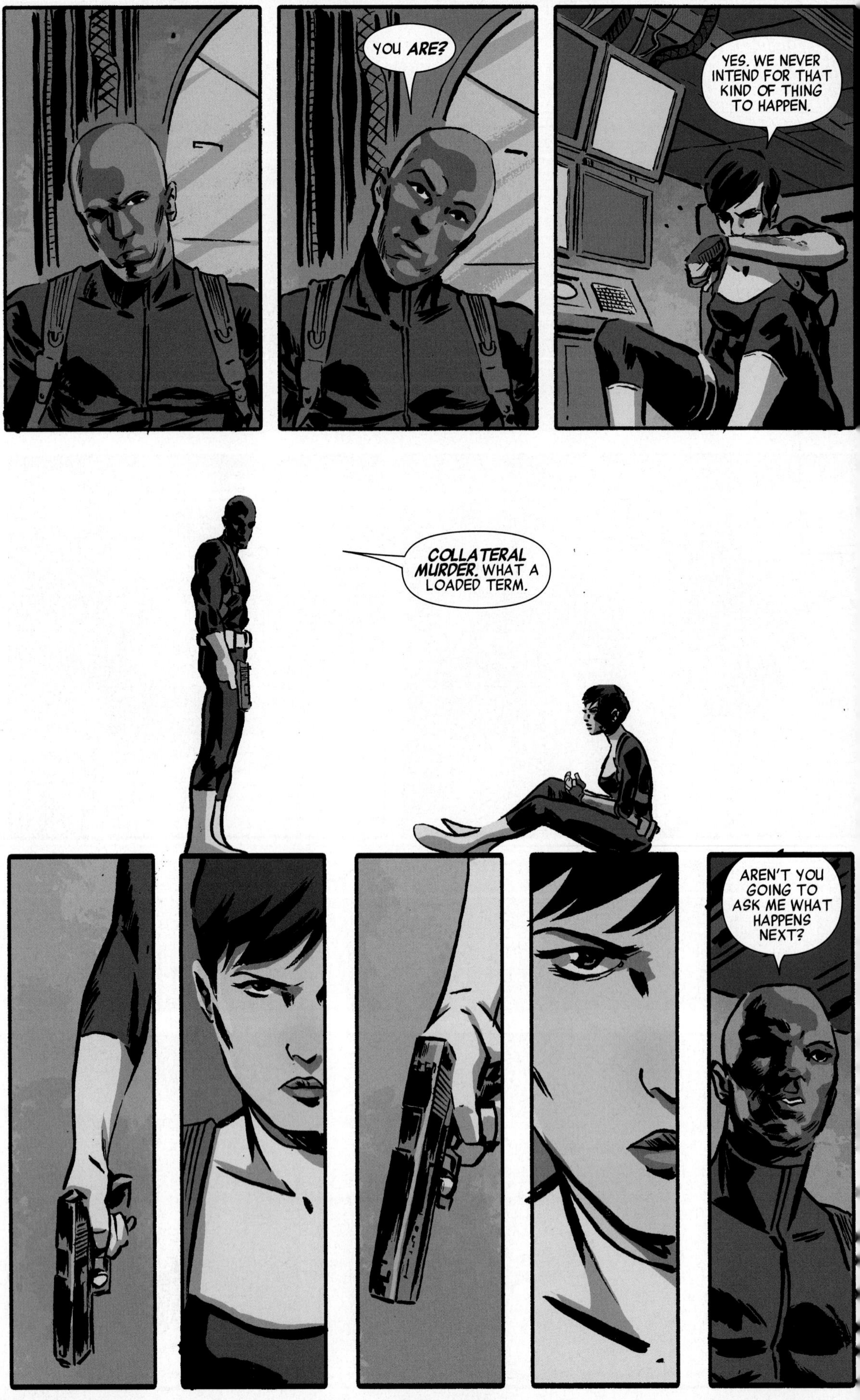

YOU ARE?
YES. WE NEVER INTEND FOR THAT KIND OF THING TO HAPPEN.
COLLATERAL MURDER. WHAT A LOADED TERM.
AREN'T YOU GOING TO ASK ME WHAT HAPPENS NEXT?

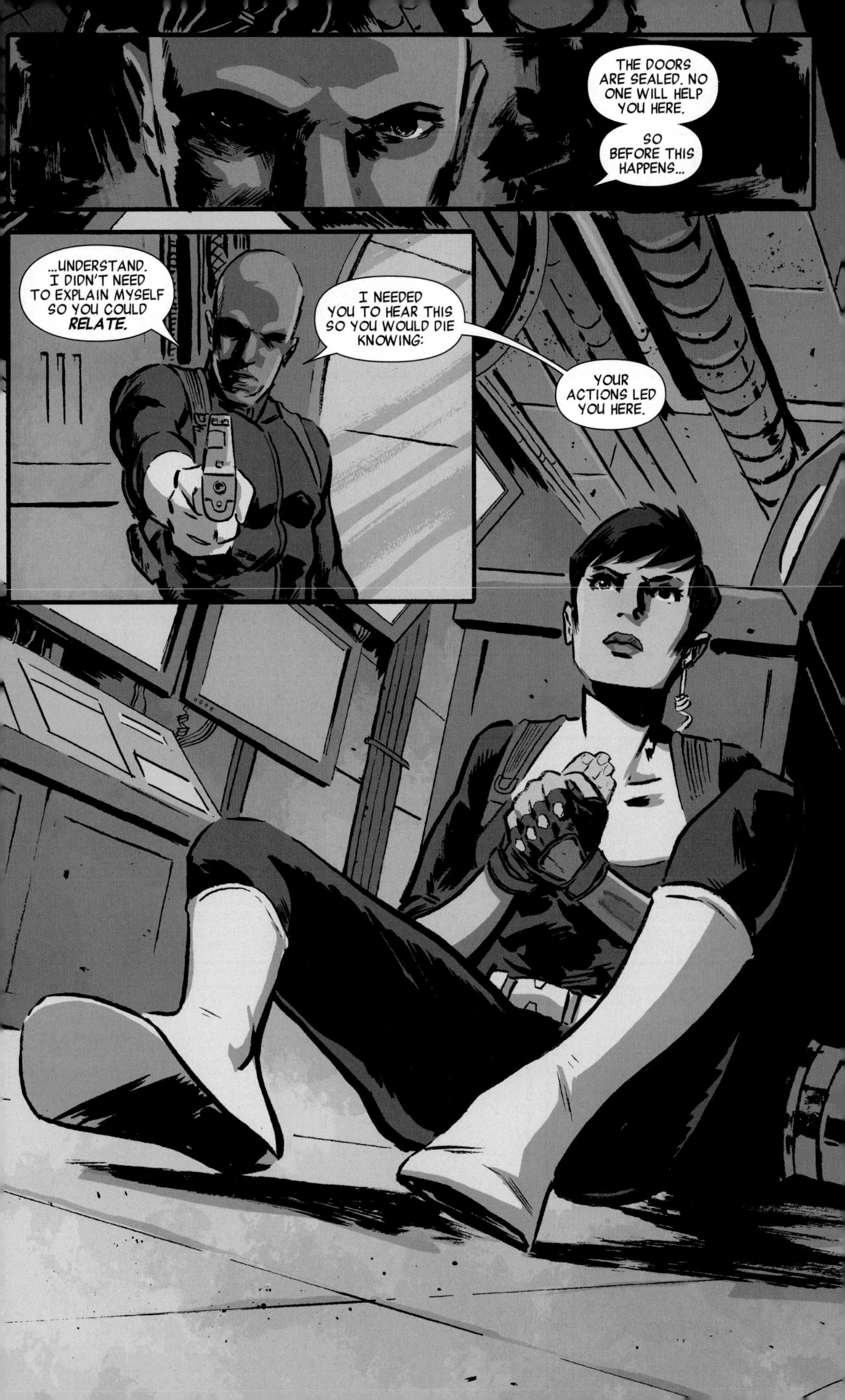
THE DOORS ARE SEALED. NO ONE WILL HELP YOU HERE.
SO BEFORE THIS HAPPENS...
...UNDERSTAND. I DIDN'T NEED TO EXPLAIN MYSELF SO YOU COULD RELATE.
I NEEDED YOU TO HEAR THIS SO YOU WOULD DIE KNOWING:
YOUR ACTIONS LED YOU HERE.

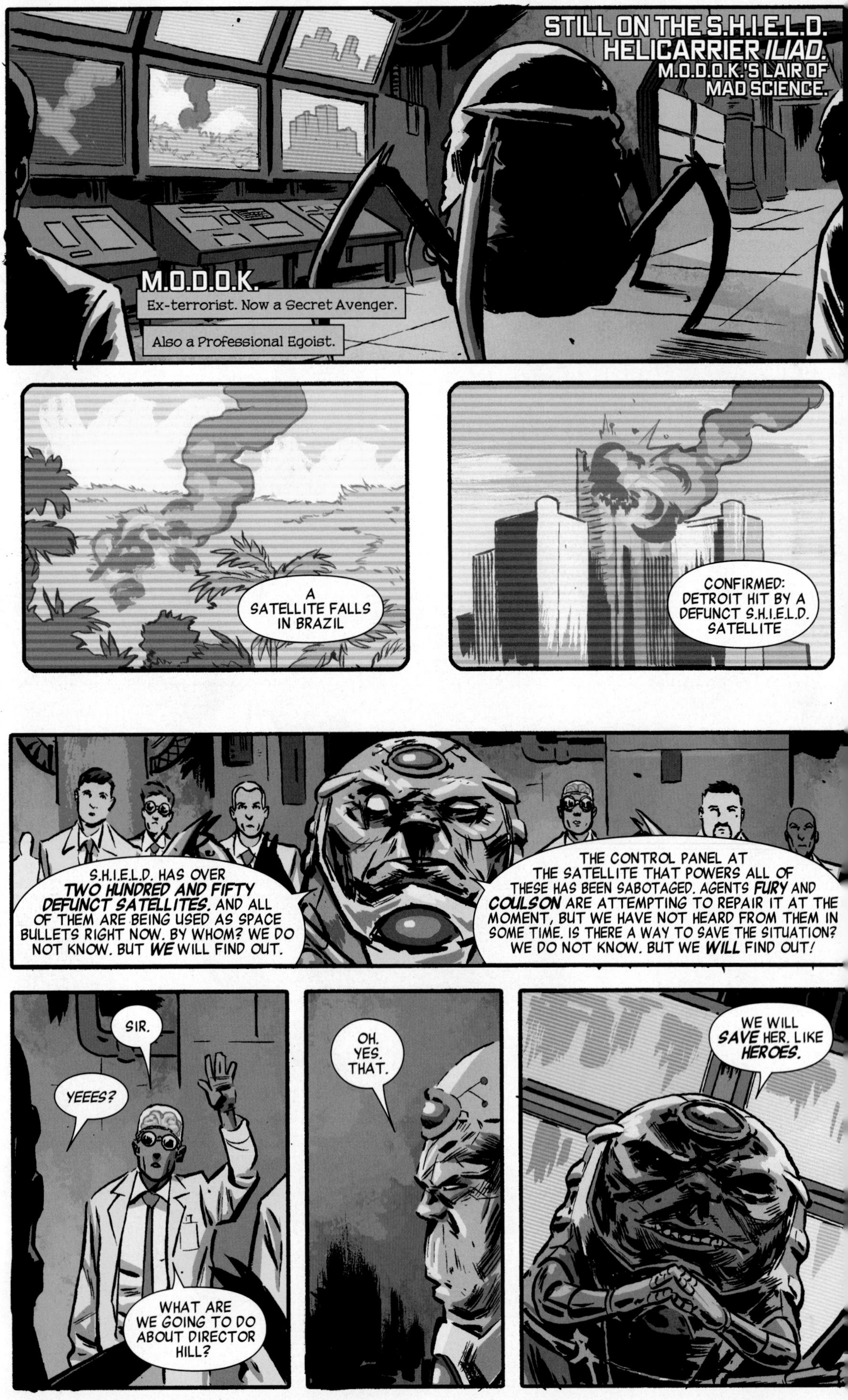

STILL ON THE S.H.I.E.L.D. HELICARRIER ILIAD.
M.O.D.O.K.'S LAIR OF MAD SCIENCE.
M.O.D.O.K.
Ex-terrorist. Now a Secret Avenger.
Also a Professional Egoist.
A SATELLITE FALLS IN BRAZIL
CONFIRMED: DETROIT HIT BY A DEFUNCT S.H.I.E.L.D. SATELLITE
S.H.I.E.L.D. HAS OVER TWO HUNDRED AND FIFTY DEFUNCT SATELLITES. AND ALL OF THEM ARE BEING USED AS SPACE BULLETS RIGHT NOW. BY WHOM? WE DO NOT KNOW. BUT WE WILL FIND OUT.
THE CONTROL PANEL AT THE SATELLITE THAT POWERS ALL OF THESE HAS BEEN SABOTAGED. AGENTS FURY AND COULSON ARE ATTEMPTING TO REPAIR IT AT THE MOMENT, BUT WE HAVE NOT HEARD FROM THEM IN SOME TIME. IS THERE A WAY TO SAVE THE SITUATION? WE DO NOT KNOW. BUT WE WILL FIND OUT!
SIR.
YEEES?
WHAT ARE WE GOING TO DO ABOUT DIRECTOR HILL?
OH. YES. THAT.
WE WILL SAVE HER. LIKE HEROES.

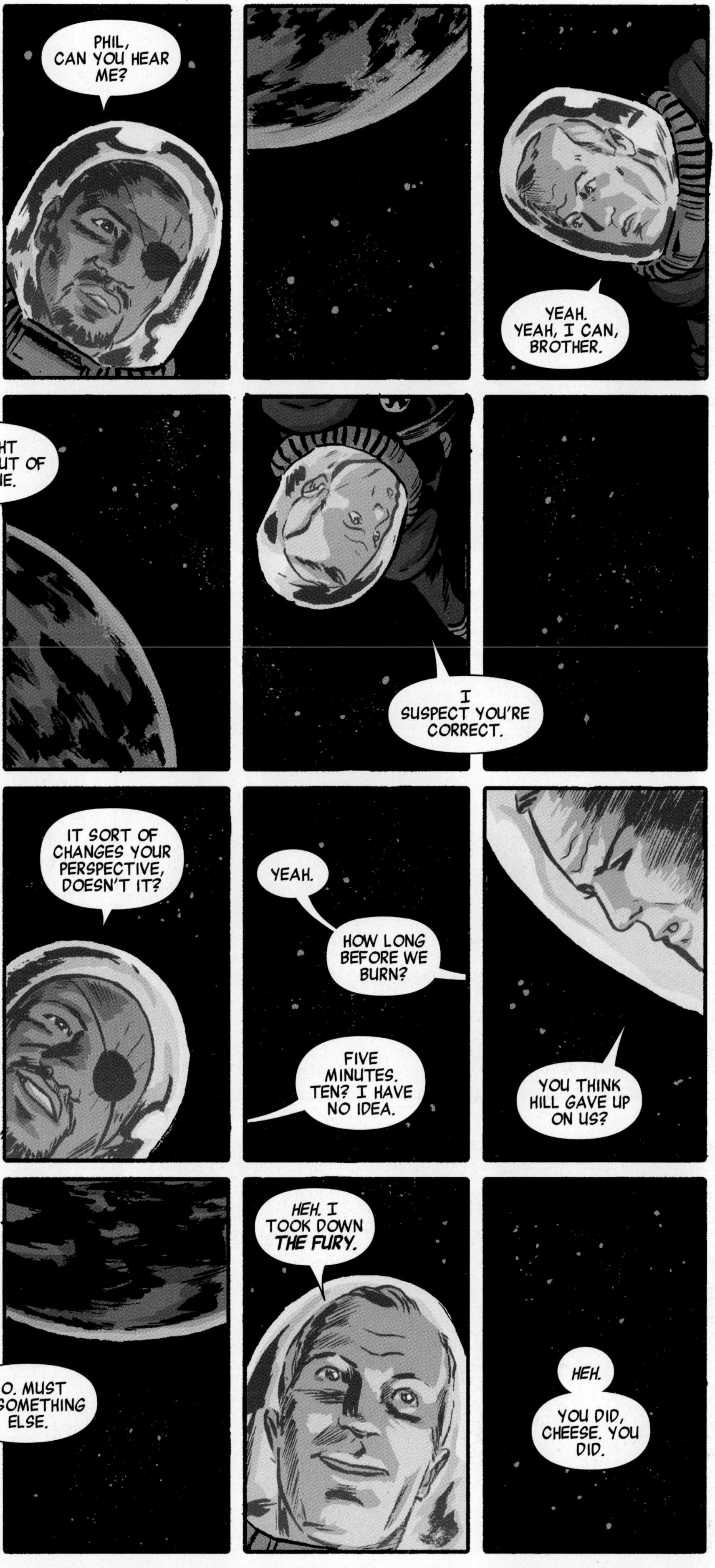
PHIL, CAN YOU HEAR ME?
YEAH. YEAH, I CAN, BROTHER.
I SUSPECT YOU'RE CORRECT.
IT SORT OF CHANGES YOUR PERSPECTIVE, DOESN'T IT?
YEAH.
HOW LONG BEFORE WE BURN?
FIVE MINUTES. TEN? I HAVE NO IDEA.
YOU THINK HILL GAVE UP ON US?
NO. MUST SOMETHING ELSE.
HEH. I TOOK DOWN *THE FURY.*
HEH.
YOU DID, CHEESE. YOU DID.

TIK-TIK-TIK-TIK

TIK-TIK-TI

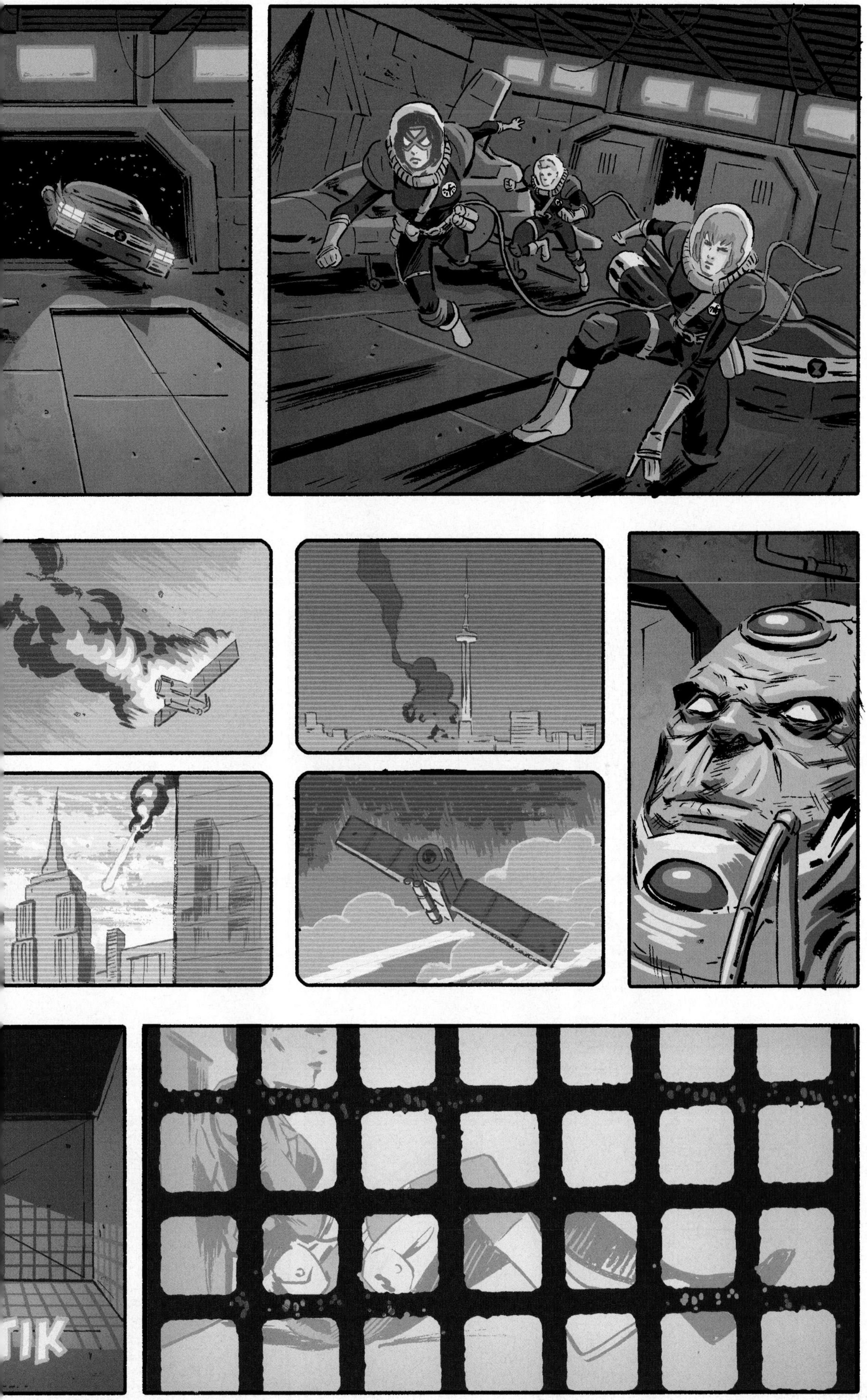
TIK

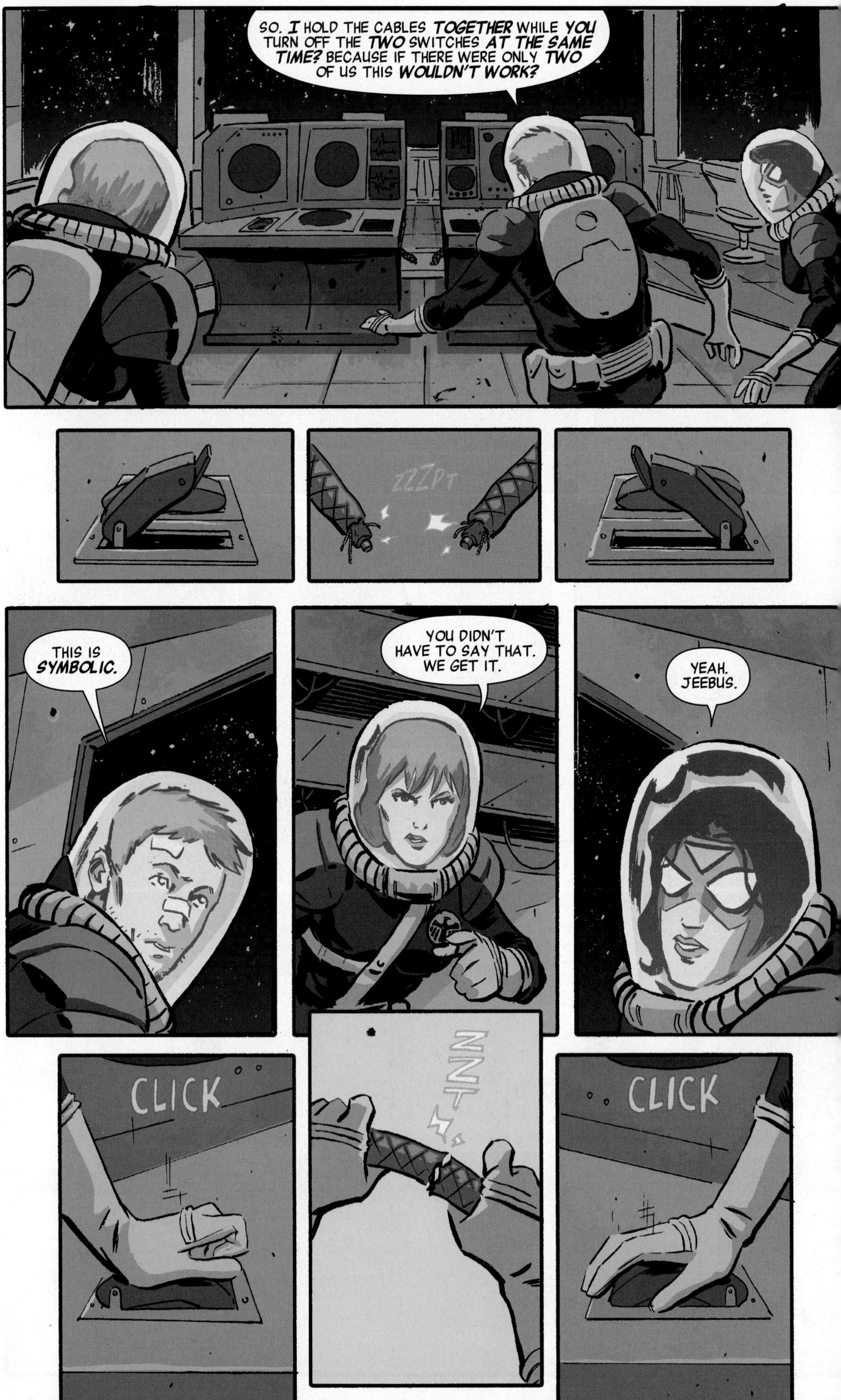
SO. I HOLD THE CABLES TOGETHER WHILE YOU TURN OFF THE TWO SWITCHES AT THE SAME TIME? BECAUSE IF THERE WERE ONLY TWO OF US THIS WOULDN'T WORK?
ZZZPT
THIS IS SYMBOLIC.
YOU DIDN'T HAVE TO SAY THAT. WE GET IT.
YEAH. JEEBUS.
CLICK
ZZNT
CLICK

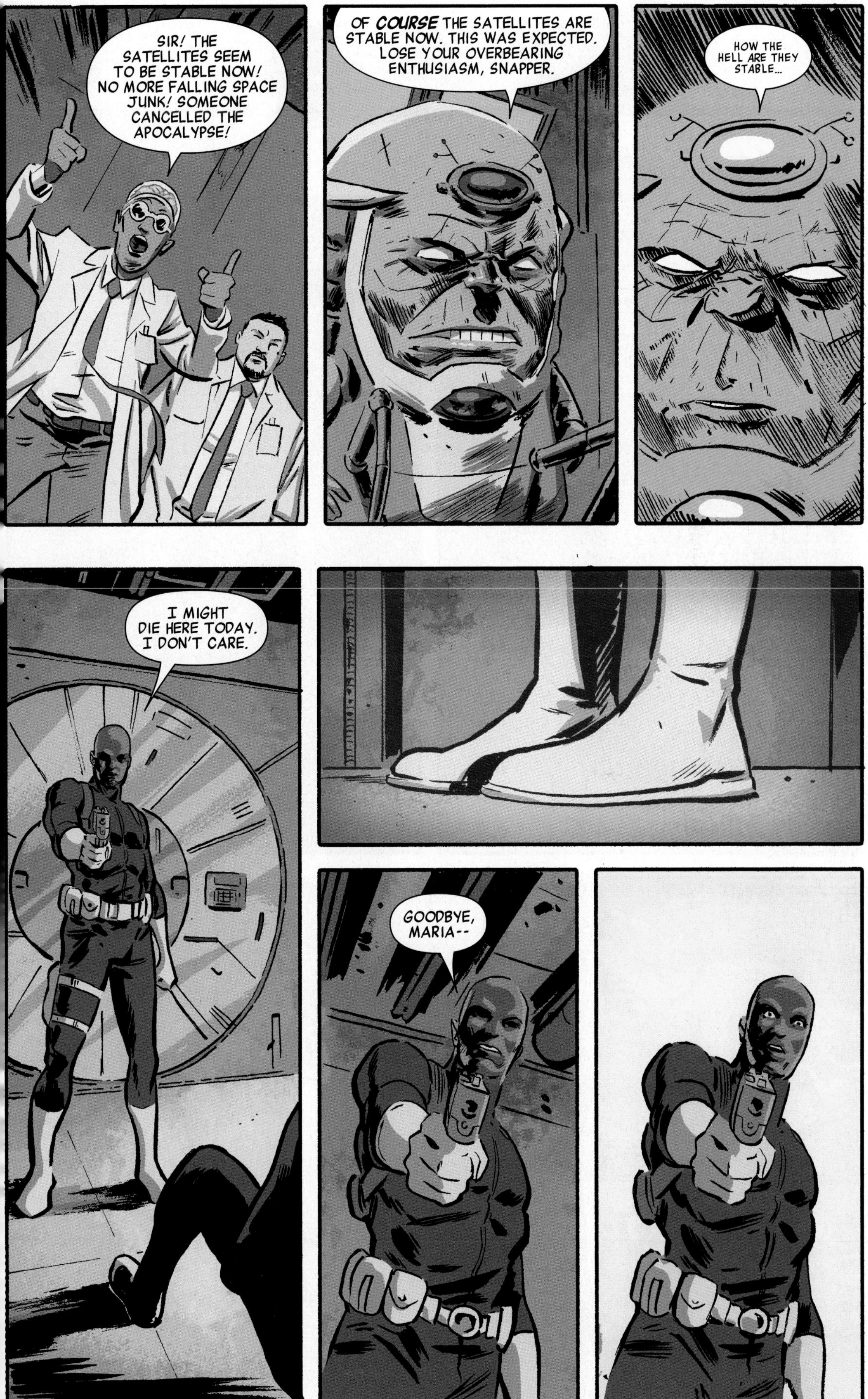
SIR! THE SATELLITES SEEM TO BE STABLE NOW! NO MORE FALLING SPACE JUNK! SOMEONE CANCELLED THE APOCALYPSE!
OF COURSE THE SATELLITES ARE STABLE NOW. THIS WAS EXPECTED. LOSE YOUR OVERBEARING ENTHUSIASM, SNAPPER.
HOW THE HELL ARE THEY STABLE...
I MIGHT DIE HERE TODAY. I DON'T CARE.
GOODBYE, MARIA--

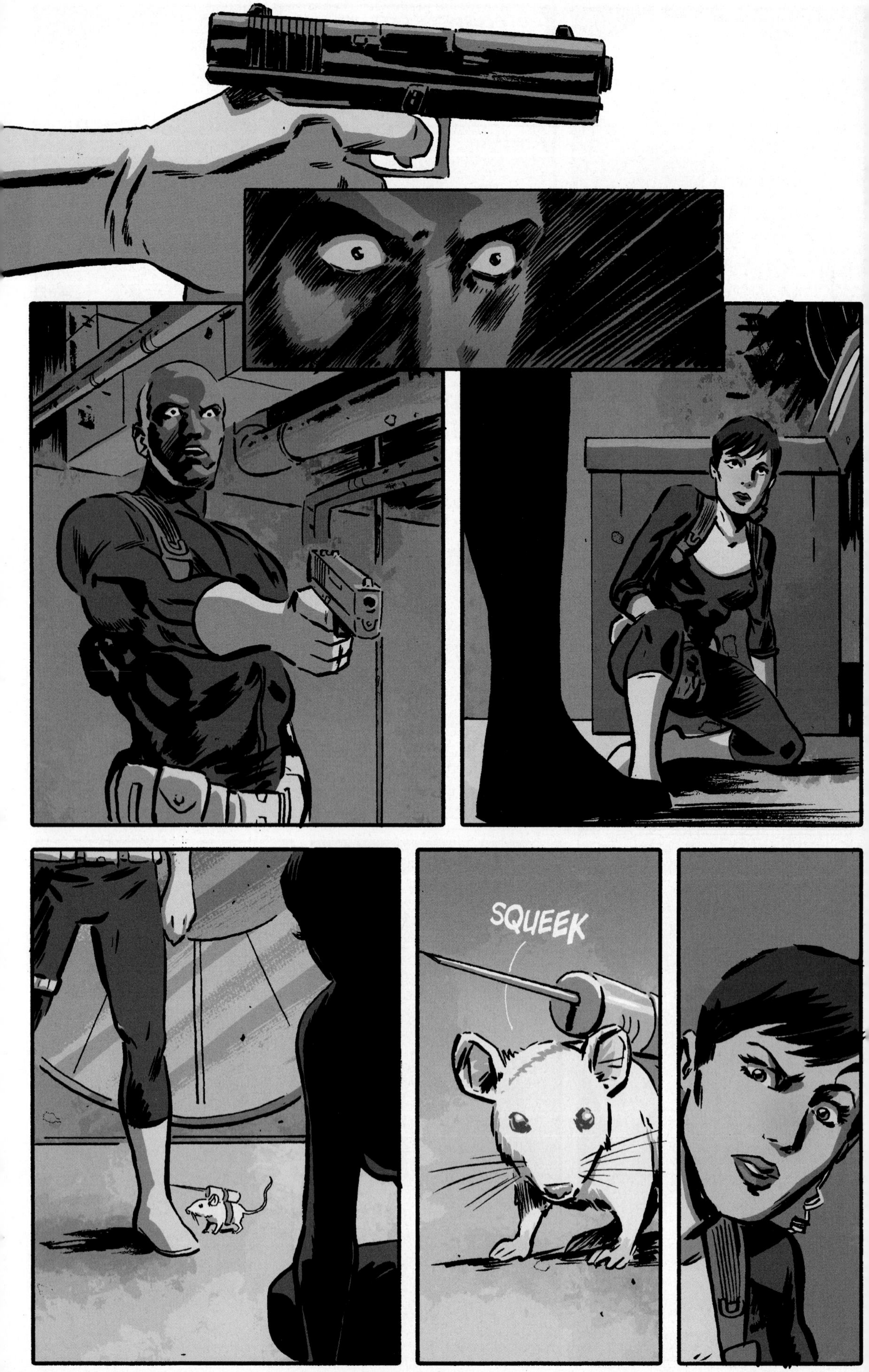
SQUEEK

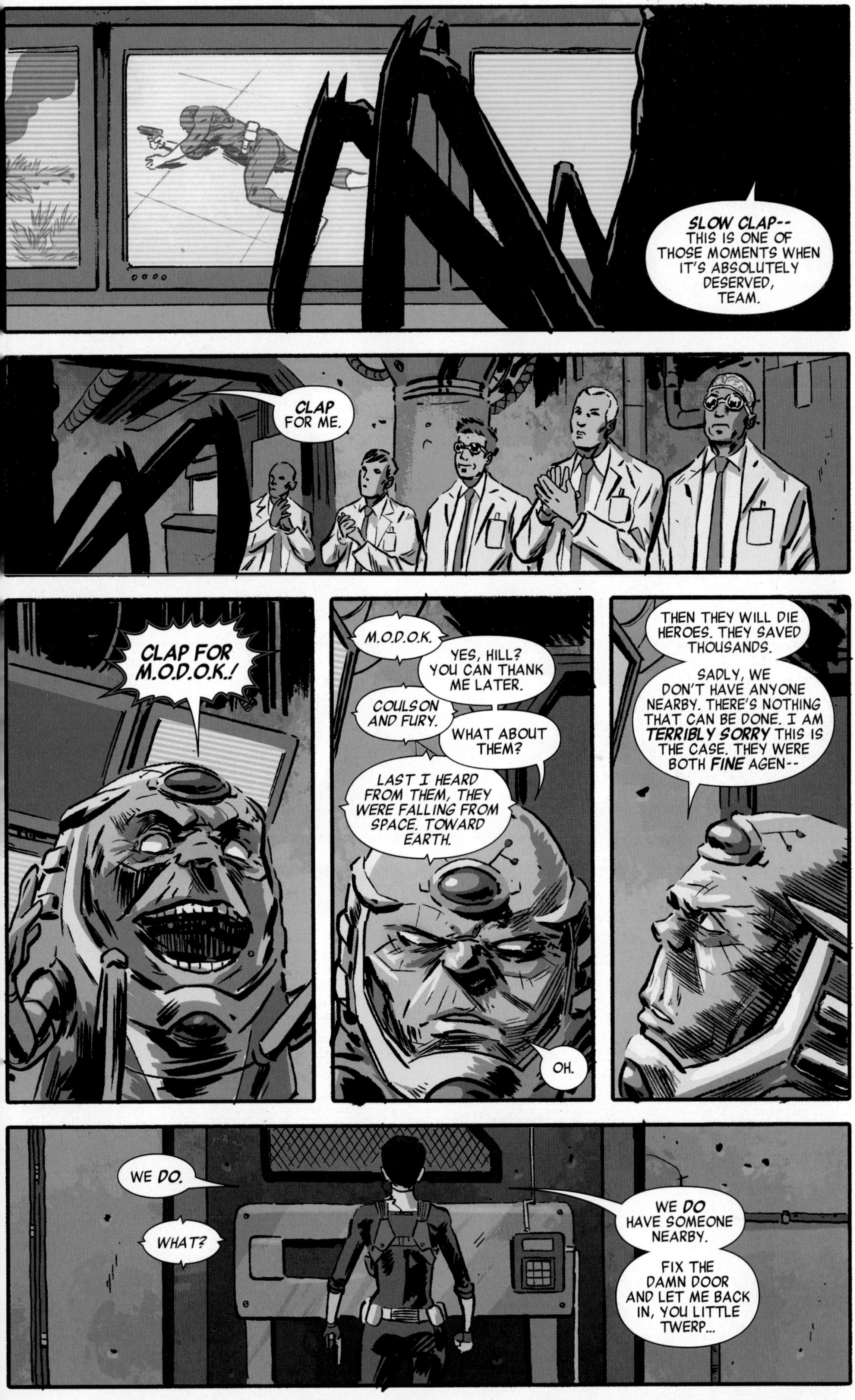
SLOW CLAP-- THIS IS ONE OF THOSE MOMENTS WHEN IT'S ABSOLUTELY DESERVED, TEAM.
CLAP FOR ME.
CLAP FOR M.O.D.O.K.!
M.O.D.O.K.
YES, HILL? YOU CAN THANK ME LATER.
COULSON AND FURY.
WHAT ABOUT THEM?
LAST I HEARD FROM THEM, THEY WERE FALLING FROM SPACE. TOWARD EARTH.
OH.
THEN THEY WILL DIE HEROES. THEY SAVED THOUSANDS.
SADLY, WE DON'T HAVE ANYONE NEARBY. THERE'S NOTHING THAT CAN BE DONE. I AM TERRIBLY SORRY THIS IS THE CASE. THEY WERE BOTH FINE AGEN--
WE DO.
WHAT?
WE DO HAVE SOMEONE NEARBY.
FIX THE DAMN DOOR AND LET ME BACK IN, YOU LITTLE TWERP...

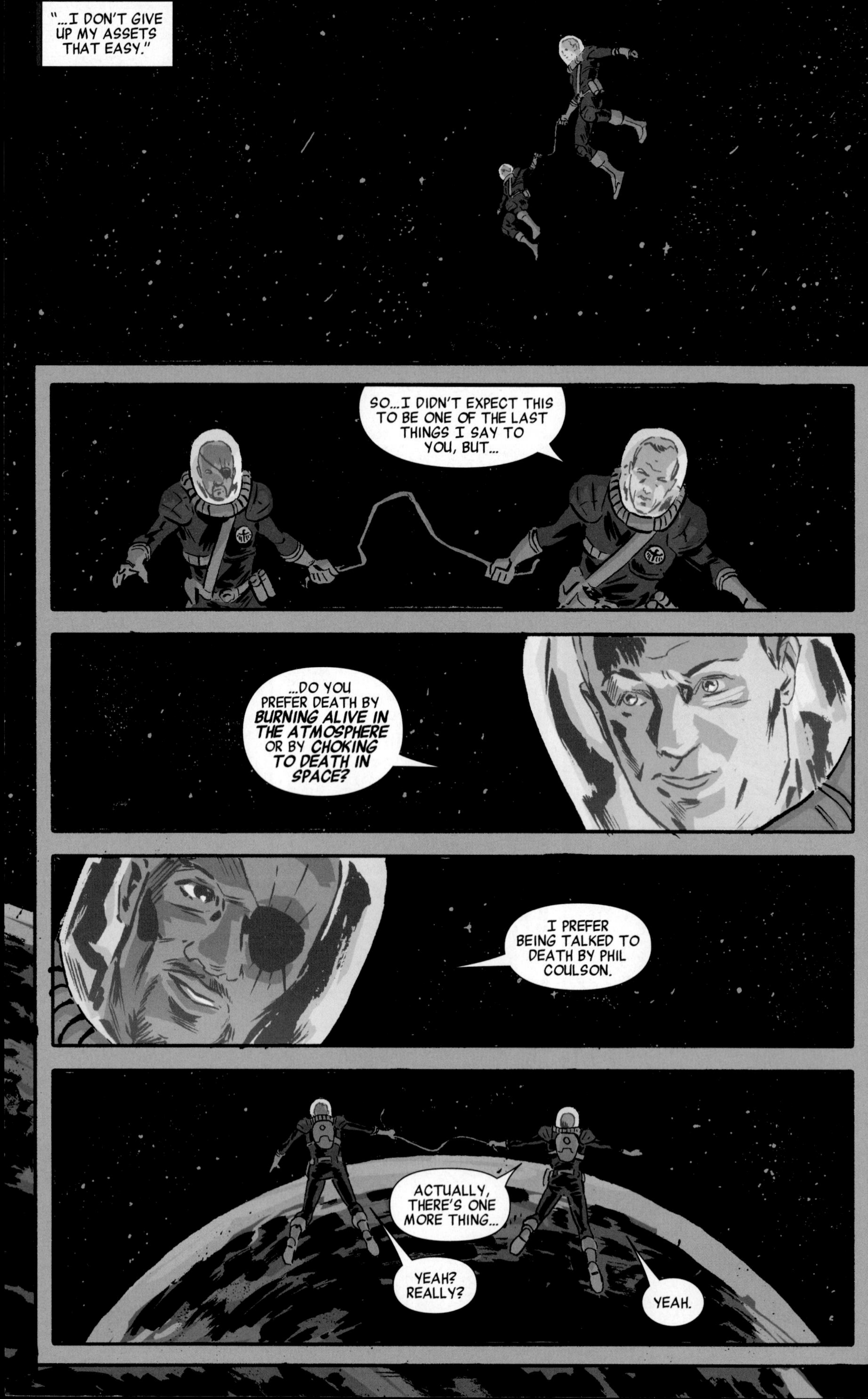
"...I DON'T GIVE UP MY ASSETS THAT EASY."
SO...I DIDN'T EXPECT THIS TO BE ONE OF THE LAST THINGS I SAY TO YOU, BUT...
...DO YOU PREFER DEATH BY BURNING ALIVE IN THE ATMOSPHERE OR BY CHOKING TO DEATH IN SPACE?
I PREFER BEING TALKED TO DEATH BY PHIL COULSON.
ACTUALLY, THERE'S ONE MORE THING...
YEAH? REALLY?
YEAH.

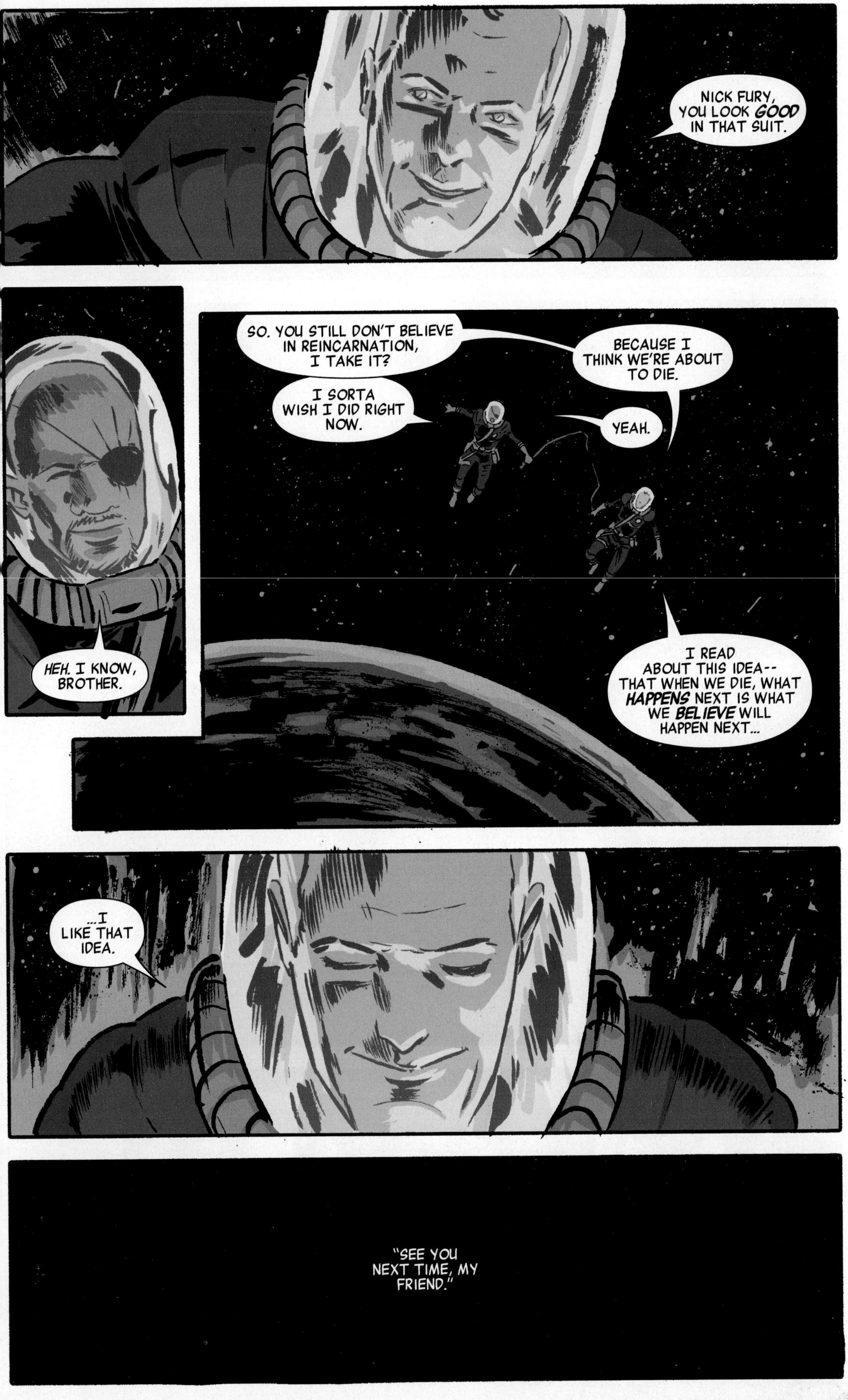
NICK FURY, YOU LOOK GOOD IN THAT SUIT.
HEH. I KNOW, BROTHER.
SO. YOU STILL DON'T BELIEVE IN REINCARNATION, I TAKE IT?
I SORTA WISH I DID RIGHT NOW.
BECAUSE I THINK WE'RE ABOUT TO DIE.
YEAH.
I READ ABOUT THIS IDEA-- THAT WHEN WE DIE, WHAT HAPPENS NEXT IS WHAT WE BELIEVE WILL HAPPEN NEXT...
...I LIKE THAT IDEA.
"SEE YOU NEXT TIME, MY FRIEND."

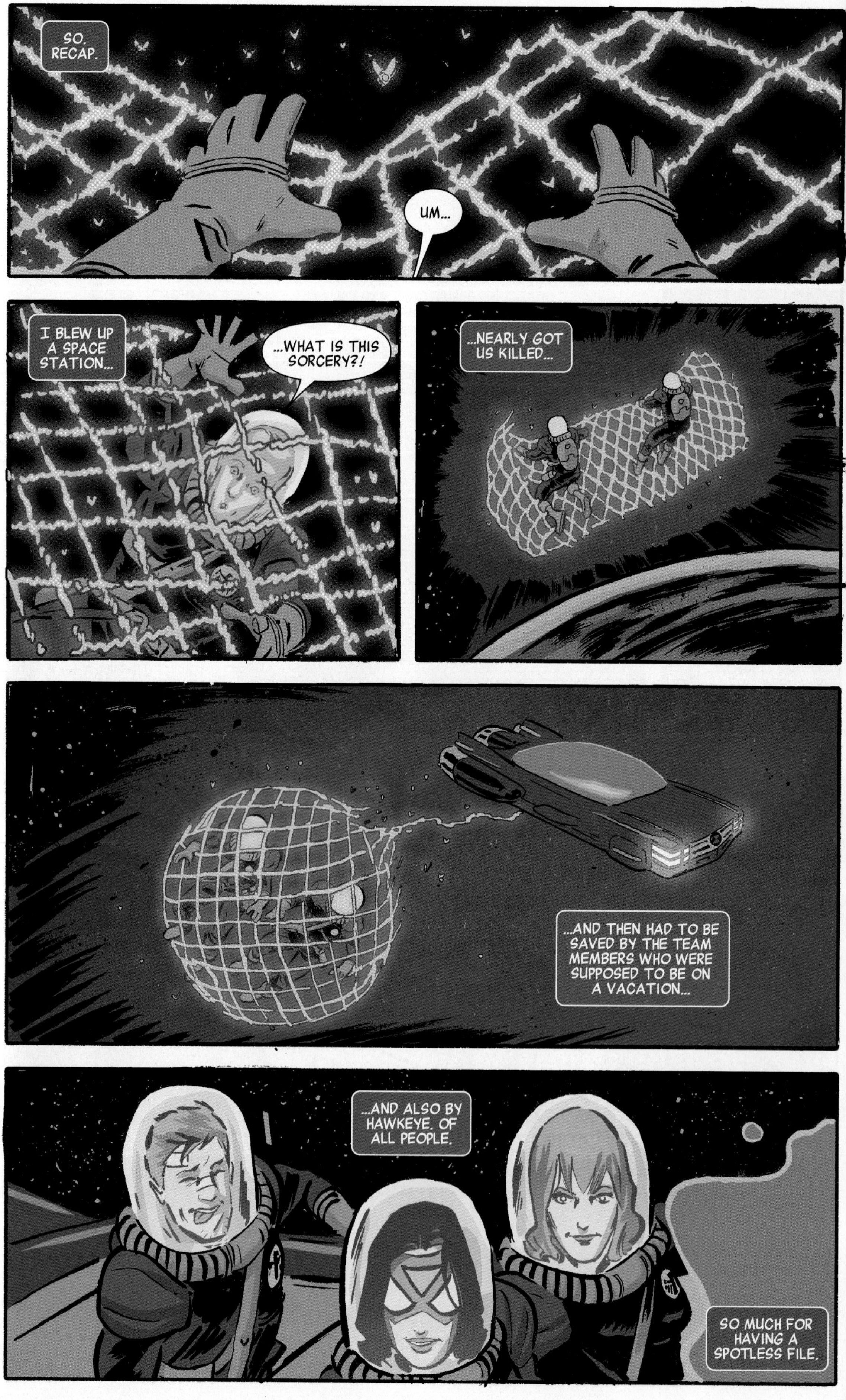
SO. RECAP.
UM...
I BLEW UP A SPACE STATION...
...WHAT IS THIS SORCERY?!
...NEARLY GOT US KILLED...
...AND THEN HAD TO BE SAVED BY THE TEAM MEMBERS WHO WERE SUPPOSED TO BE ON A VACATION...
...AND ALSO BY HAWKEYE. OF ALL PEOPLE.
SO MUCH FOR HAVING A SPOTLESS FILE.

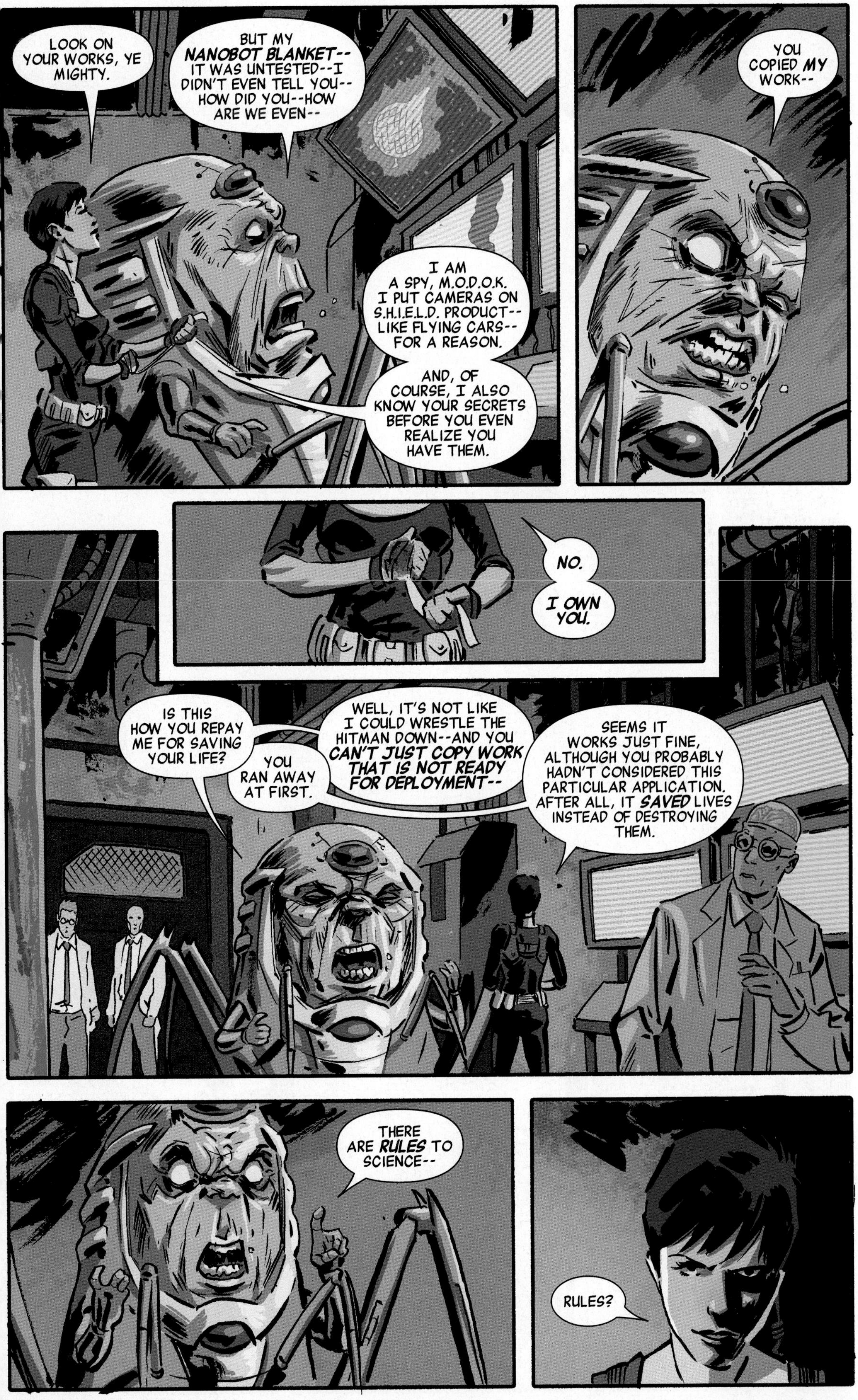
LOOK ON YOUR WORKS, YE MIGHTY.
BUT MY NANOBOT BLANKET-- IT WAS UNTESTED--I DIDN'T EVEN TELL YOU-- HOW DID YOU--HOW ARE WE EVEN--
I AM A SPY, M.O.D.O.K. I PUT CAMERAS ON S.H.I.E.L.D. PRODUCT-- LIKE FLYING CARS-- FOR A REASON.
AND, OF COURSE, I ALSO KNOW YOUR SECRETS BEFORE YOU EVEN REALIZE YOU HAVE THEM.
YOU COPIED MY WORK--
NO.
I OWN YOU.
IS THIS HOW YOU REPAY ME FOR SAVING YOUR LIFE?
YOU RAN AWAY AT FIRST.
WELL, IT'S NOT LIKE I COULD WRESTLE THE HITMAN DOWN--AND YOU CAN'T JUST COPY WORK THAT IS NOT READY FOR DEPLOYMENT--
SEEMS IT WORKS JUST FINE, ALTHOUGH YOU PROBABLY HADN'T CONSIDERED THIS PARTICULAR APPLICATION. AFTER ALL, IT SAVED LIVES INSTEAD OF DESTROYING THEM.
THERE ARE RULES TO SCIENCE--
RULES?

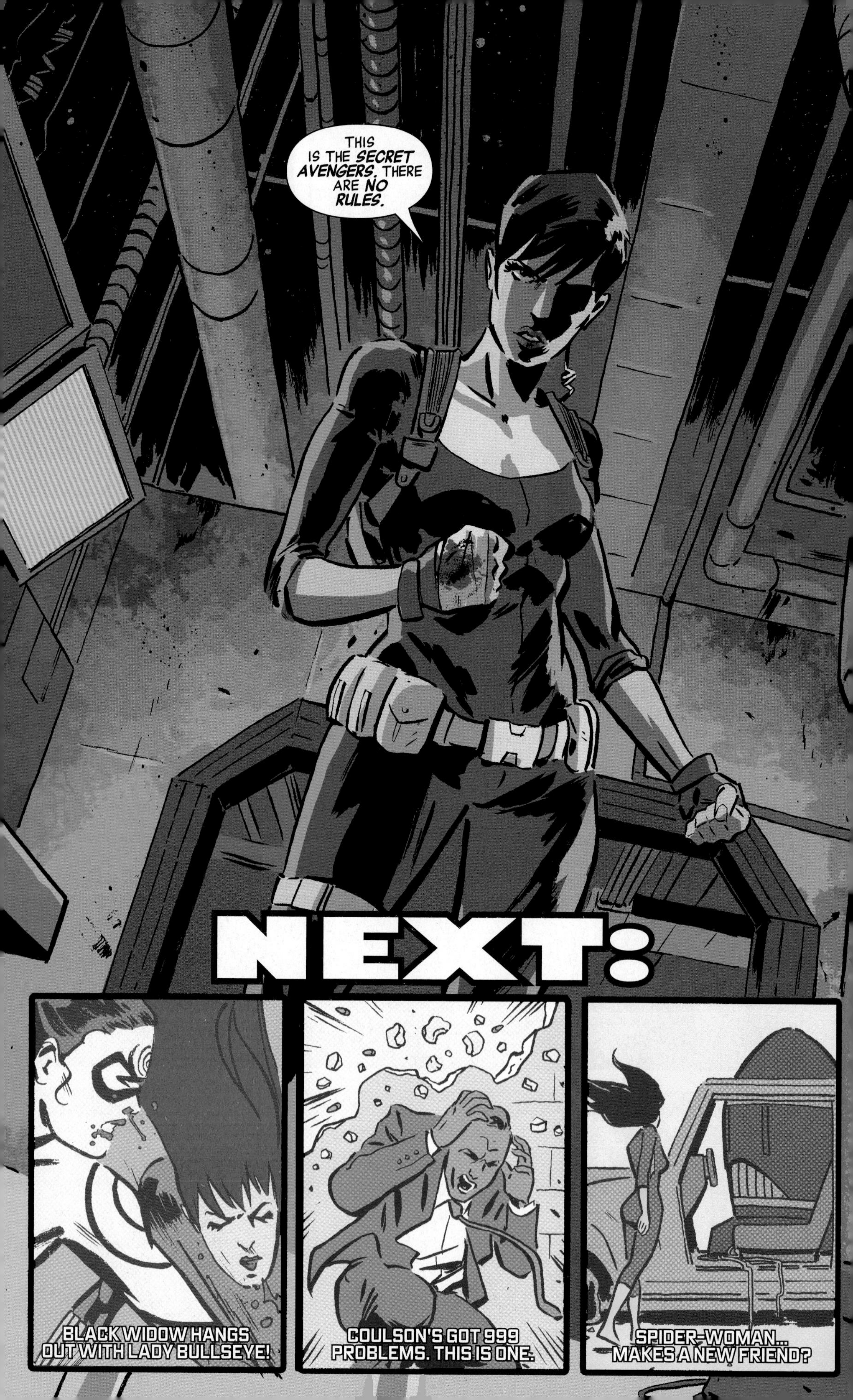
THIS IS THE SECRET AVENGERS. THERE ARE NO RULES.
NEXT:
BLACK WIDOW HANGS OUT WITH LADY BULLSEYE!
COULSON'S GOT 999 PROBLEMS. THIS IS ONE.
SPIDER-WOMAN... MAKES A NEW FRIEND?

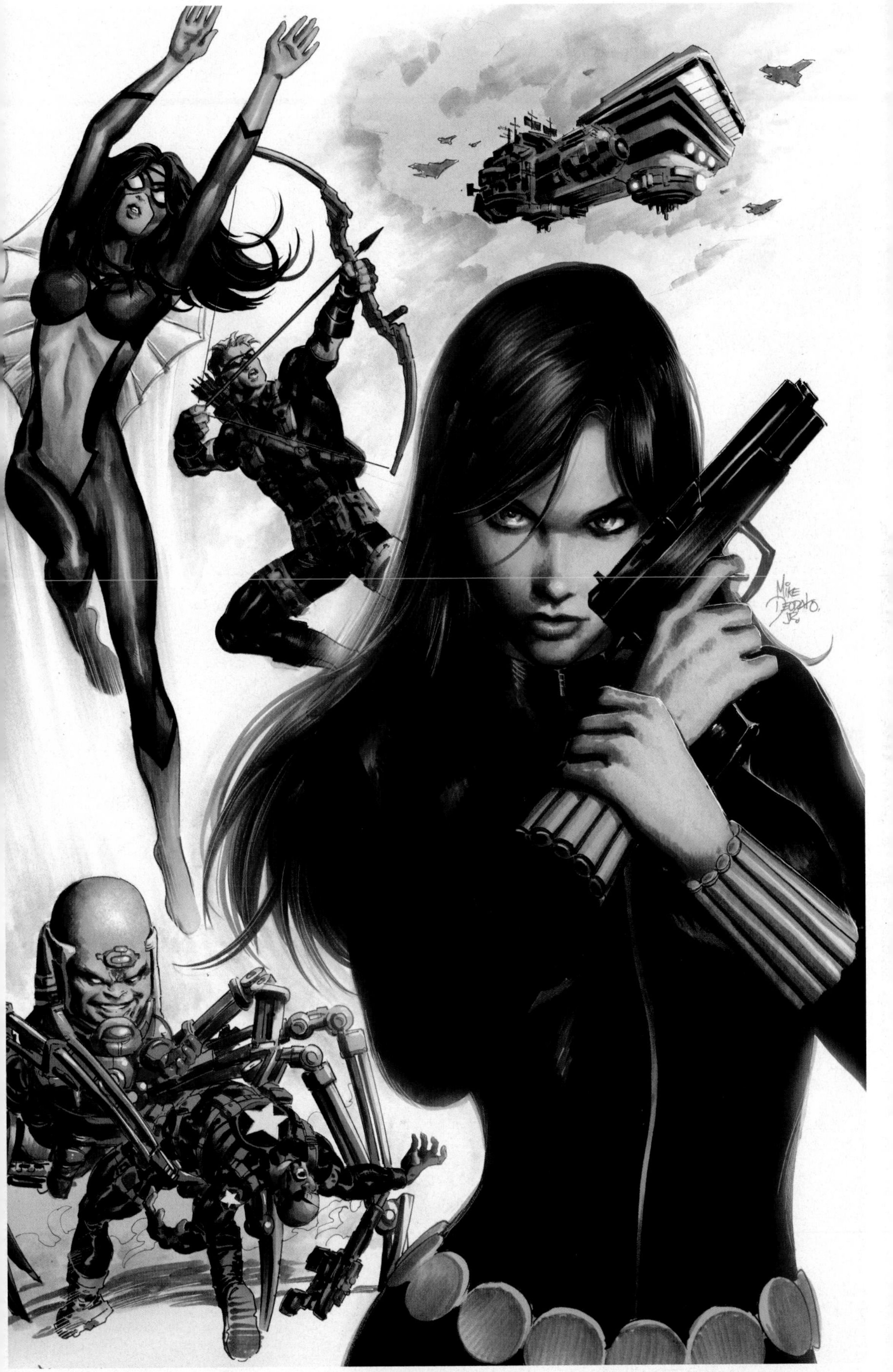

#1 VARIANT BY MIKE DEODATO & FRANK MARTIN

3

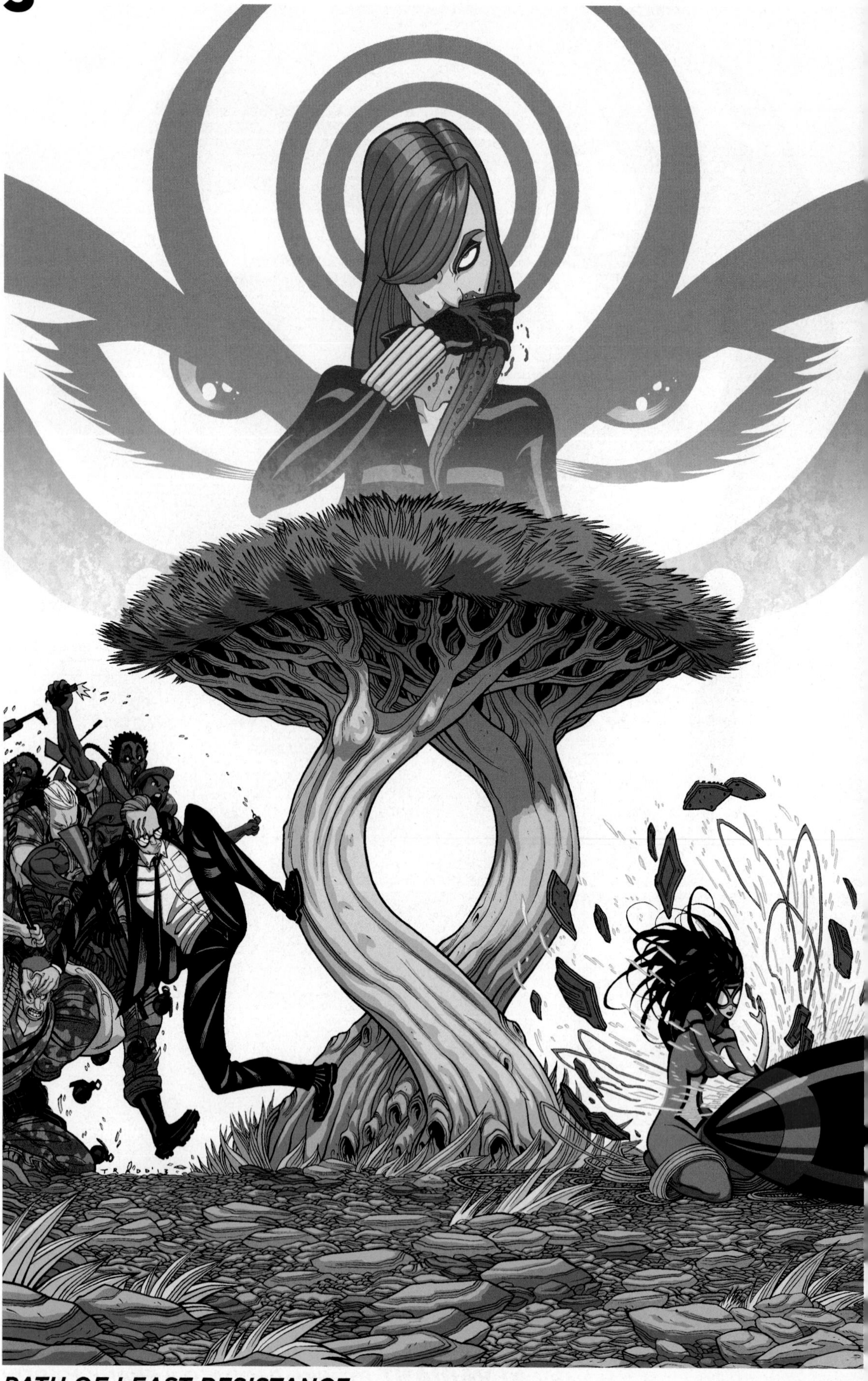

PATH OF LEAST RESISTANCE

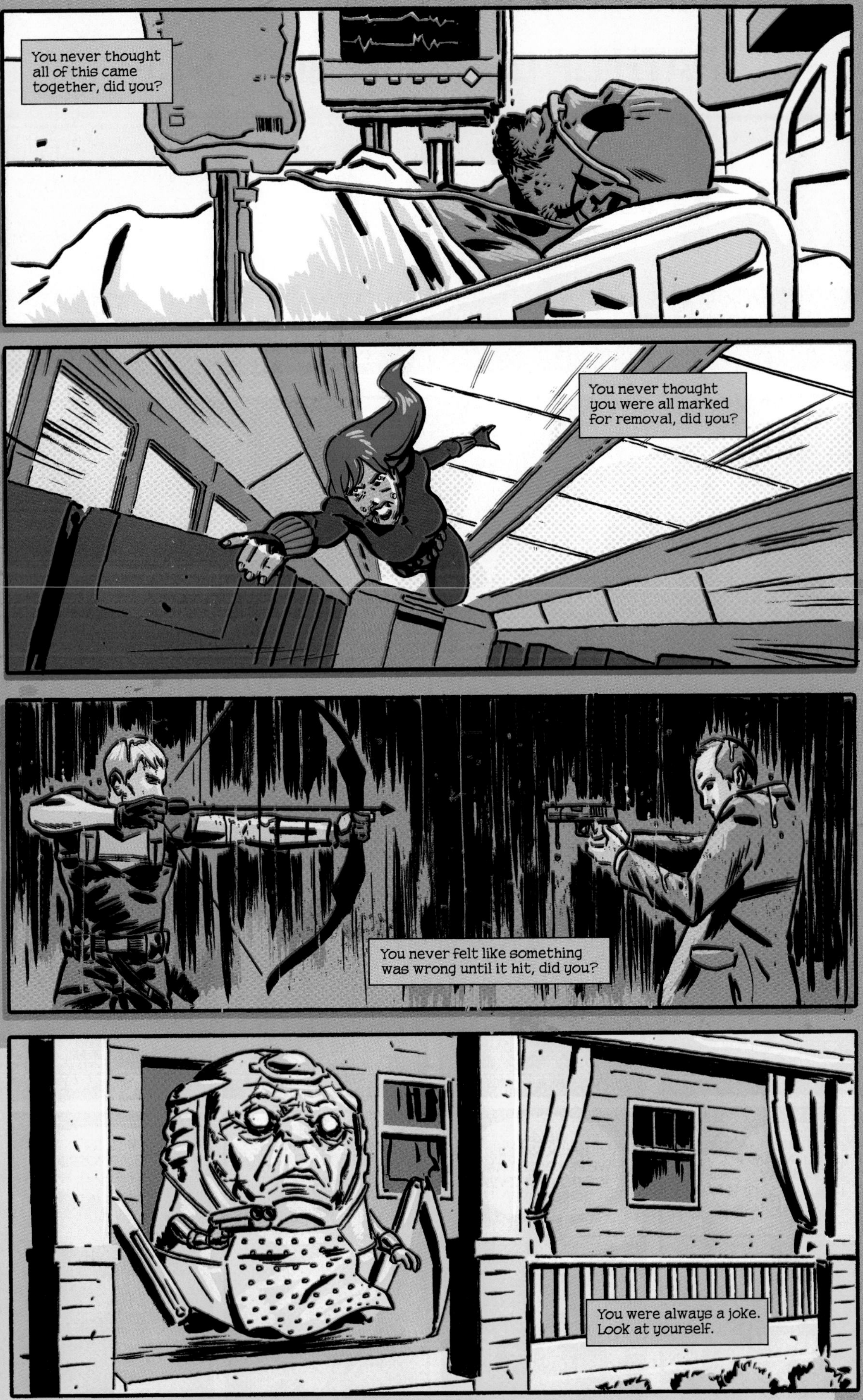
You never thought all of this came together, did you?
You never thought you were all marked for removal, did you?
You never felt like something was wrong until it hit, did you?
You were always a joke. Look at yourself.

"PATH OF LEAST RESISTANCE"

AS OF NOW, YOU ARE OFFICIALLY *SECRET AVENGERS.*

THEN.
S.H.I.E.L.D. HELICARRIER
ILIAD.

MARIA HILL.
Micromanages the Secret Avengers.

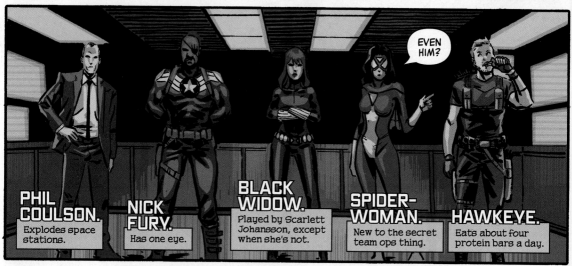

EVEN HIM?

PHIL COULSON.
Explodes space stations.

NICK FURY.
Has one eye.

BLACK WIDOW.
Played by Scarlett Johansson, except when she's not.

SPIDER-WOMAN.
New to the secret team ops thing.

HAWKEYE.
Eats about four protein bars a day.

EVEN THE *TROUBLED ONE,* YES.

HH. "TROUBLED."

DOES *EVERYONE* UNDERSTAND WHAT WE DO?

HAWKEYE?

UM. UMUMMMHMENTT.

WE GO AND DO THE THINGS THE *THUNDERBOLTS* WERE DOING WHEN NORMAN OSBORN WAS IN CHARGE. *BUT* WE'RE THE *GOOD GUYS.*

THANK YOU, NOAM CHOMSKY. FURY. PLEASE.

WE GO IN WHEREVER WE'RE NEEDED AND WE DO WHATEVER IS REQUIRED.

MINIMAL NOISE. MAXIMAL EFFECTIVITY.

KILL AS LITTLE AS POSSIBLE. THINK ABOUT P.R.

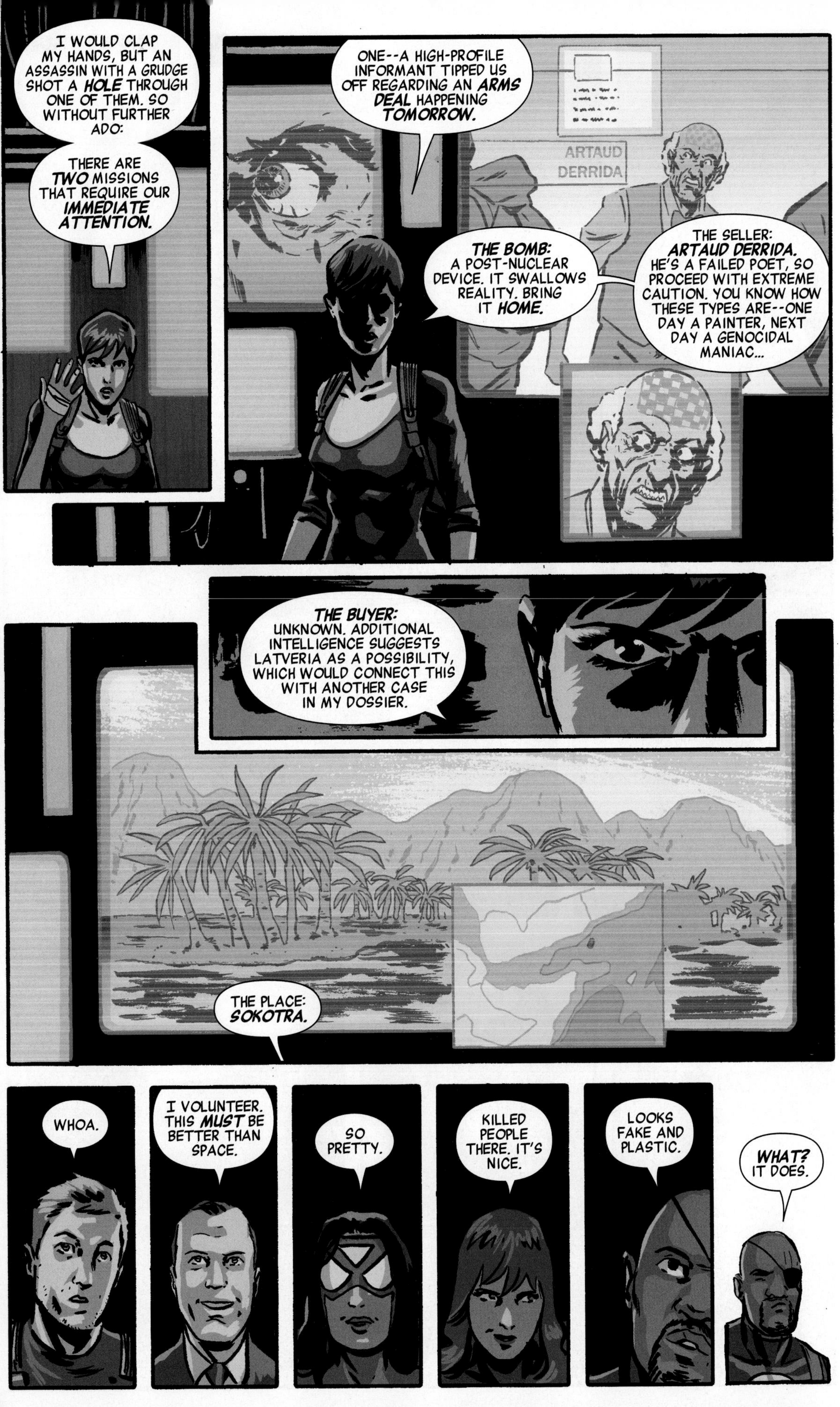
I WOULD CLAP MY HANDS, BUT AN ASSASSIN WITH A GRUDGE SHOT A HOLE THROUGH ONE OF THEM. SO WITHOUT FURTHER ADO:
THERE ARE TWO MISSIONS THAT REQUIRE OUR IMMEDIATE ATTENTION.
ONE--A HIGH-PROFILE INFORMANT TIPPED US OFF REGARDING AN ARMS DEAL HAPPENING TOMORROW.
ARTAUD DERRIDA
THE BOMB: A POST-NUCLEAR DEVICE. IT SWALLOWS REALITY. BRING IT HOME.
THE SELLER: ARTAUD DERRIDA. HE'S A FAILED POET, SO PROCEED WITH EXTREME CAUTION. YOU KNOW HOW THESE TYPES ARE--ONE DAY A PAINTER, NEXT DAY A GENOCIDAL MANIAC...
THE BUYER: UNKNOWN. ADDITIONAL INTELLIGENCE SUGGESTS LATVERIA AS A POSSIBILITY, WHICH WOULD CONNECT THIS WITH ANOTHER CASE IN MY DOSSIER.
THE PLACE: SOKOTRA.
WHOA.
I VOLUNTEER. THIS MUST BE BETTER THAN SPACE.
SO PRETTY.
KILLED PEOPLE THERE. IT'S NICE.
LOOKS FAKE AND PLASTIC.
WHAT? IT DOES.

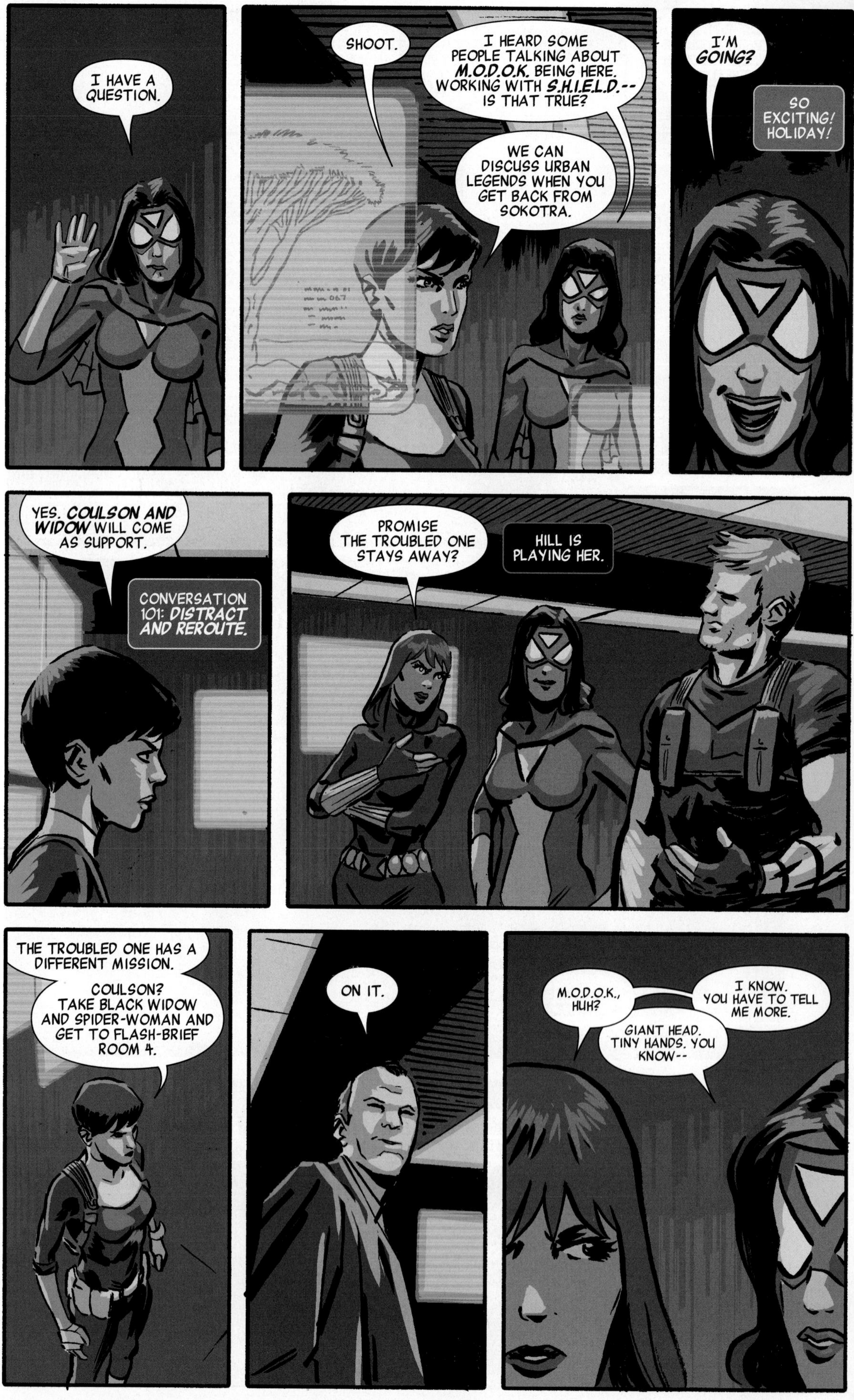
I HAVE A QUESTION.
SHOOT.
I HEARD SOME PEOPLE TALKING ABOUT M.O.D.O.K. BEING HERE. WORKING WITH S.H.I.E.L.D.-- IS THAT TRUE?
WE CAN DISCUSS URBAN LEGENDS WHEN YOU GET BACK FROM SOKOTRA.
I'M GOING?
SO EXCITING! HOLIDAY!
YES. COULSON AND WIDOW WILL COME AS SUPPORT.
CONVERSATION 101: DISTRACT AND REROUTE.
PROMISE THE TROUBLED ONE STAYS AWAY?
HILL IS PLAYING HER.
THE TROUBLED ONE HAS A DIFFERENT MISSION.
COULSON? TAKE BLACK WIDOW AND SPIDER-WOMAN AND GET TO FLASH-BRIEF ROOM 4.
ON IT.
M.O.D.O.K., HUH?
I KNOW. YOU HAVE TO TELL ME MORE.
GIANT HEAD. TINY HANDS. YOU KNOW--

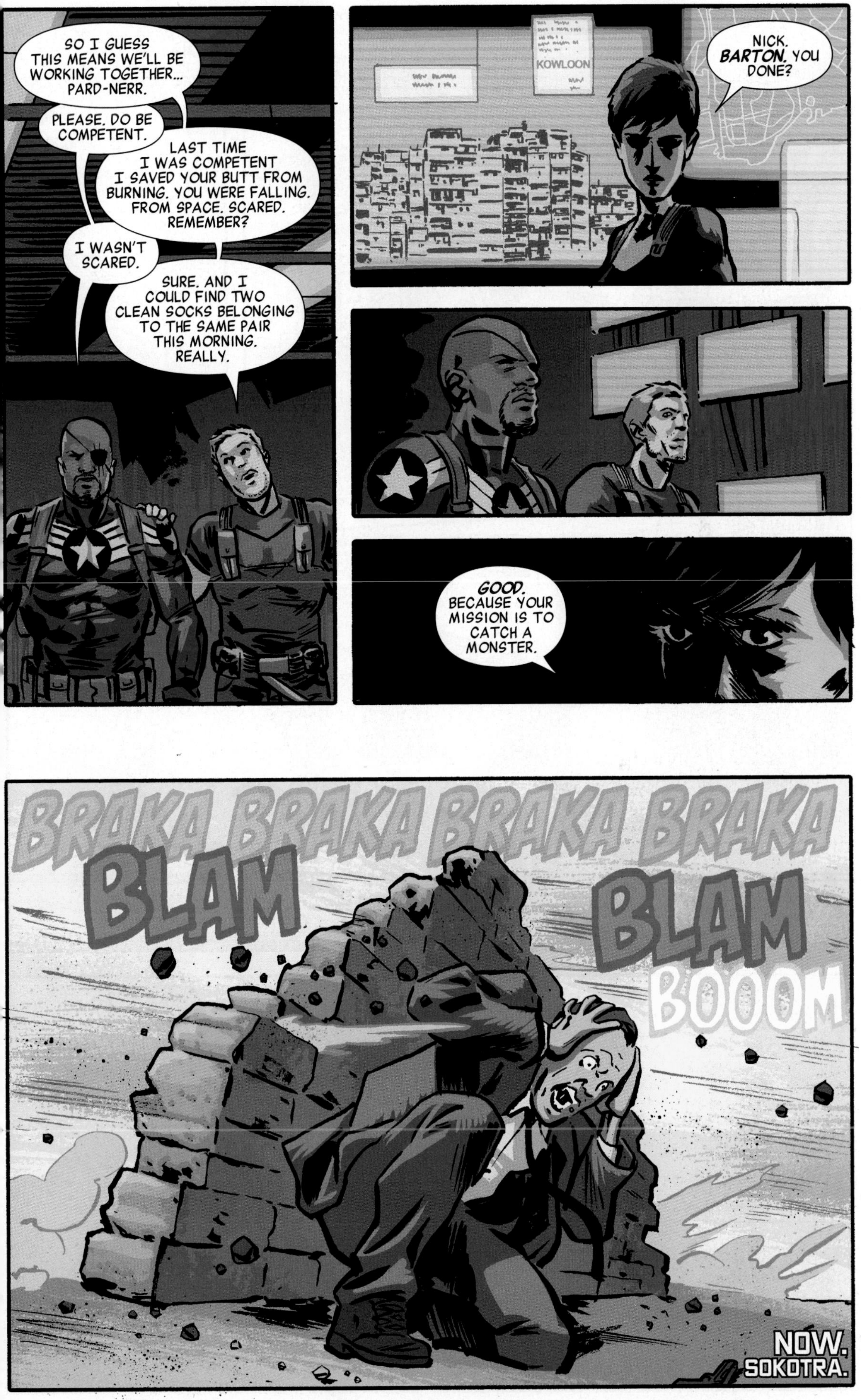
SO I GUESS THIS MEANS WE'LL BE WORKING TOGETHER... PARD-NERR.
PLEASE. DO BE COMPETENT.
LAST TIME I WAS COMPETENT I SAVED YOUR BUTT FROM BURNING. YOU WERE FALLING. FROM SPACE. SCARED. REMEMBER?
I WASN'T SCARED.
SURE. AND I COULD FIND TWO CLEAN SOCKS BELONGING TO THE SAME PAIR THIS MORNING. REALLY.
KOWLOON
NICK. BARTON. YOU DONE?
GOOD. BECAUSE YOUR MISSION IS TO CATCH A MONSTER.
BRAKA BRAKA BRAKA BRAKA
BLAM
BLAM
BOOOM
NOW. SOKOTRA.

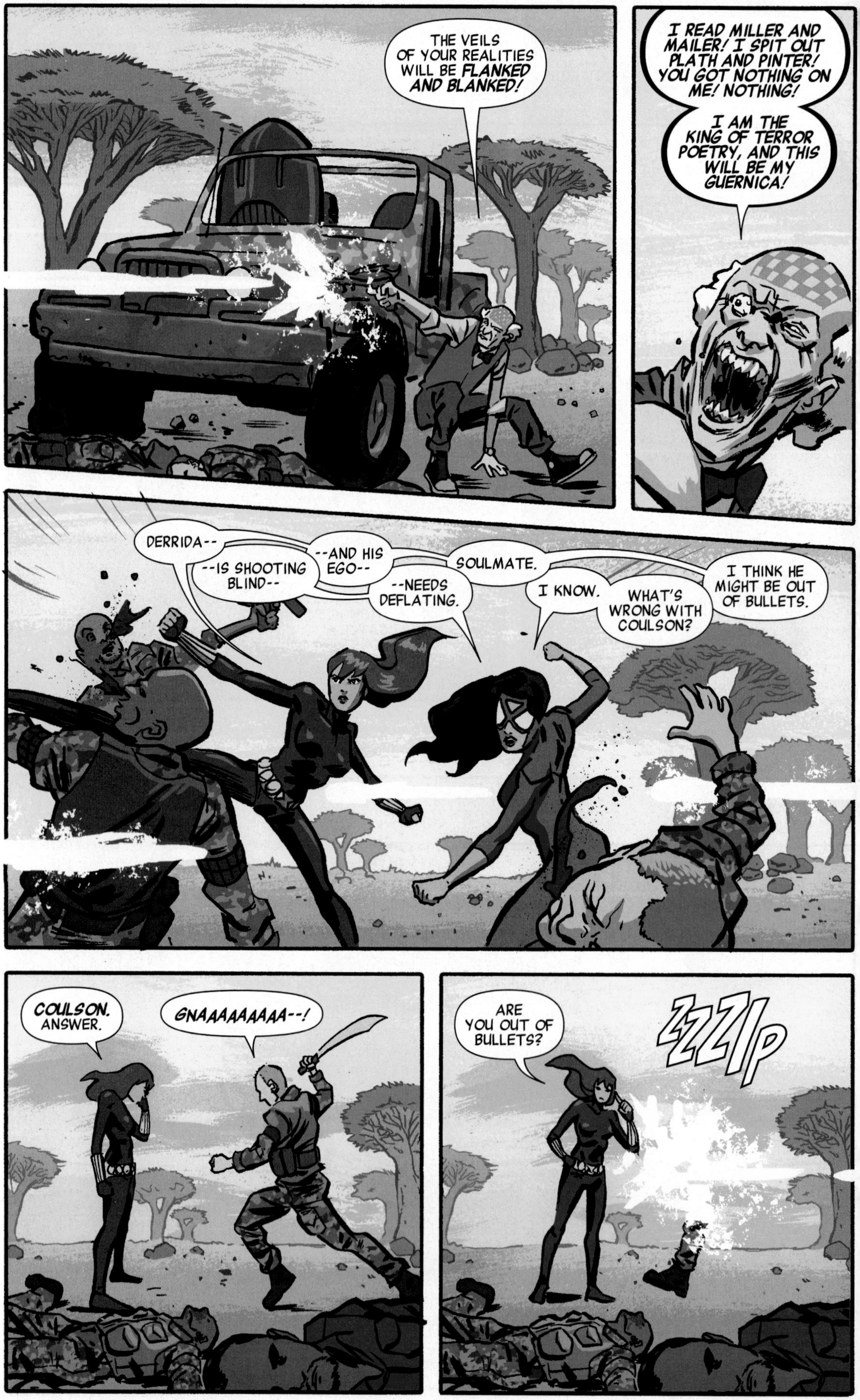
THE VEILS OF YOUR REALITIES WILL BE FLANKED AND BLANKED!
I READ MILLER AND MAILER! I SPIT OUT PLATH AND PINTER! YOU GOT NOTHING ON ME! NOTHING!
I AM THE KING OF TERROR POETRY, AND THIS WILL BE MY GUERNICA!
DERRIDA--
--IS SHOOTING BLIND--
--AND HIS EGO--
--NEEDS DEFLATING.
SOULMATE.
I KNOW.
WHAT'S WRONG WITH COULSON?
I THINK HE MIGHT BE OUT OF BULLETS.
COULSON. ANSWER.
GNAAAAAAAAA--!
ARE YOU OUT OF BULLETS?
ZZZIP

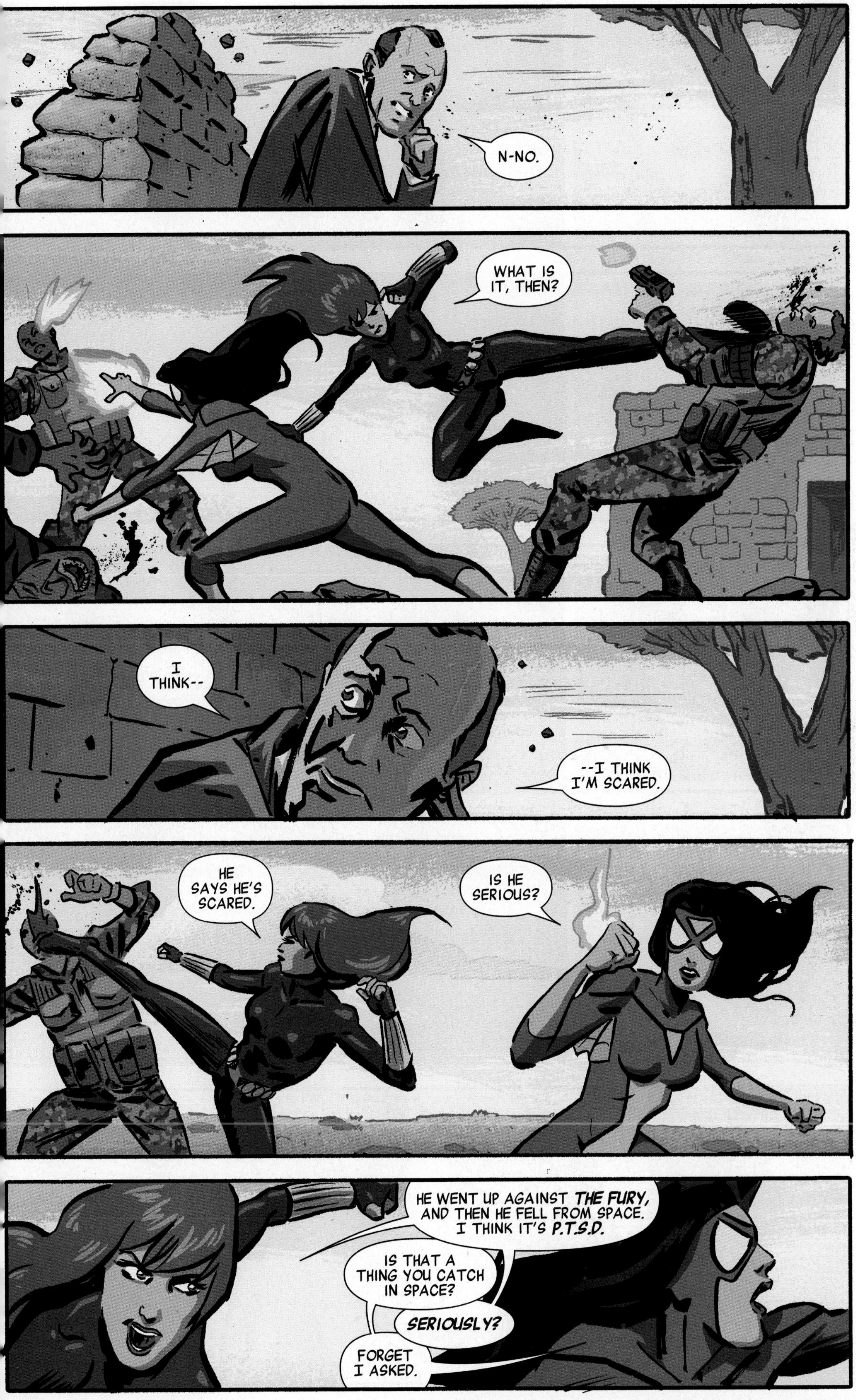
N-NO.
WHAT IS IT, THEN?
I THINK--
--I THINK I'M SCARED.
HE SAYS HE'S SCARED.
IS HE SERIOUS?
HE WENT UP AGAINST THE FURY, AND THEN HE FELL FROM SPACE. I THINK IT'S P.T.S.D.
IS THAT A THING YOU CATCH IN SPACE?
SERIOUSLY?
FORGET I ASKED.

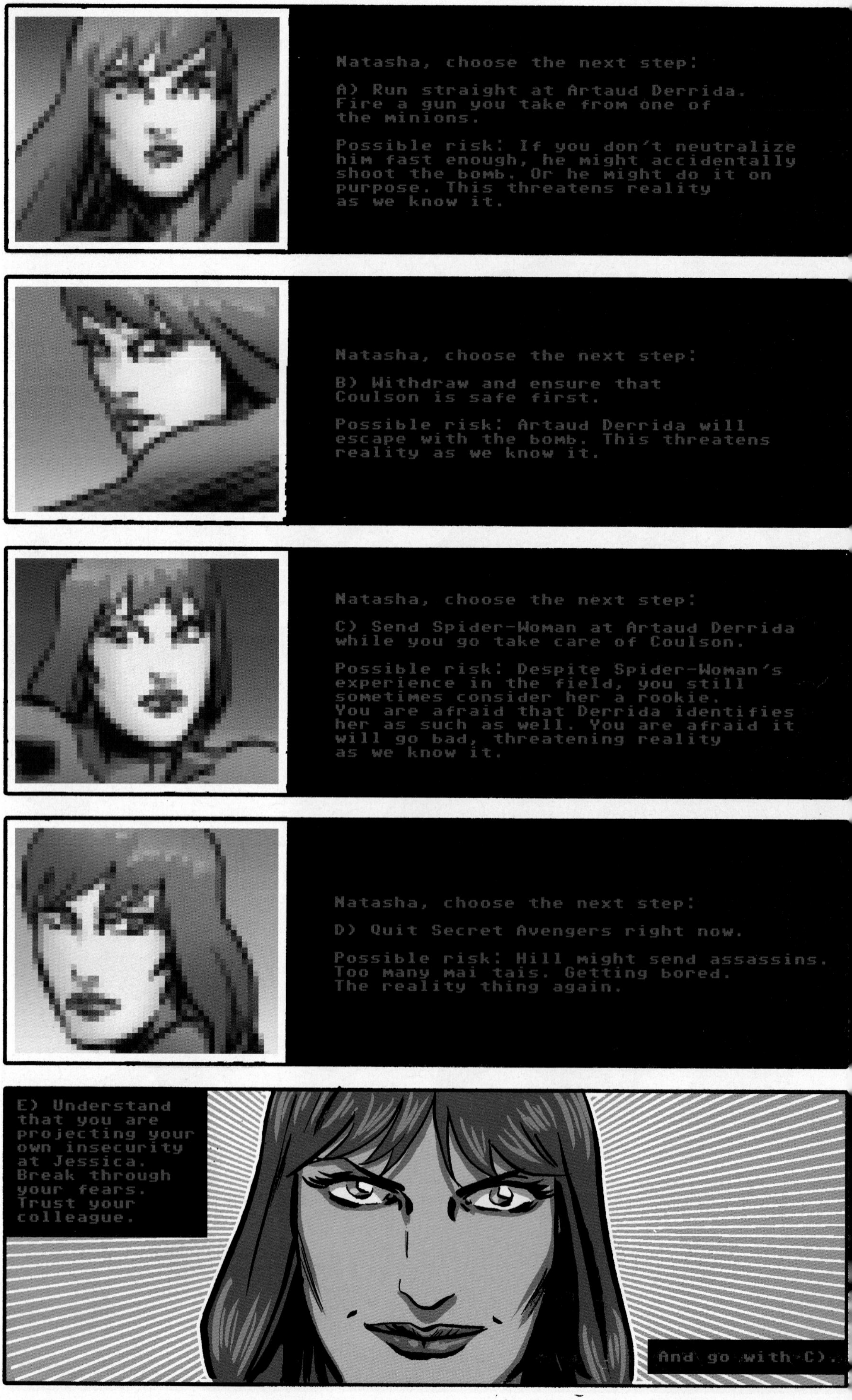
Natasha, choose the next step:
A) Run straight at Artaud Derrida. Fire a gun you take from one of the minions.
Possible risk: If you don't neutralize him fast enough, he might accidentally shoot the bomb. Or he might do it on purpose. This threatens reality as we know it.
Natasha, choose the next step:
B) Withdraw and ensure that Coulson is safe first.
Possible risk: Artaud Derrida will escape with the bomb. This threatens reality as we know it.
Natasha, choose the next step:
C) Send Spider-Woman at Artaud Derrida while you go take care of Coulson.
Possible risk: Despite Spider-Woman's experience in the field, you still sometimes consider her a rookie. You are afraid that Derrida identifies her as such as well. You are afraid it will go bad, threatening reality as we know it.
Natasha, choose the next step:
D) Quit Secret Avengers right now.
Possible risk: Hill might send assassins. Too many mai tais. Getting bored. The reality thing again.
E) Understand that you are projecting your own insecurity at Jessica. Break through your fears. Trust your colleague.
And go with C).

JESSICA! GET HIM!

ON IT!

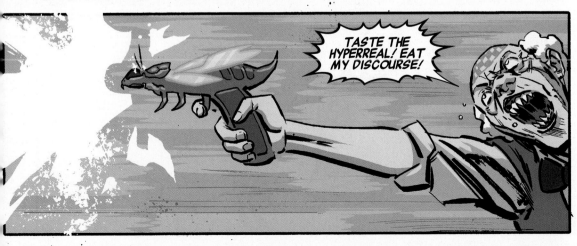

TASTE THE HYPERREAL! EAT MY DISCOURSE!

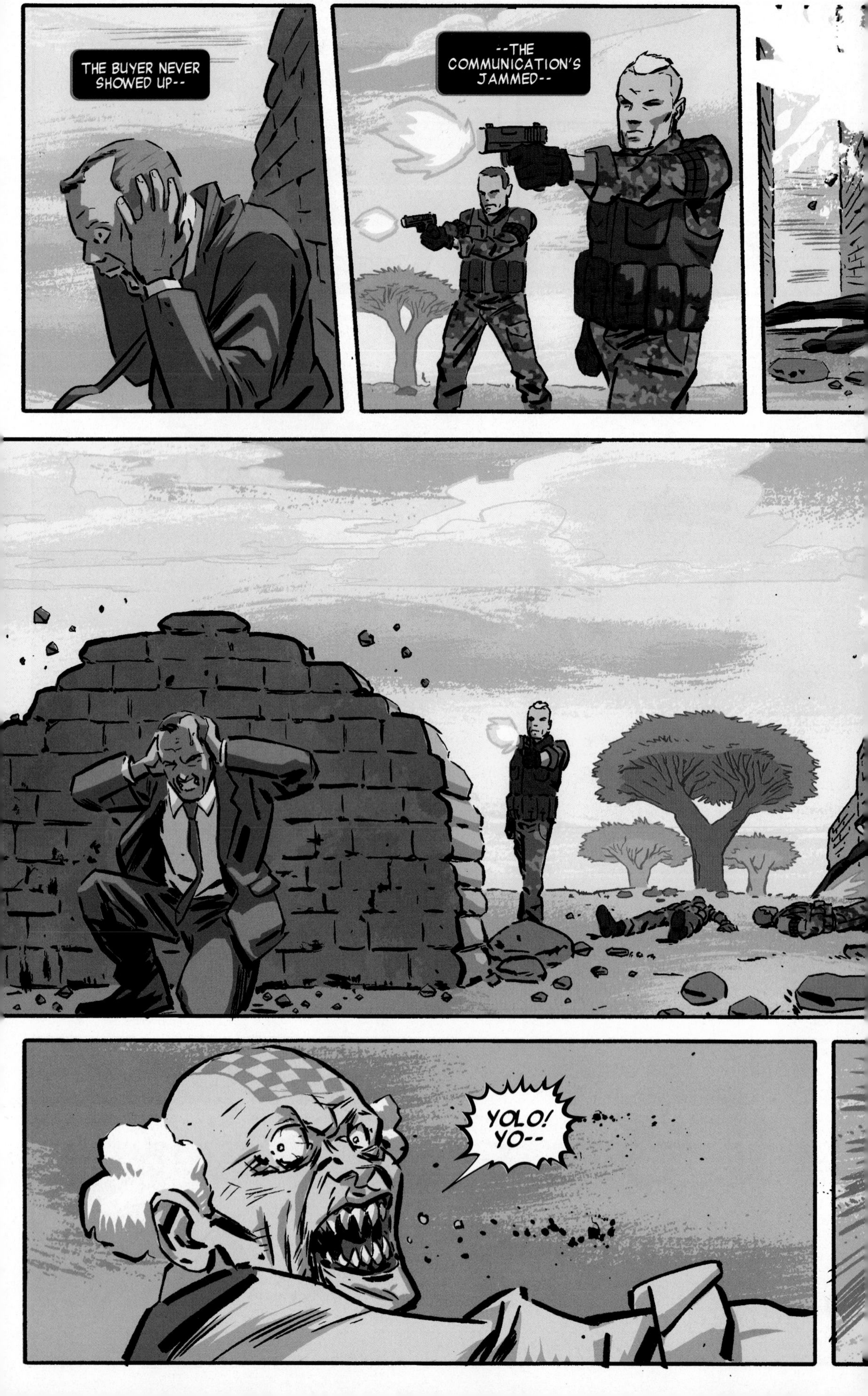
THE BUYER NEVER SHOWED UP--
--THE COMMUNICATION'S JAMMED--
YOLO! YO--

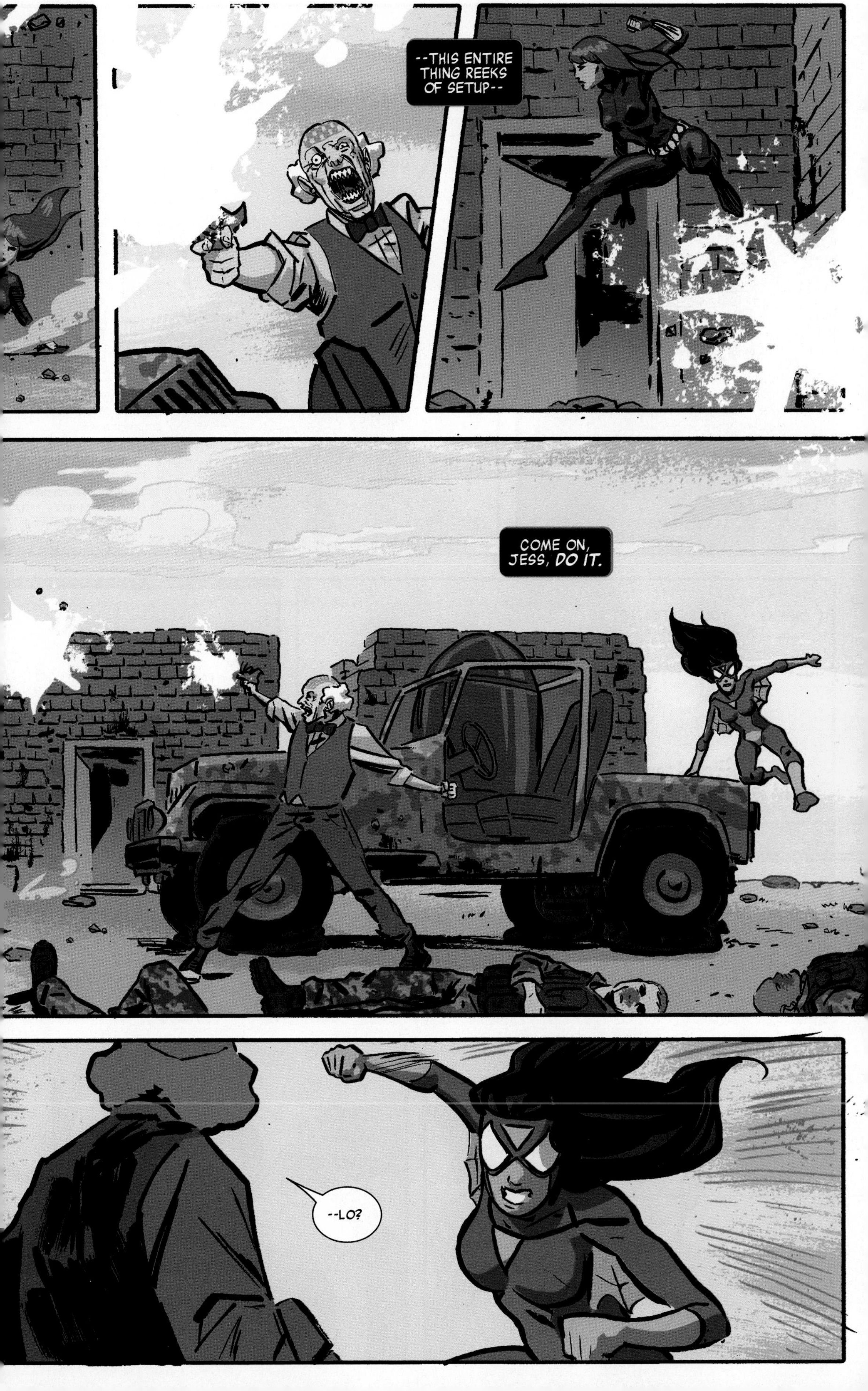
--THIS ENTIRE THING REEKS OF SETUP--
COME ON, JESS, DO IT.
--LO?

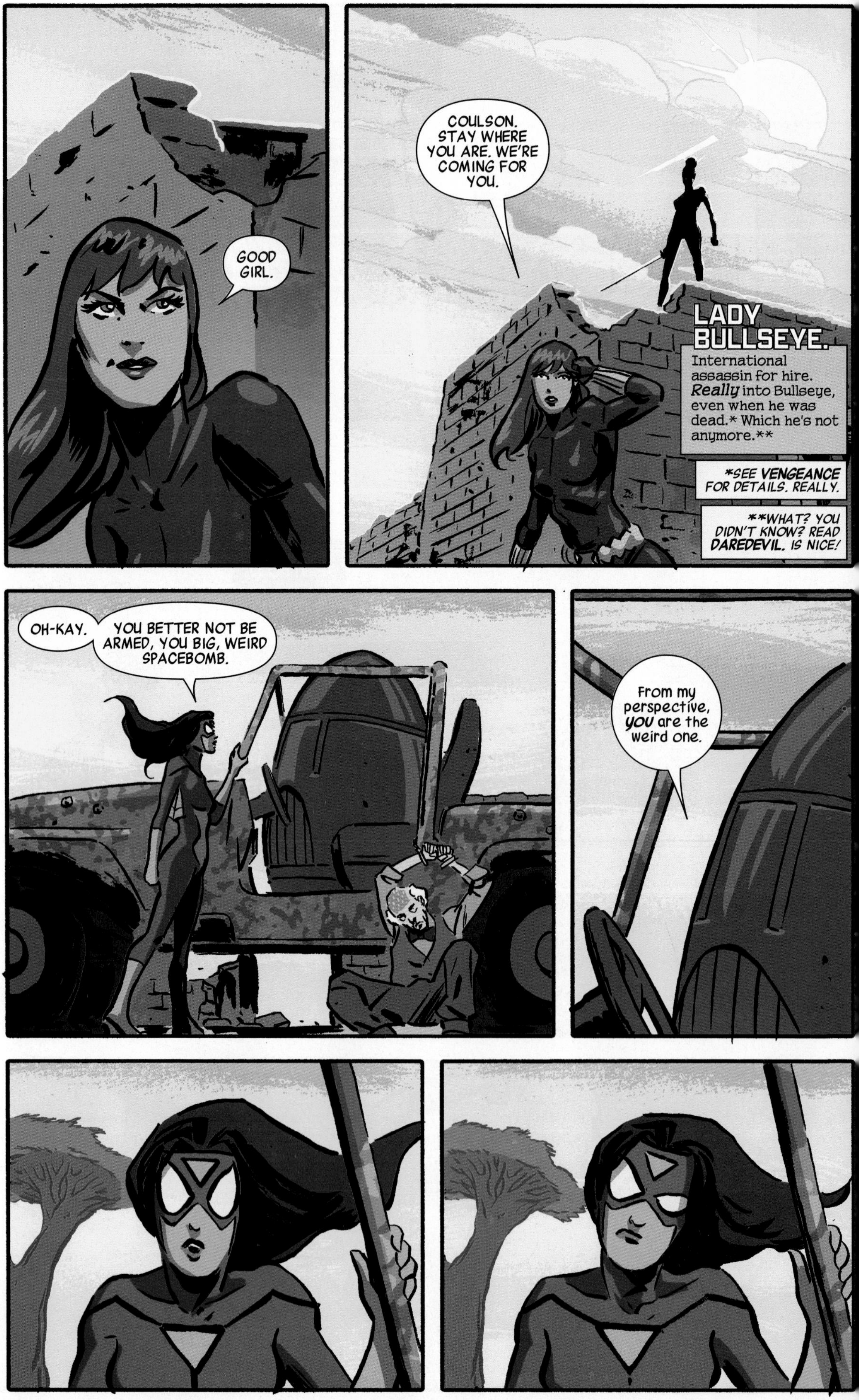
GOOD GIRL.
COULSON. STAY WHERE YOU ARE. WE'RE COMING FOR YOU.
LADY BULLSEYE.
International assassin for hire. Really into Bullseye, even when he was dead.* Which he's not anymore.**
*SEE VENGEANCE FOR DETAILS. REALLY.
**WHAT? YOU DIDN'T KNOW? READ DAREDEVIL. IS NICE!
OH-KAY.
YOU BETTER NOT BE ARMED, YOU BIG, WEIRD SPACEBOMB.
From my perspective, YOU are the weird one.

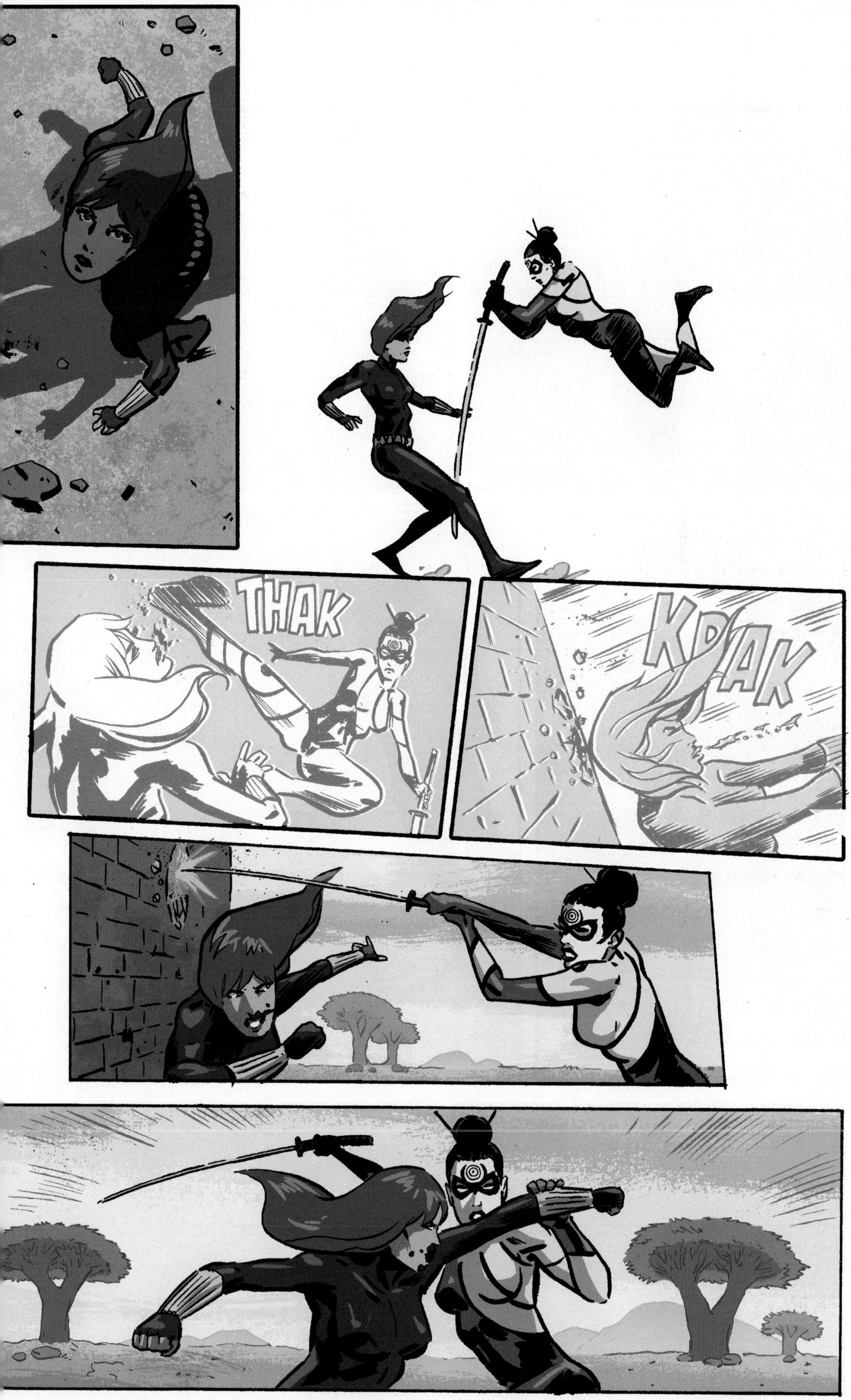
THAK
KRAK

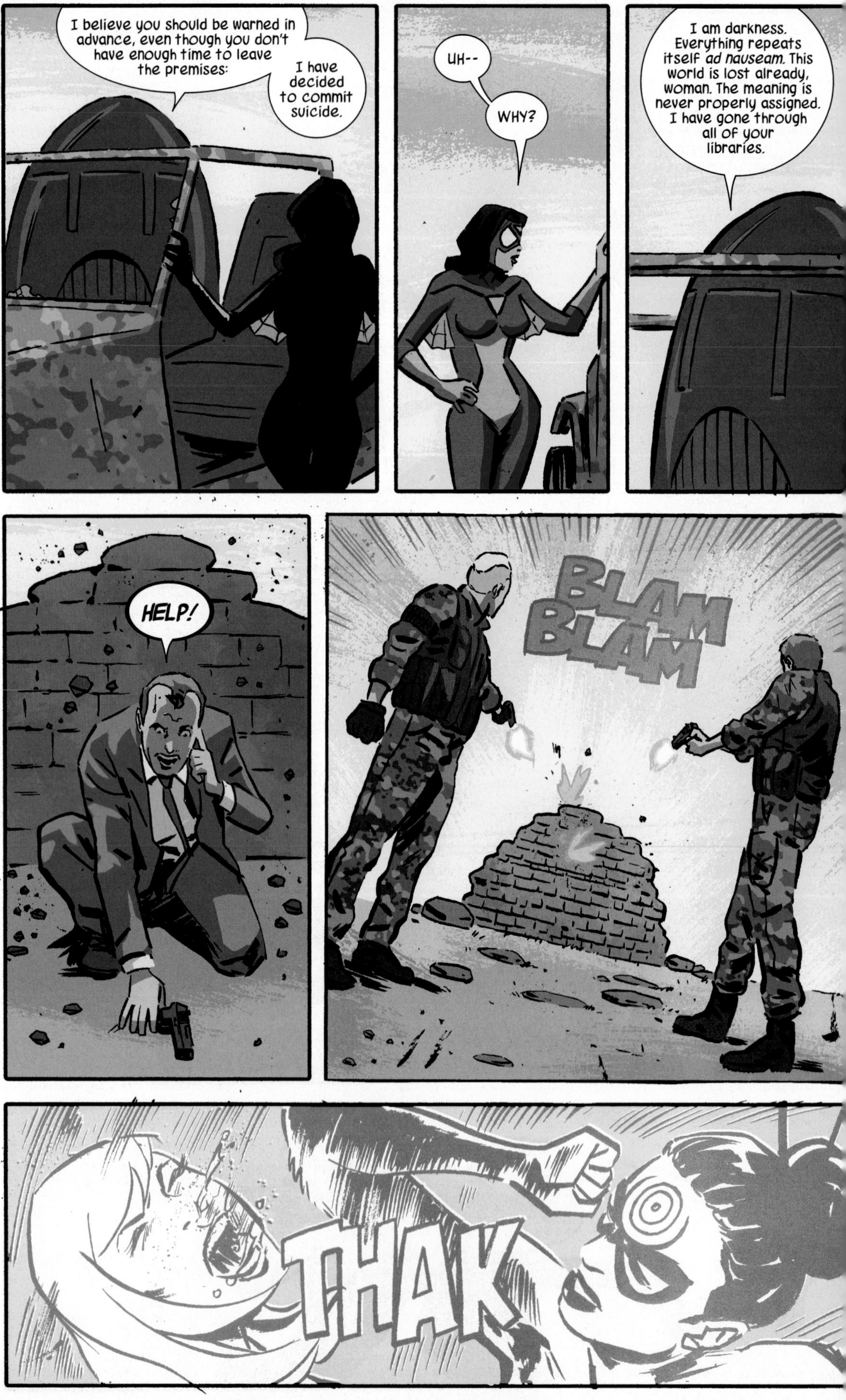
I believe you should be warned in advance, even though you don't have enough time to leave the premises:
I have decided to commit suicide.
UH--
WHY?
I am darkness. Everything repeats itself *ad nauseam*. This world is lost already, woman. The meaning is never properly assigned. I have gone through all of your libraries.
HELP!
BLAM BLAM
THAK

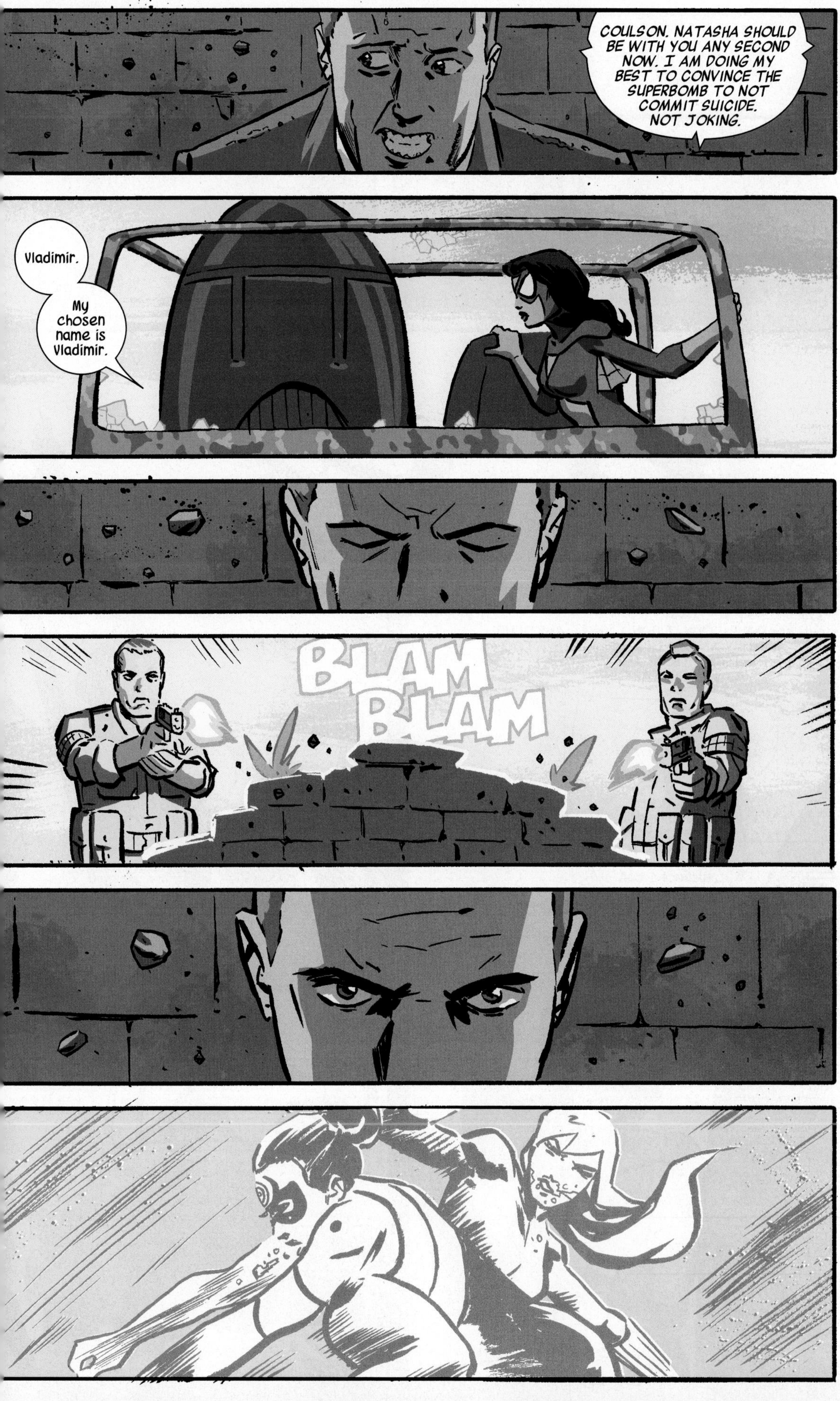
COULSON. NATASHA SHOULD BE WITH YOU ANY SECOND NOW. I AM DOING MY BEST TO CONVINCE THE SUPERBOMB TO NOT COMMIT SUICIDE. NOT JOKING.
Vladimir.
My chosen name is Vladimir.
BLAM
BLAM

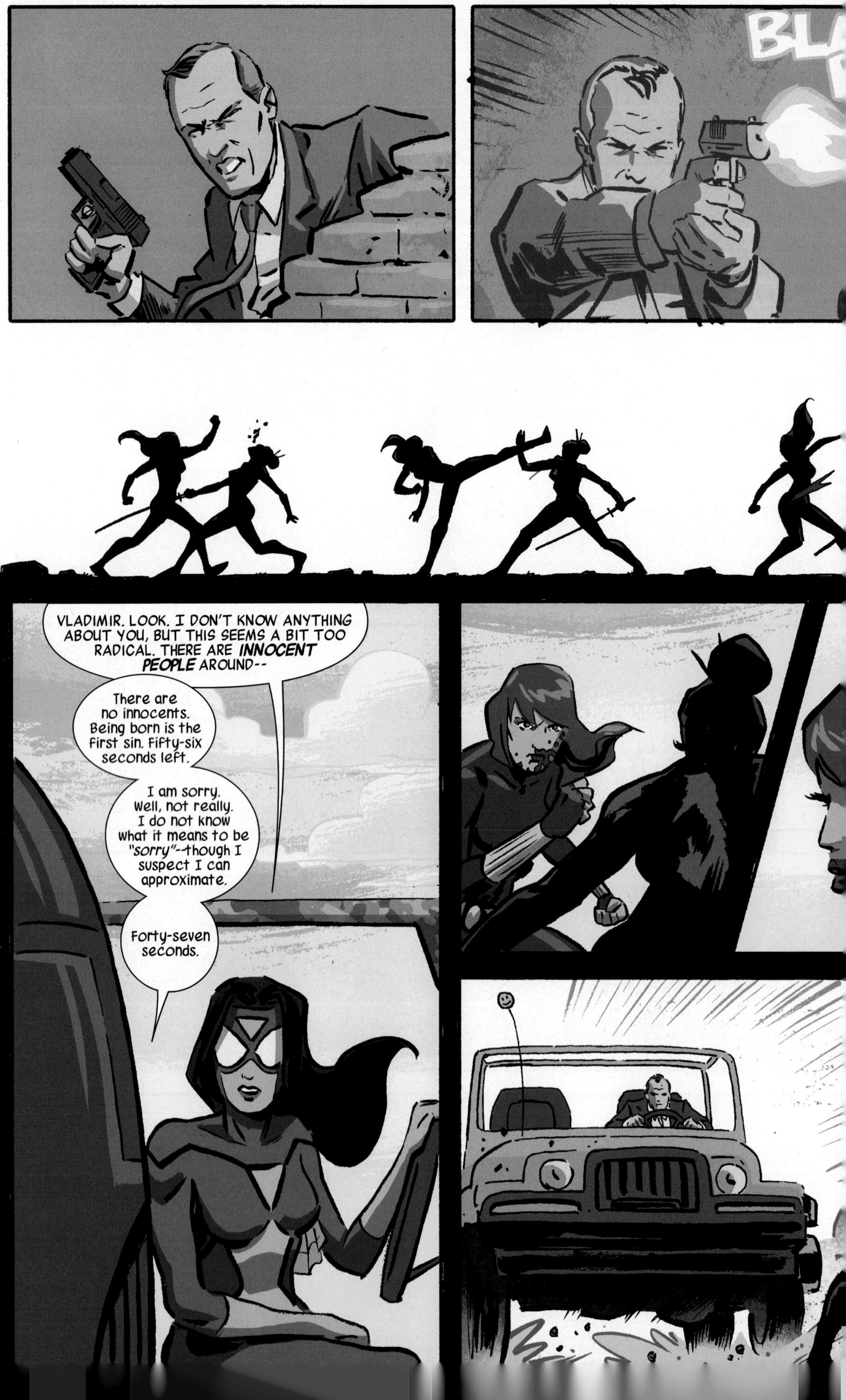
VLADIMIR. LOOK. I DON'T KNOW ANYTHING ABOUT YOU, BUT THIS SEEMS A BIT TOO RADICAL. THERE ARE INNOCENT PEOPLE AROUND--
There are no innocents. Being born is the first sin. Fifty-six seconds left.
I am sorry. Well, not really. I do not know what it means to be "sorry"--though I suspect I can approximate.
Forty-seven seconds.

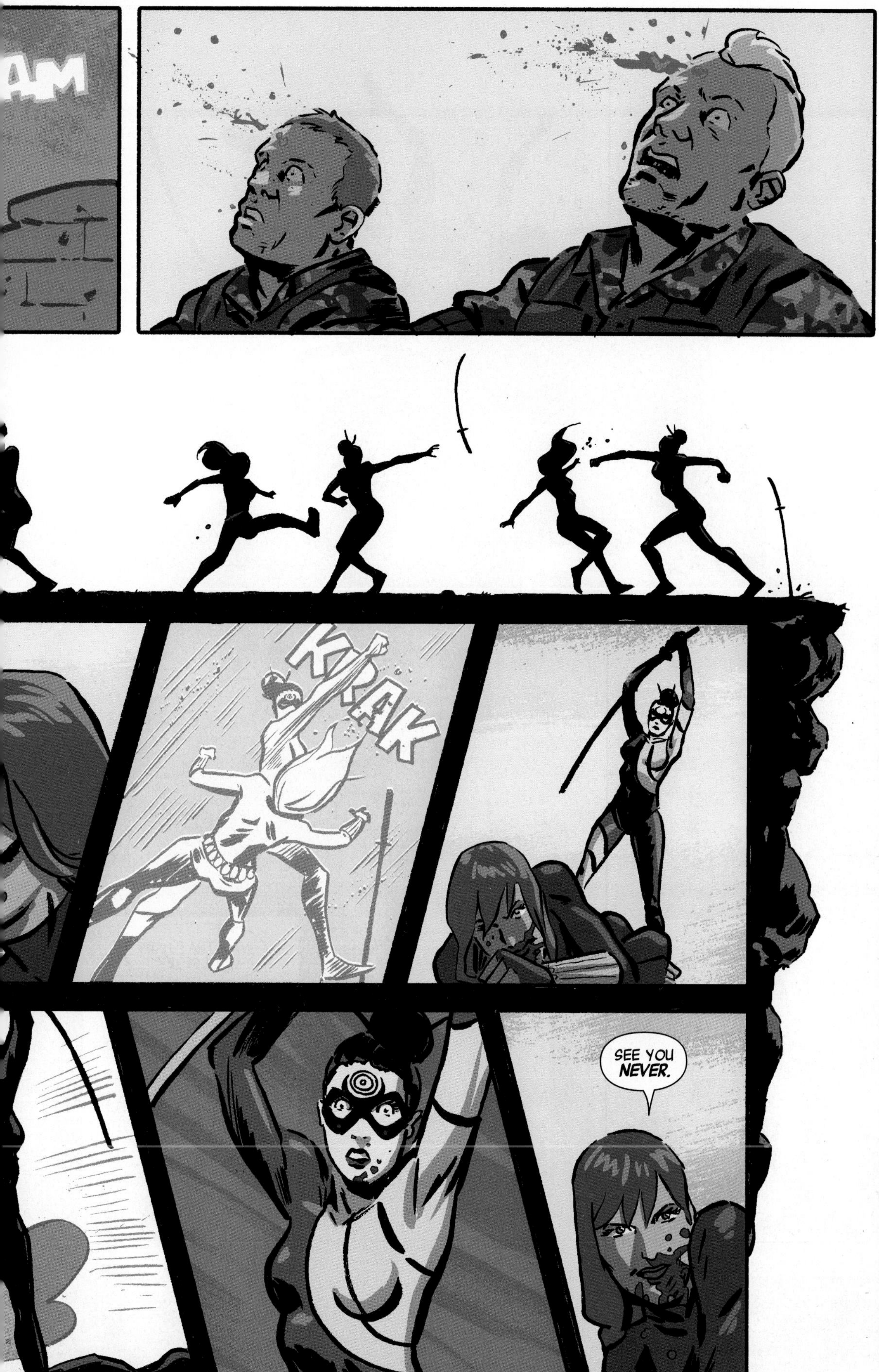
KRAK
SEE YOU NEVER.

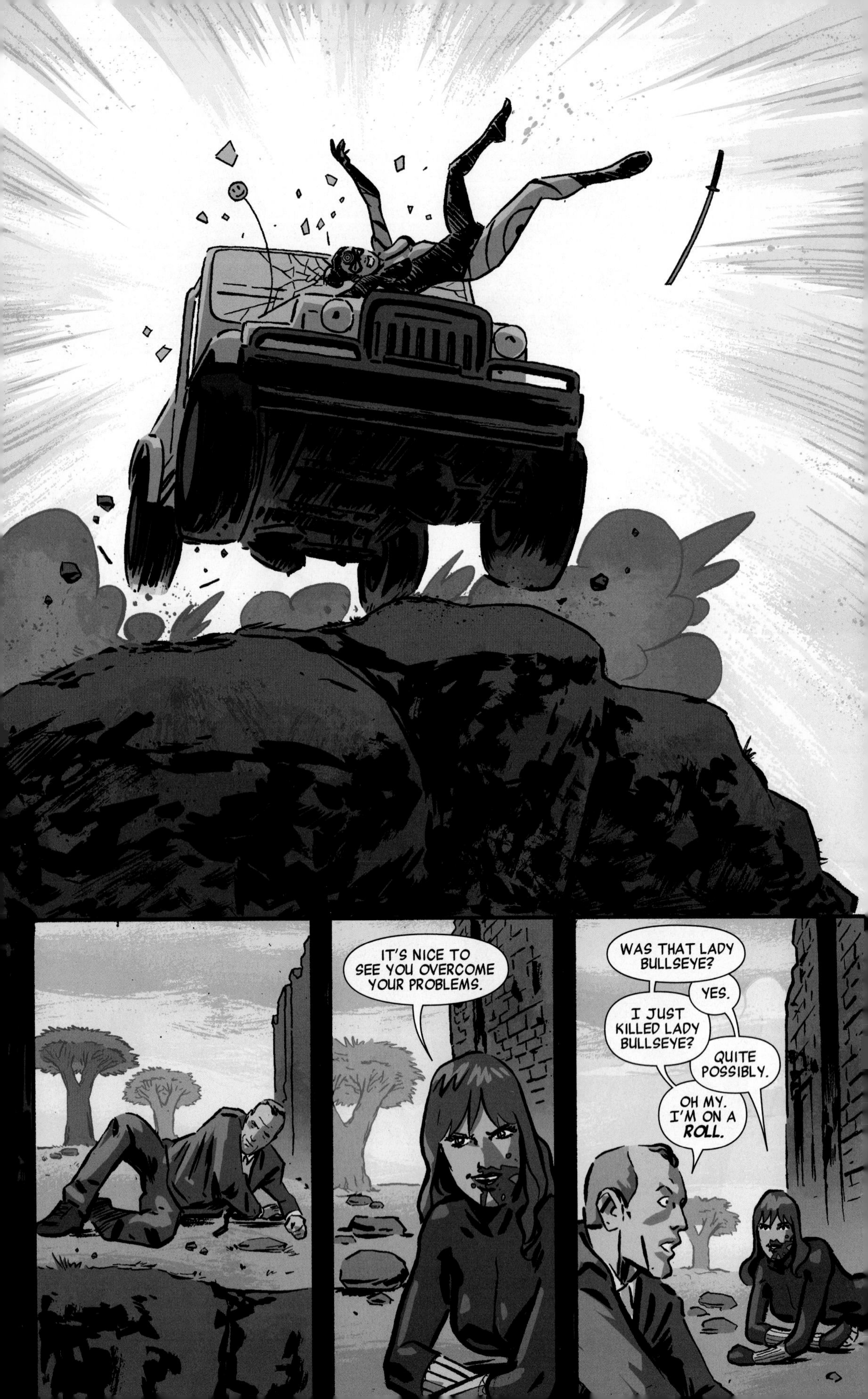
IT'S NICE TO SEE YOU OVERCOME YOUR PROBLEMS.
WAS THAT LADY BULLSEYE?
YES.
I JUST KILLED LADY BULLSEYE?
QUITE POSSIBLY.
OH MY. I'M ON A ROLL.

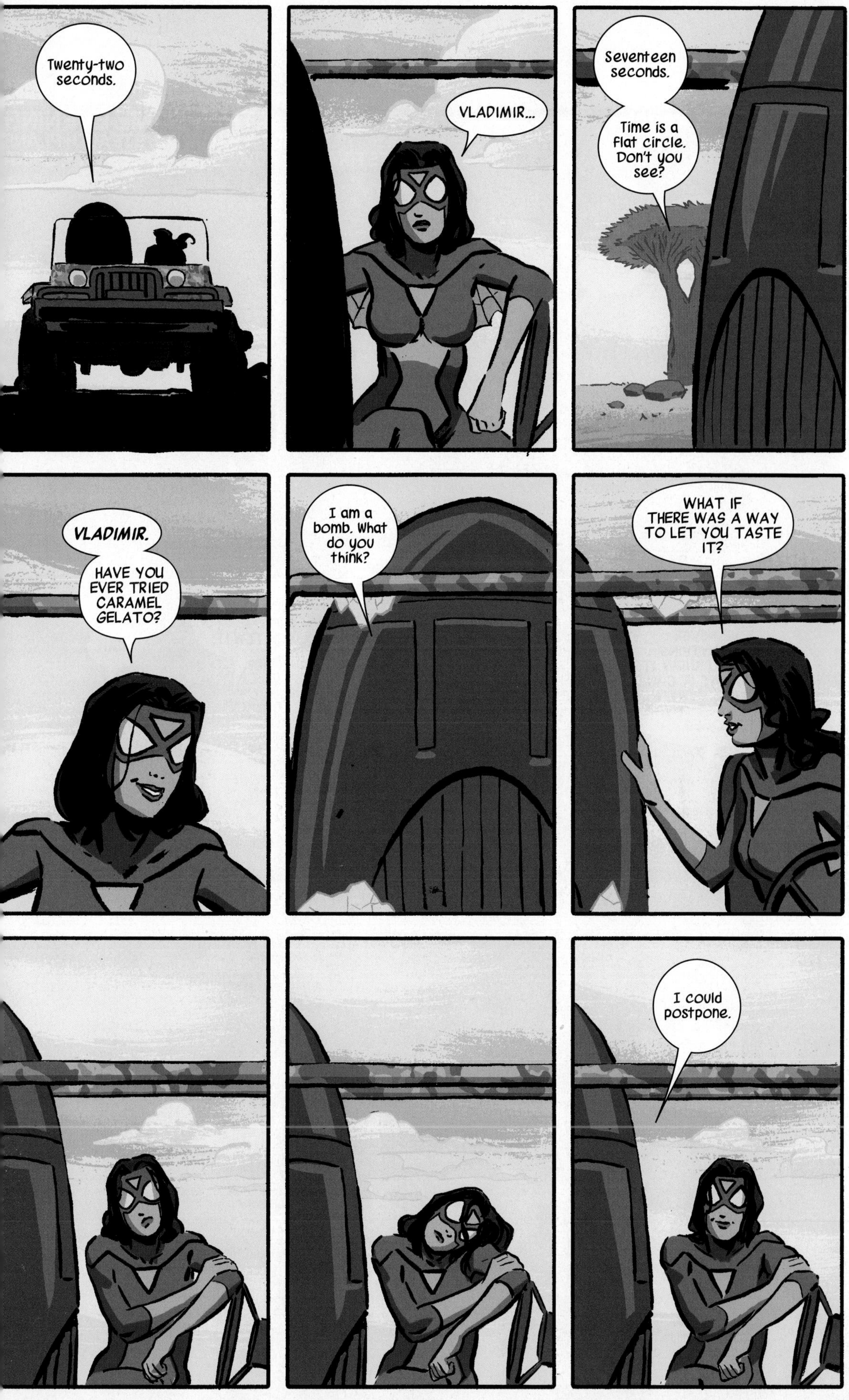

Twenty-two seconds.
VLADIMIR...
Seventeen seconds.
Time is a flat circle. Don't you see?
VLADIMIR.
HAVE YOU EVER TRIED CARAMEL GELATO?
I am a bomb. What do you think?
WHAT IF THERE WAS A WAY TO LET YOU TASTE IT?
I could postpone.

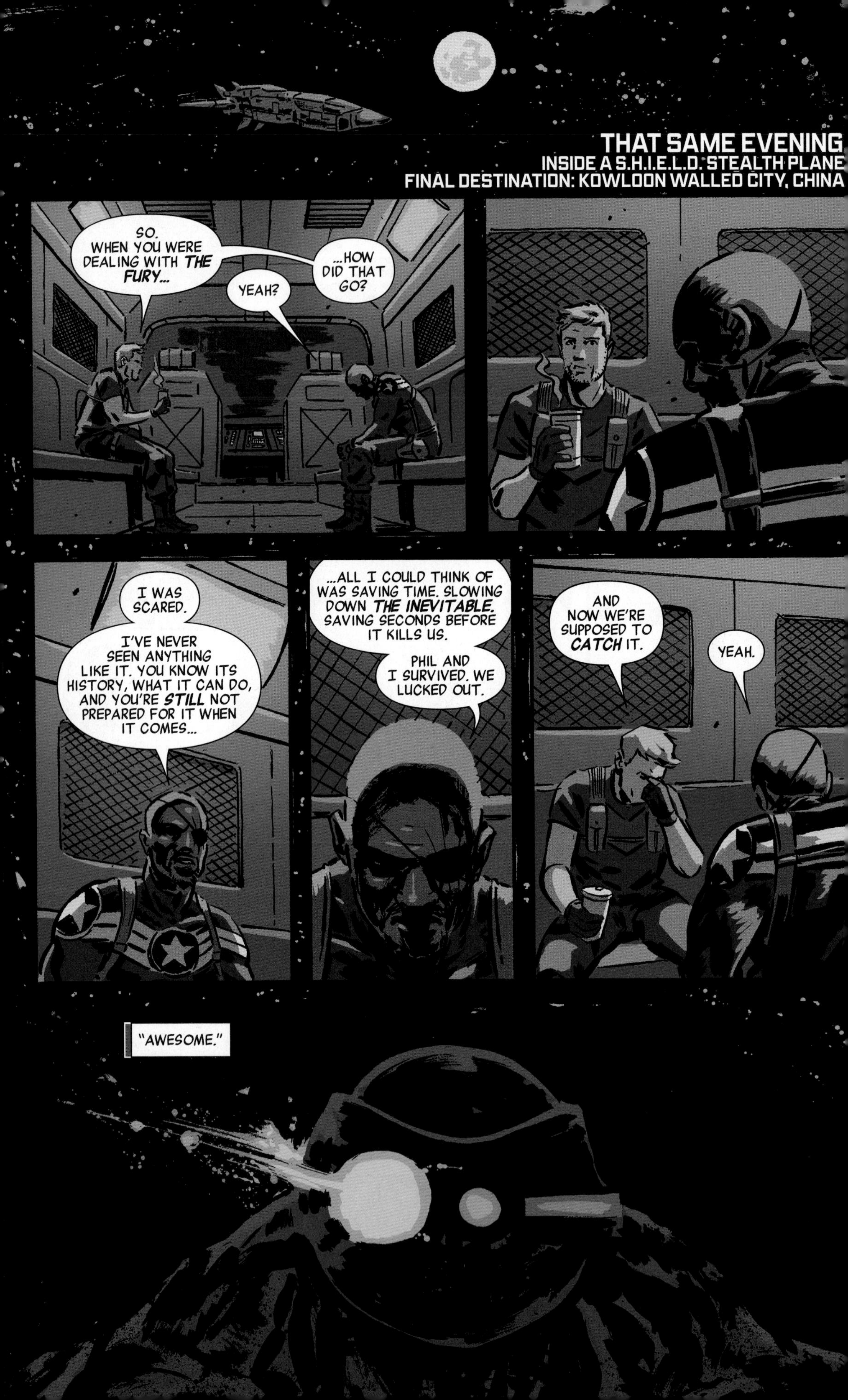
THAT SAME EVENING
INSIDE A S.H.I.E.L.D. STEALTH PLANE
FINAL DESTINATION: KOWLOON WALLED CITY, CHINA
SO. WHEN YOU WERE DEALING WITH THE FURY...
YEAH?
...HOW DID THAT GO?
I WAS SCARED.
I'VE NEVER SEEN ANYTHING LIKE IT. YOU KNOW ITS HISTORY, WHAT IT CAN DO, AND YOU'RE STILL NOT PREPARED FOR IT WHEN IT COMES...
...ALL I COULD THINK OF WAS SAVING TIME. SLOWING DOWN THE INEVITABLE. SAVING SECONDS BEFORE IT KILLS US.
PHIL AND I SURVIVED. WE LUCKED OUT.
AND NOW WE'RE SUPPOSED TO CATCH IT.
YEAH.
"AWESOME."

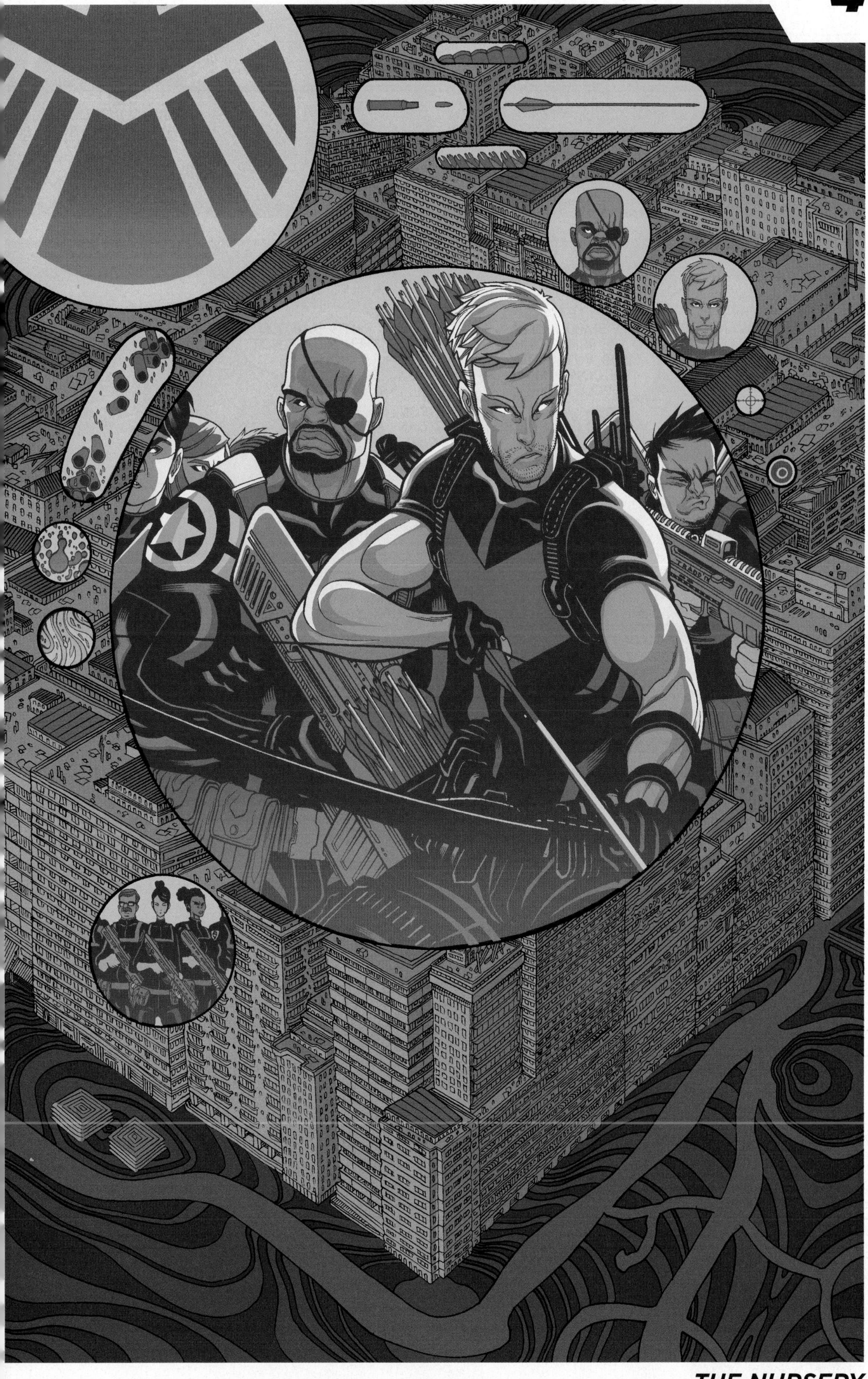

4

THE NURSERY

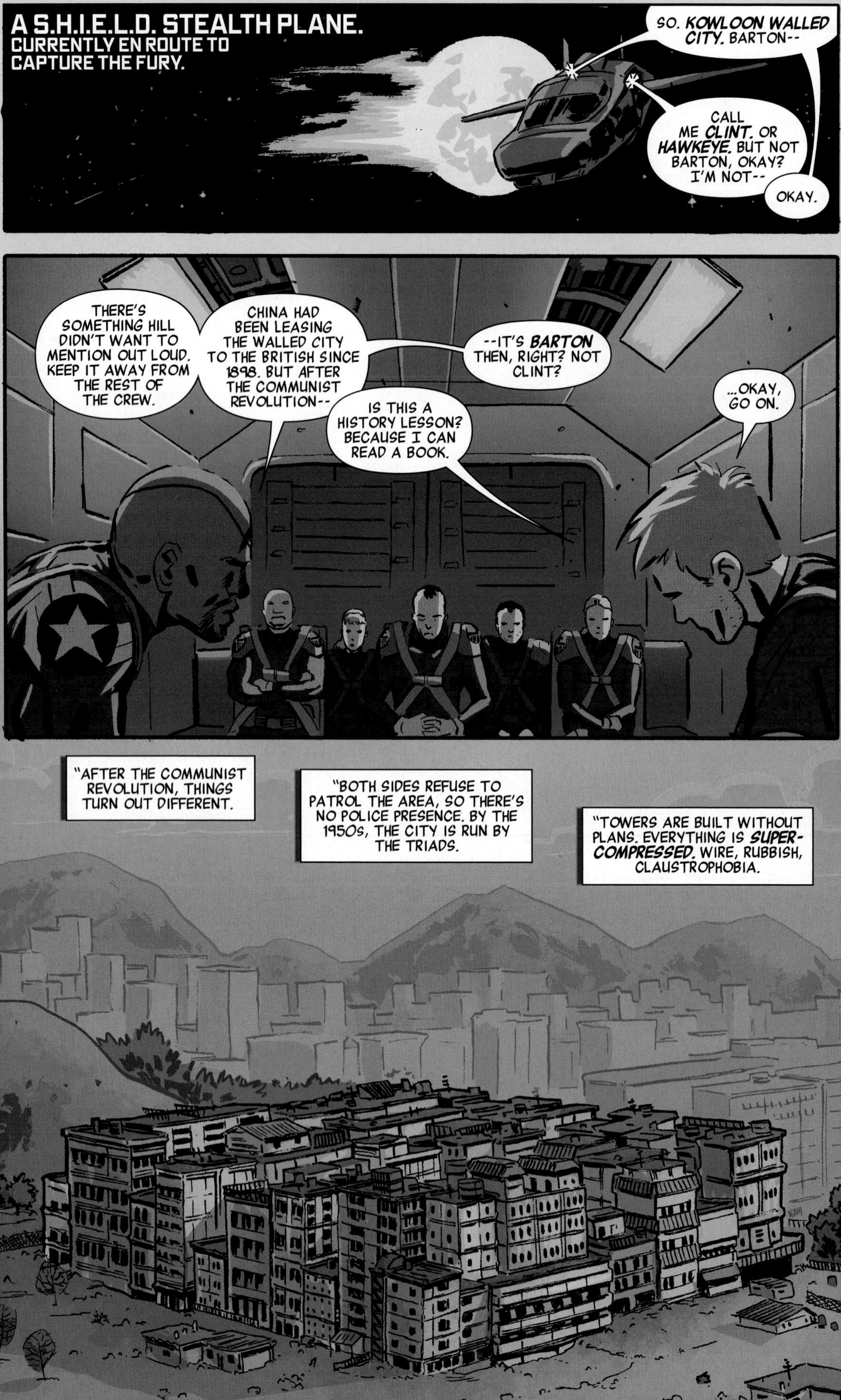
A S.H.I.E.L.D. STEALTH PLANE.
CURRENTLY EN ROUTE TO CAPTURE THE FURY.
SO. KOWLOON WALLED CITY. BARTON--
CALL ME CLINT. OR HAWKEYE. BUT NOT BARTON, OKAY? I'M NOT--
OKAY.
THERE'S SOMETHING HILL DIDN'T WANT TO MENTION OUT LOUD. KEEP IT AWAY FROM THE REST OF THE CREW.
CHINA HAD BEEN LEASING THE WALLED CITY TO THE BRITISH SINCE 1898. BUT AFTER THE COMMUNIST REVOLUTION--
--IT'S BARTON THEN, RIGHT? NOT CLINT?
IS THIS A HISTORY LESSON? BECAUSE I CAN READ A BOOK.
...OKAY, GO ON.
"AFTER THE COMMUNIST REVOLUTION, THINGS TURN OUT DIFFERENT.
"BOTH SIDES REFUSE TO PATROL THE AREA, SO THERE'S NO POLICE PRESENCE. BY THE 1950s, THE CITY IS RUN BY THE TRIADS.
"TOWERS ARE BUILT WITHOUT PLANS. EVERYTHING IS SUPER-COMPRESSED. WIRE, RUBBISH, CLAUSTROPHOBIA.

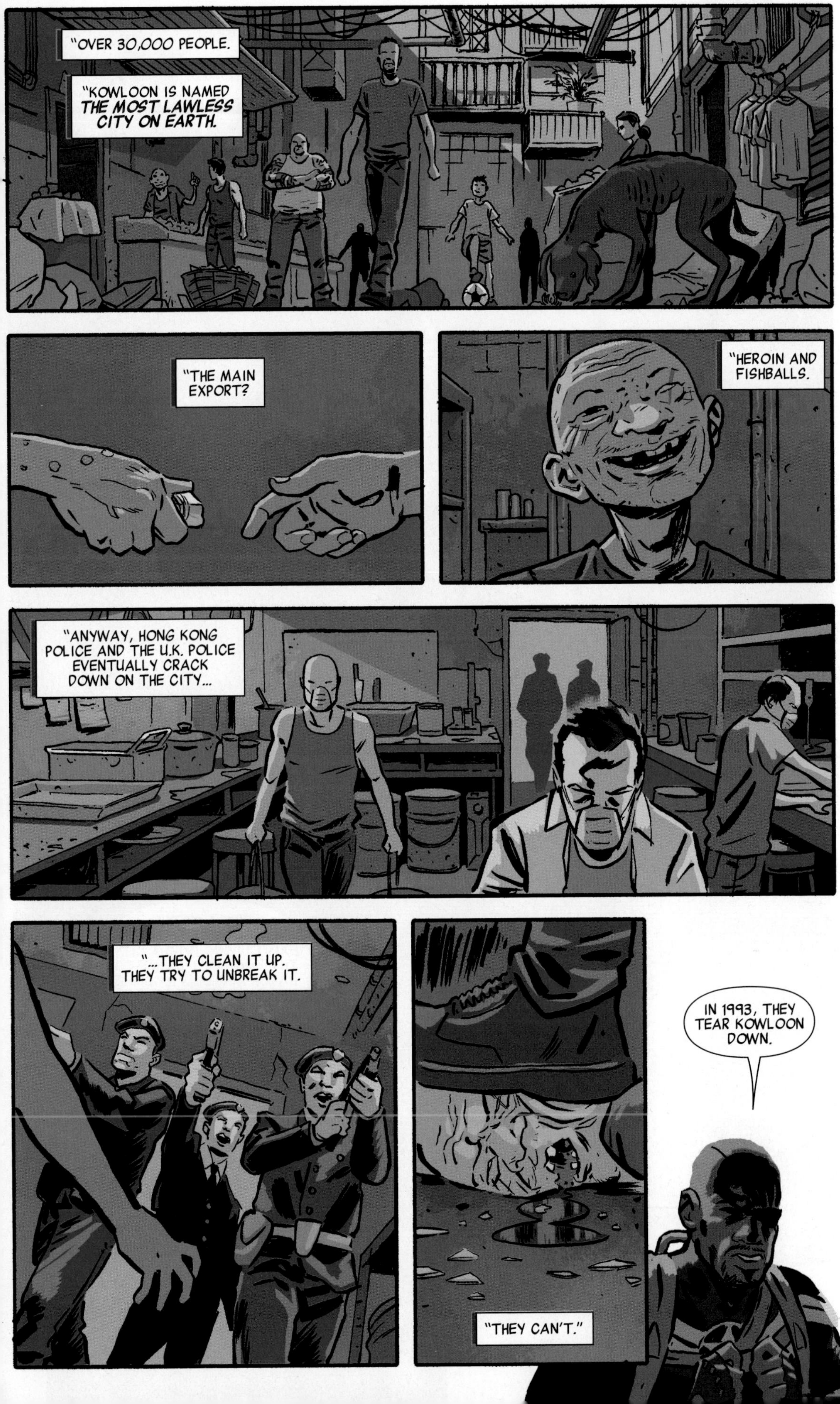
"OVER 30,000 PEOPLE.
"KOWLOON IS NAMED THE MOST LAWLESS CITY ON EARTH.
"THE MAIN EXPORT?
"HEROIN AND FISHBALLS.
"ANYWAY, HONG KONG POLICE AND THE U.K. POLICE EVENTUALLY CRACK DOWN ON THE CITY...
"...THEY CLEAN IT UP. THEY TRY TO UNBREAK IT.
"THEY CAN'T."
IN 1993, THEY TEAR KOWLOON DOWN.

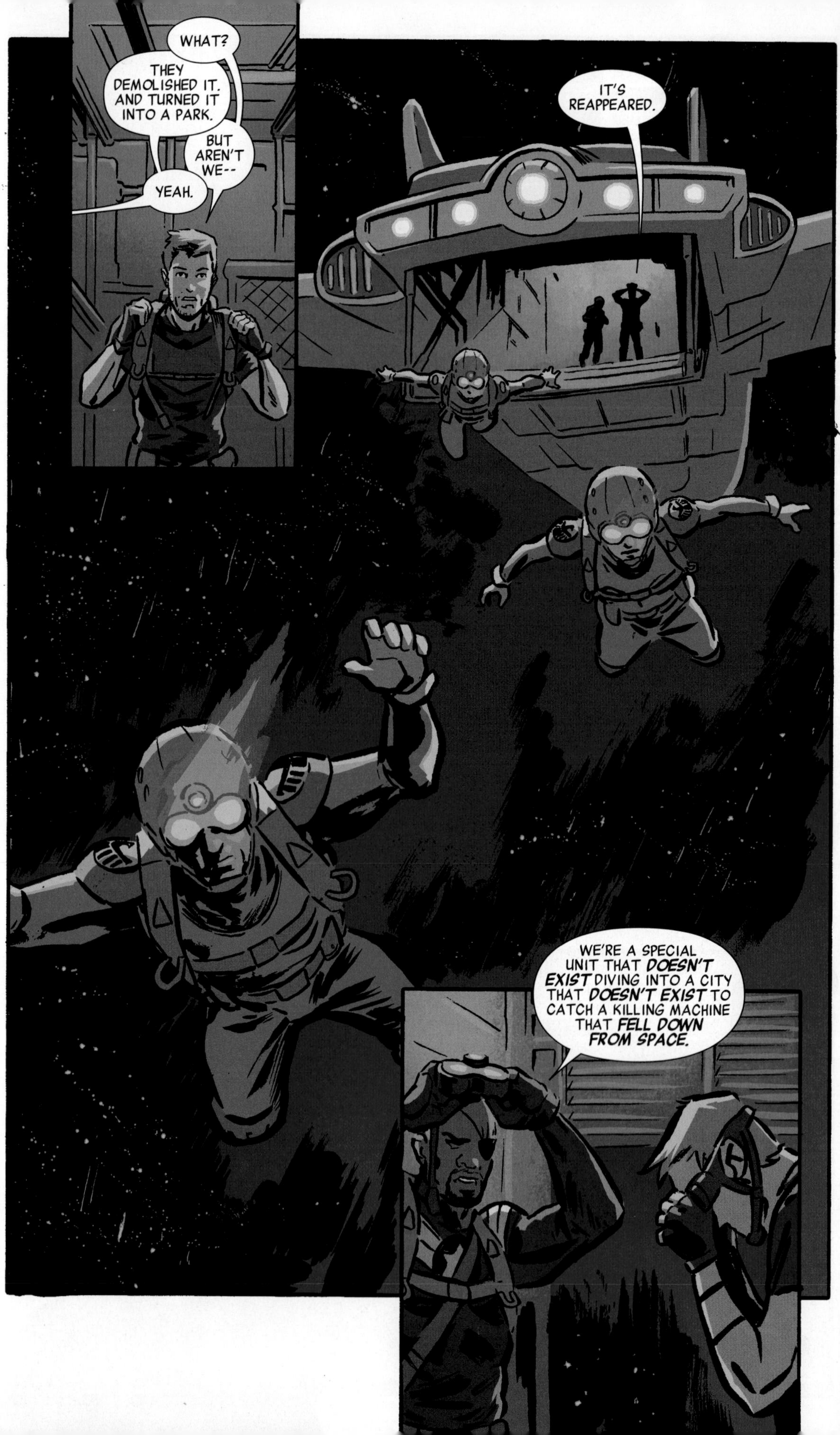
WHAT?
THEY DEMOLISHED IT. AND TURNED IT INTO A PARK.
BUT AREN'T WE--
YEAH.
IT'S REAPPEARED.
WE'RE A SPECIAL UNIT THAT **DOESN'T EXIST** DIVING INTO A CITY THAT **DOESN'T EXIST** TO CATCH A KILLING MACHINE THAT **FELL DOWN FROM SPACE.**

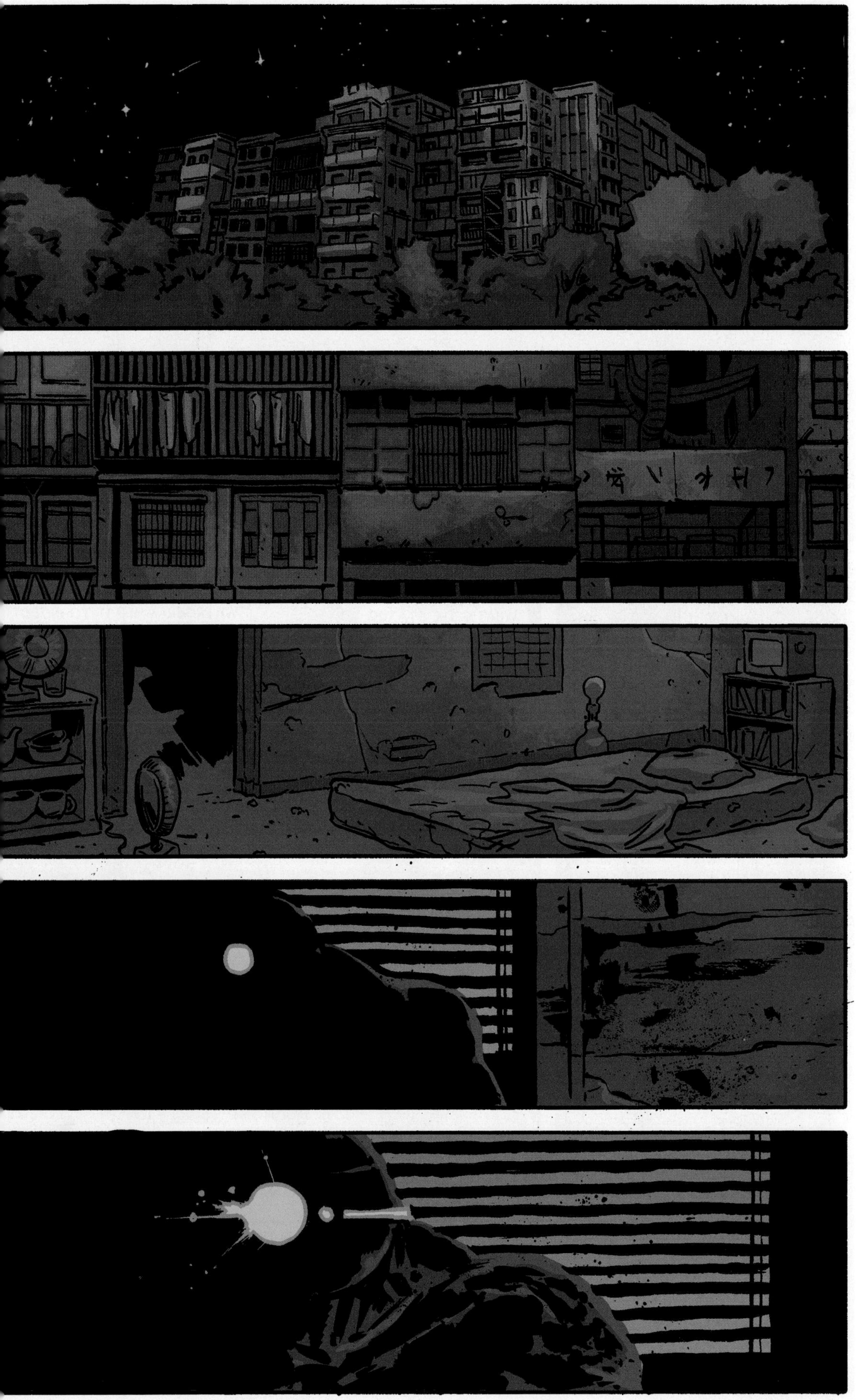

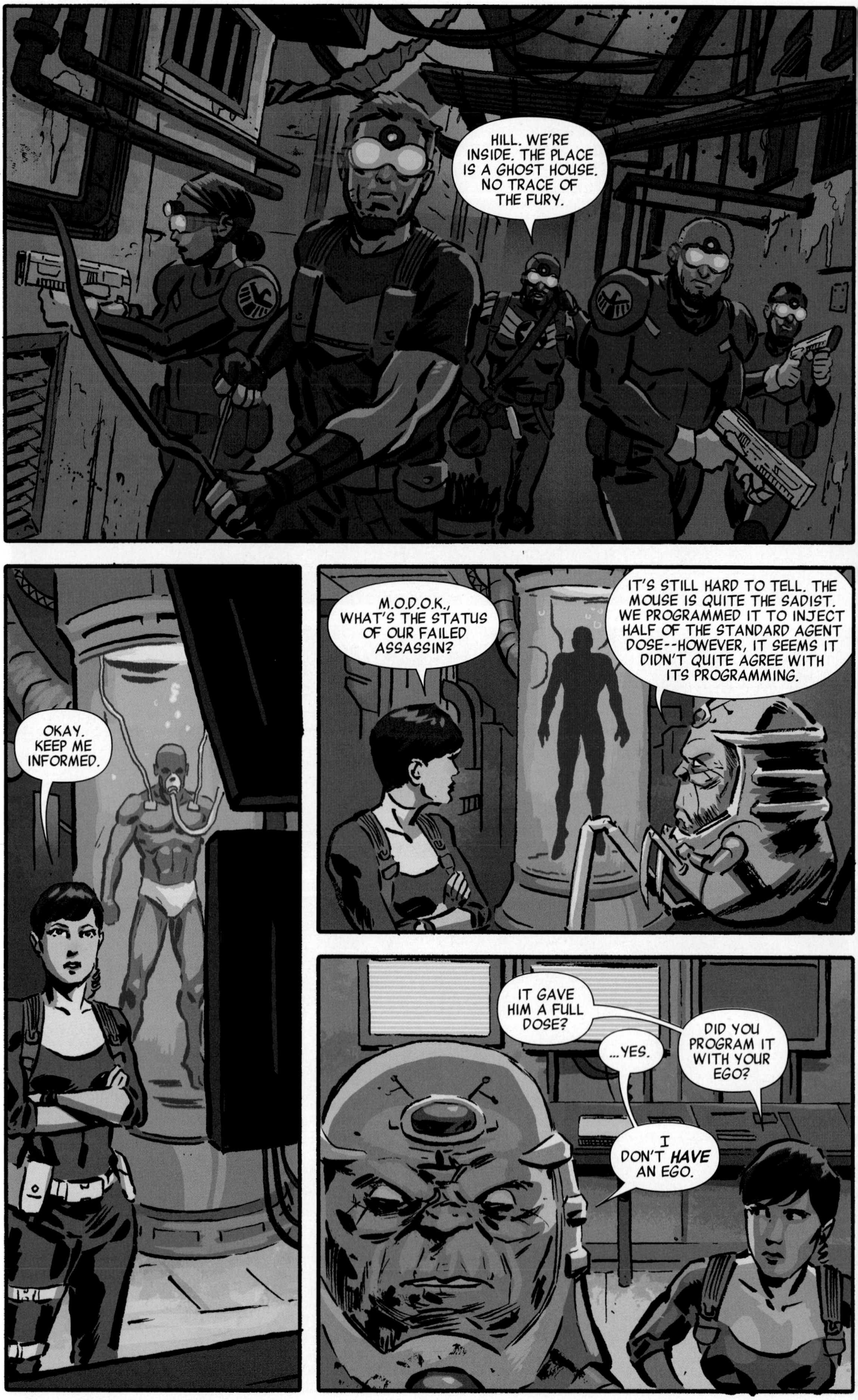
HILL. WE'RE INSIDE. THE PLACE IS A GHOST HOUSE. NO TRACE OF THE FURY.
OKAY. KEEP ME INFORMED.
M.O.D.O.K., WHAT'S THE STATUS OF OUR FAILED ASSASSIN?
IT'S STILL HARD TO TELL. THE MOUSE IS QUITE THE SADIST. WE PROGRAMMED IT TO INJECT HALF OF THE STANDARD AGENT DOSE--HOWEVER, IT SEEMS IT DIDN'T QUITE AGREE WITH ITS PROGRAMMING.
IT GAVE HIM A FULL DOSE?
DID YOU PROGRAM IT WITH YOUR EGO?
...YES.
I DON'T HAVE AN EGO.

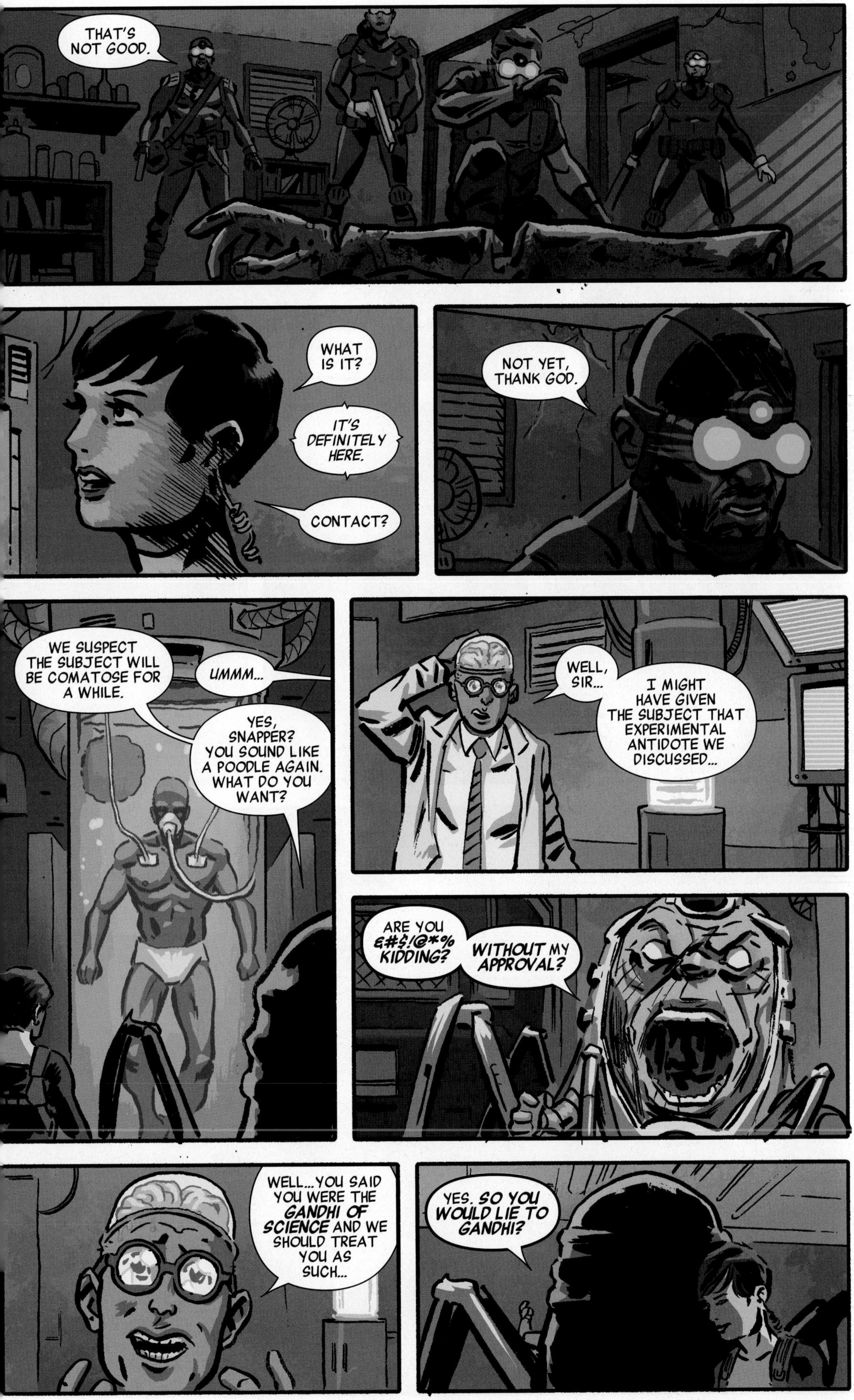
THAT'S NOT GOOD.
WHAT IS IT?
IT'S DEFINITELY HERE.
CONTACT?
NOT YET, THANK GOD.
WE SUSPECT THE SUBJECT WILL BE COMATOSE FOR A WHILE.
UMMM...
YES, SNAPPER? YOU SOUND LIKE A POODLE AGAIN. WHAT DO YOU WANT?
WELL, SIR...
I MIGHT HAVE GIVEN THE SUBJECT THAT EXPERIMENTAL ANTIDOTE WE DISCUSSED...
ARE YOU &#$!@*% KIDDING?
WITHOUT MY APPROVAL?
WELL...YOU SAID YOU WERE THE GANDHI OF SCIENCE AND WE SHOULD TREAT YOU AS SUCH...
YES. SO YOU WOULD LIE TO GANDHI?

WELL, GANDHI SAID THAT WE SHOULD BELIEVE NOTHING, NOT EVEN *HIM*, UNLESS WE TEST IT AND JUDGE IT TO BE TRUE OURSELVES...

HILL, CAN I USE SNAPPER FOR MY NEXT EXPERIMENT? I ALWAYS WANTED A LAMPSHADE MADE OF HUMAN SKIN.

OVERRULED.

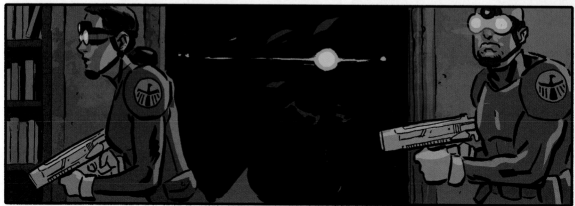

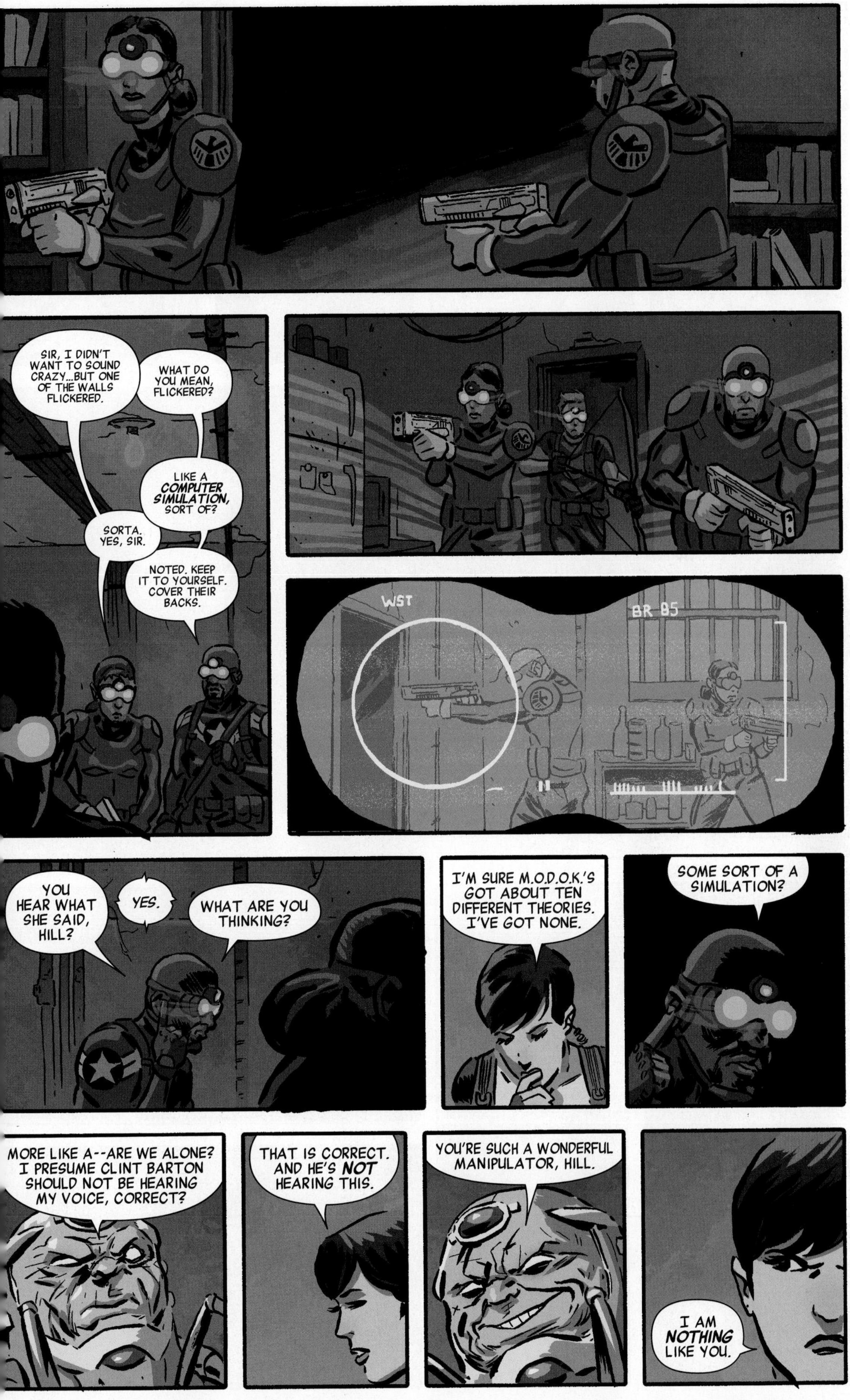

SIR, I DIDN'T WANT TO SOUND CRAZY...BUT ONE OF THE WALLS FLICKERED.
WHAT DO YOU MEAN, FLICKERED?
LIKE A COMPUTER SIMULATION, SORT OF?
SORTA. YES, SIR.
NOTED. KEEP IT TO YOURSELF. COVER THEIR BACKS.
WST
BR 85
YOU HEAR WHAT SHE SAID, HILL?
YES.
WHAT ARE YOU THINKING?
I'M SURE M.O.D.O.K.'S GOT ABOUT TEN DIFFERENT THEORIES. I'VE GOT NONE.
SOME SORT OF A SIMULATION?
MORE LIKE A--ARE WE ALONE? I PRESUME CLINT BARTON SHOULD NOT BE HEARING MY VOICE, CORRECT?
THAT IS CORRECT. AND HE'S NOT HEARING THIS.
YOU'RE SUCH A WONDERFUL MANIPULATOR, HILL.
I AM NOTHING LIKE YOU.

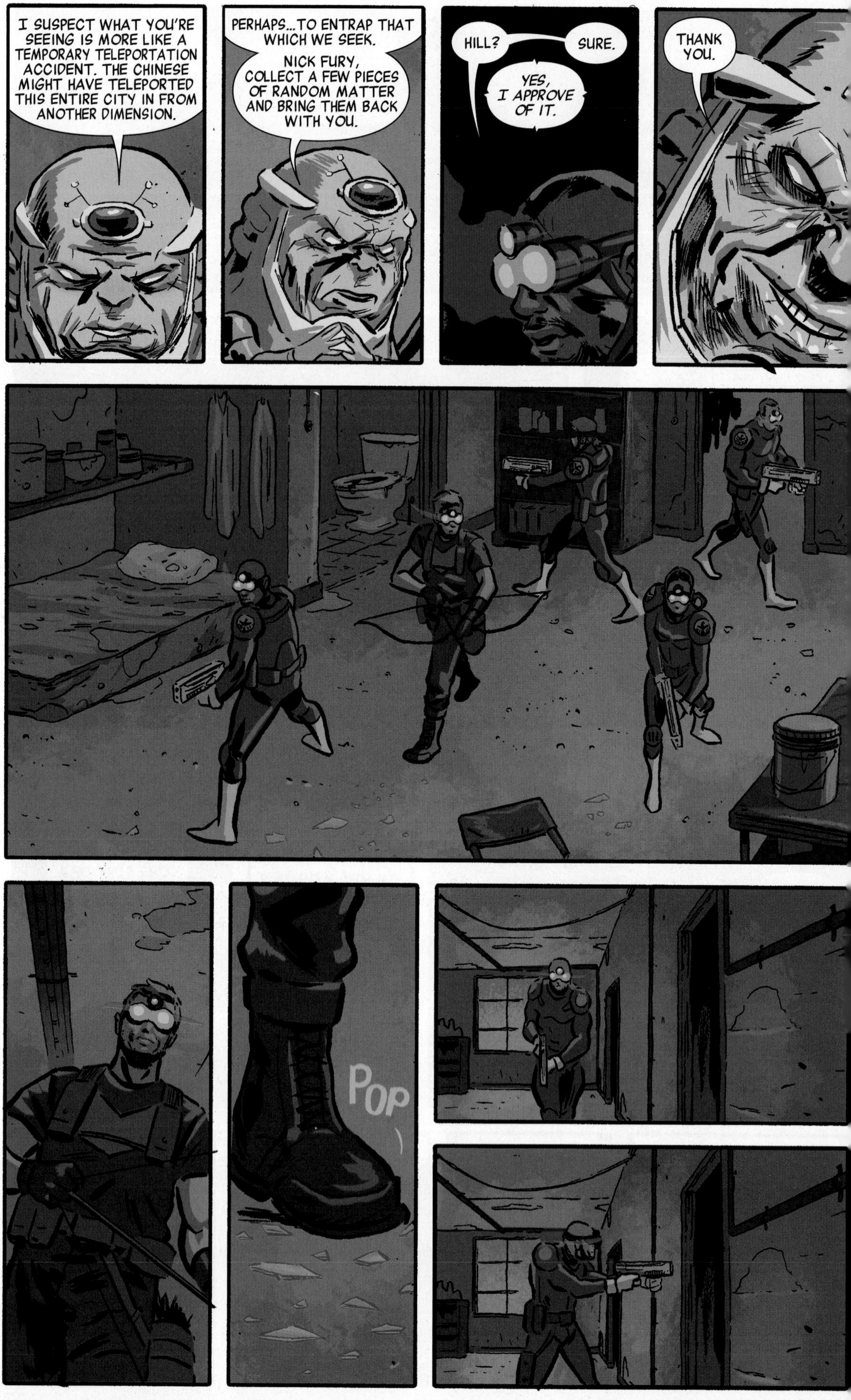
I SUSPECT WHAT YOU'RE SEEING IS MORE LIKE A TEMPORARY TELEPORTATION ACCIDENT. THE CHINESE MIGHT HAVE TELEPORTED THIS ENTIRE CITY IN FROM ANOTHER DIMENSION.
PERHAPS...TO ENTRAP THAT WHICH WE SEEK.
NICK FURY, COLLECT A FEW PIECES OF RANDOM MATTER AND BRING THEM BACK WITH YOU.
HILL?
SURE.
YES, I APPROVE OF IT.
THANK YOU.
POP

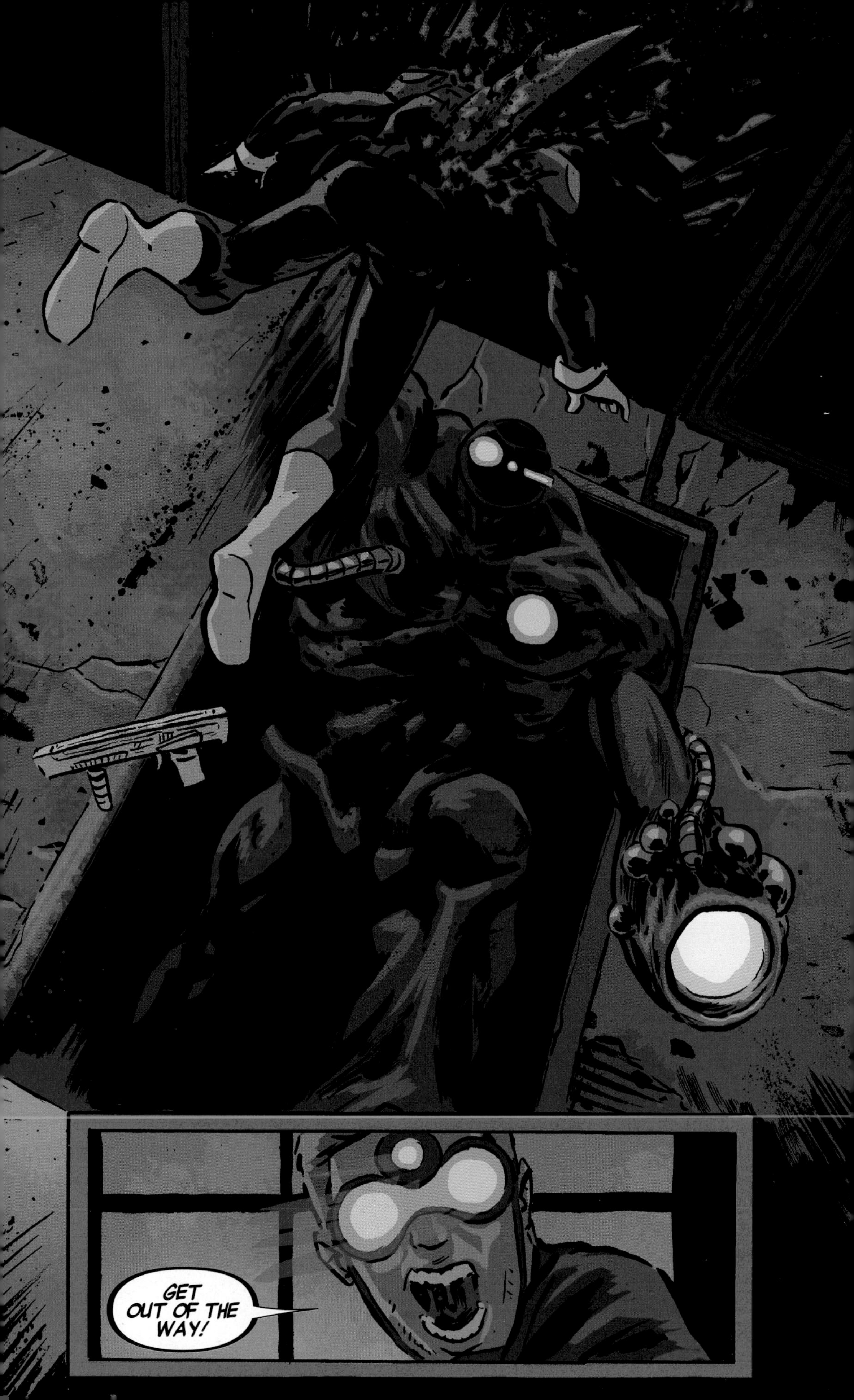
GET OUT OF THE WAY!

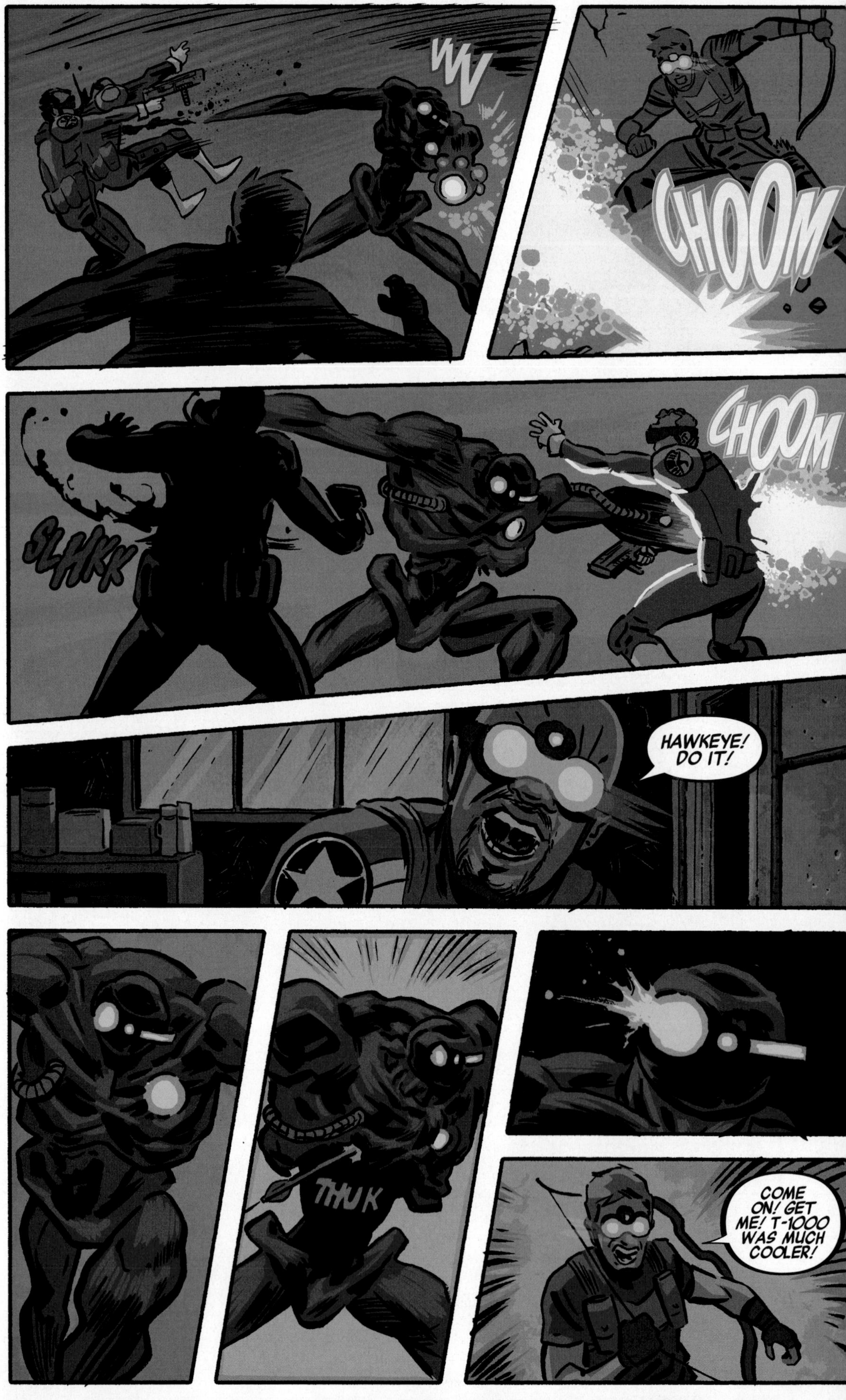
VVV
CHOOM
CHOOM
SLHKK
HAWKEYE! DO IT!
THUK
COME ON! GET ME! T-1000 WAS MUCH COOLER!

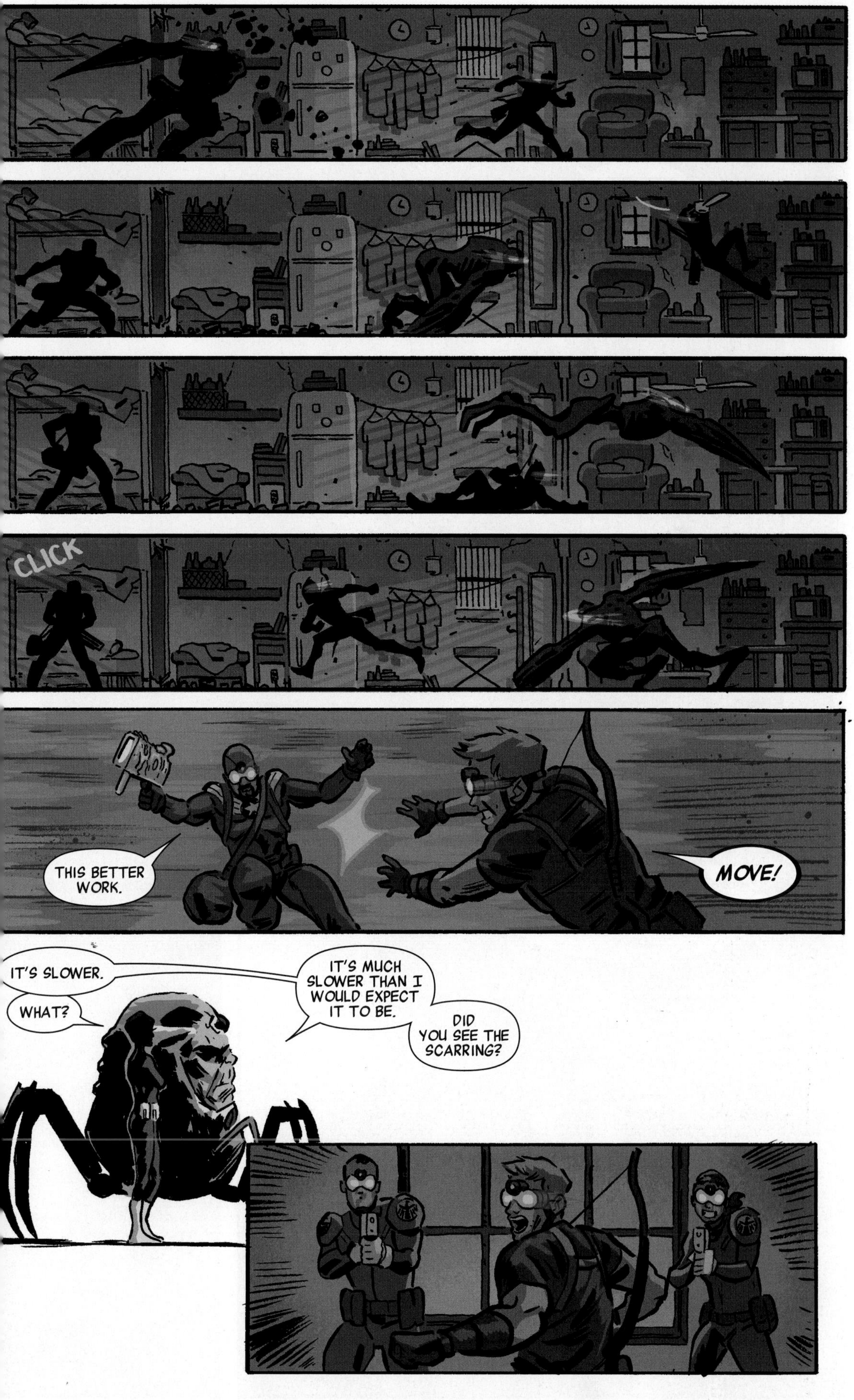
CLICK
THIS BETTER WORK.
MOVE!
IT'S SLOWER.
WHAT?
IT'S MUCH SLOWER THAN I WOULD EXPECT IT TO BE.
DID YOU SEE THE SCARRING?

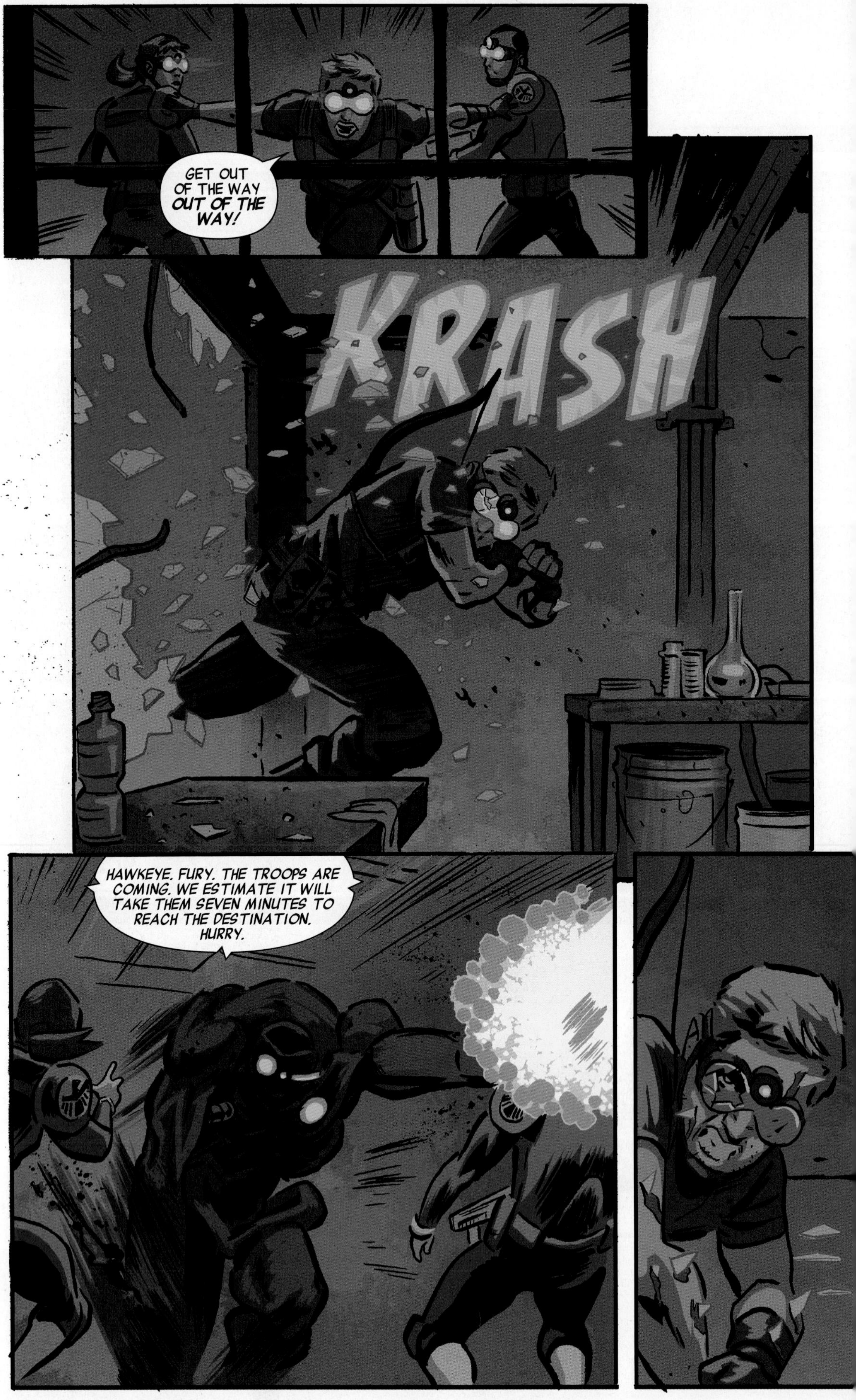
GET OUT OF THE WAY OUT OF THE WAY!
KRASH
HAWKEYE. FURY. THE TROOPS ARE COMING. WE ESTIMATE IT WILL TAKE THEM SEVEN MINUTES TO REACH THE DESTINATION. HURRY.

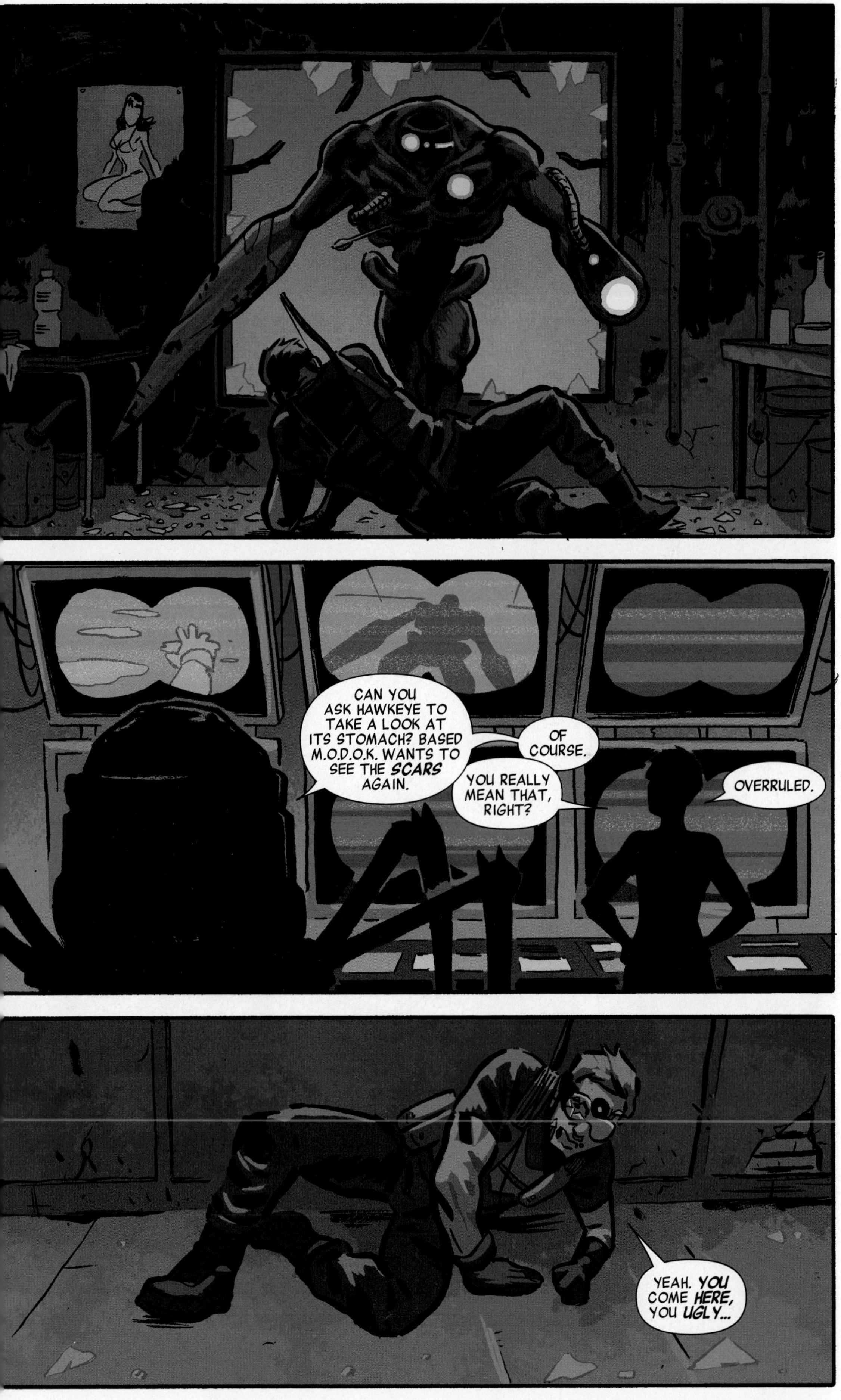
CAN YOU ASK HAWKEYE TO TAKE A LOOK AT ITS STOMACH? BASED M.O.D.O.K. WANTS TO SEE THE SCARS AGAIN.
OF COURSE.
YOU REALLY MEAN THAT, RIGHT?
OVERRULED.
YEAH. YOU COME HERE, YOU UGLY...

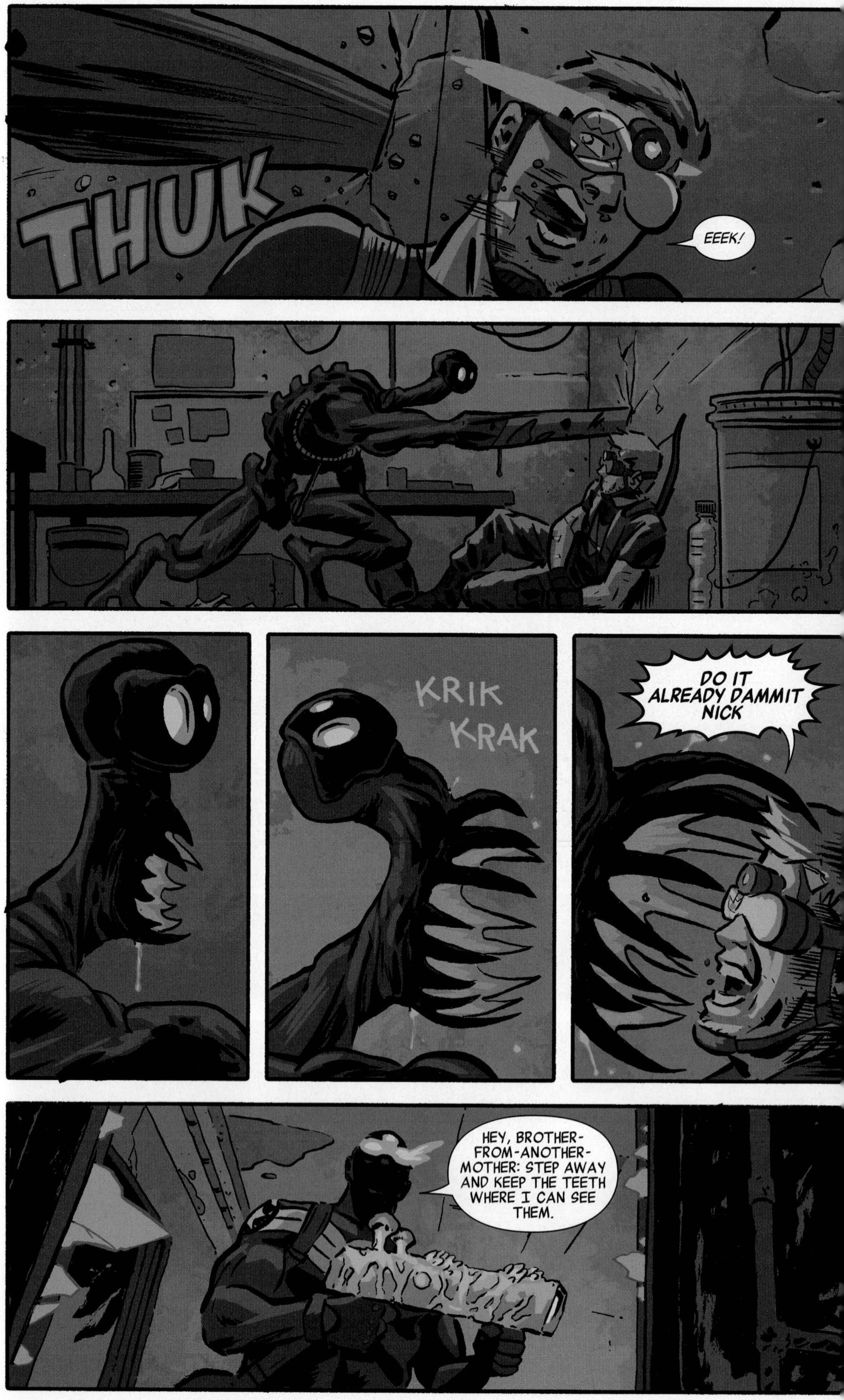
THUK
EEEK!
KRIK
KRAK
DO IT ALREADY DAMMIT NICK
HEY, BROTHER-FROM-ANOTHER-MOTHER: STEP AWAY AND KEEP THE TEETH WHERE I CAN SEE THEM.

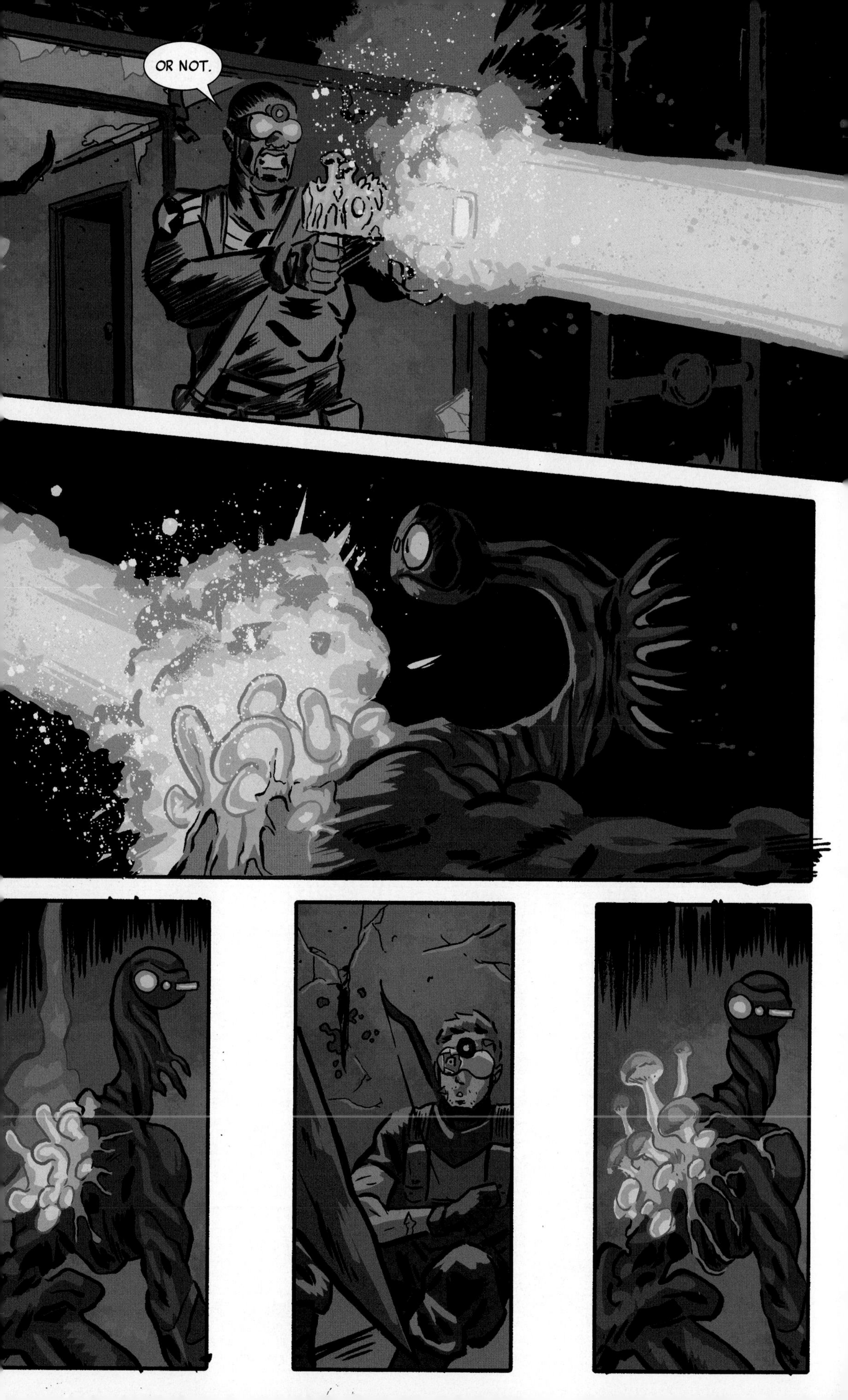
OR NOT.

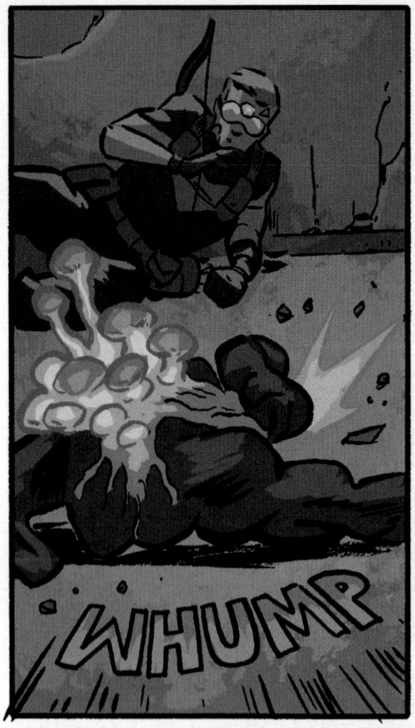
WHUMP

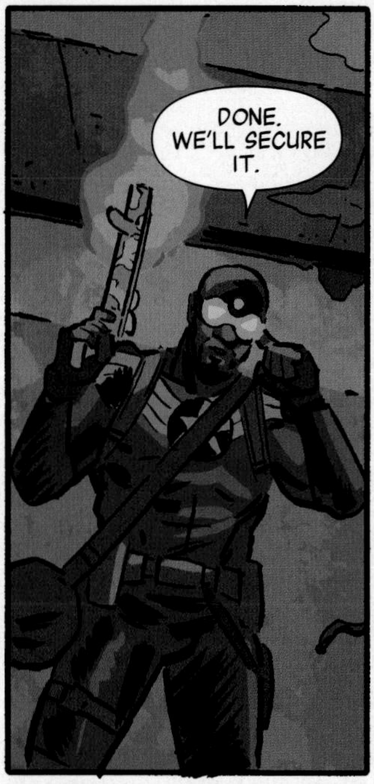
DONE. WE'LL SECURE IT.

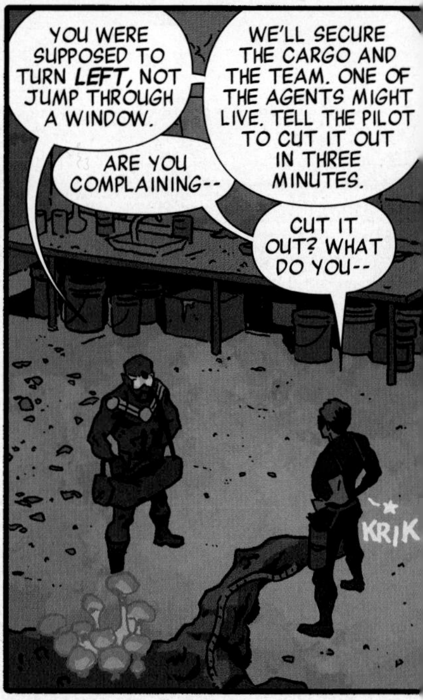
YOU WERE SUPPOSED TO TURN LEFT, NOT JUMP THROUGH A WINDOW.
WE'LL SECURE THE CARGO AND THE TEAM. ONE OF THE AGENTS MIGHT LIVE. TELL THE PILOT TO CUT IT OUT IN THREE MINUTES.
ARE YOU COMPLAINING--
CUT IT OUT? WHAT DO YOU--
KRIK

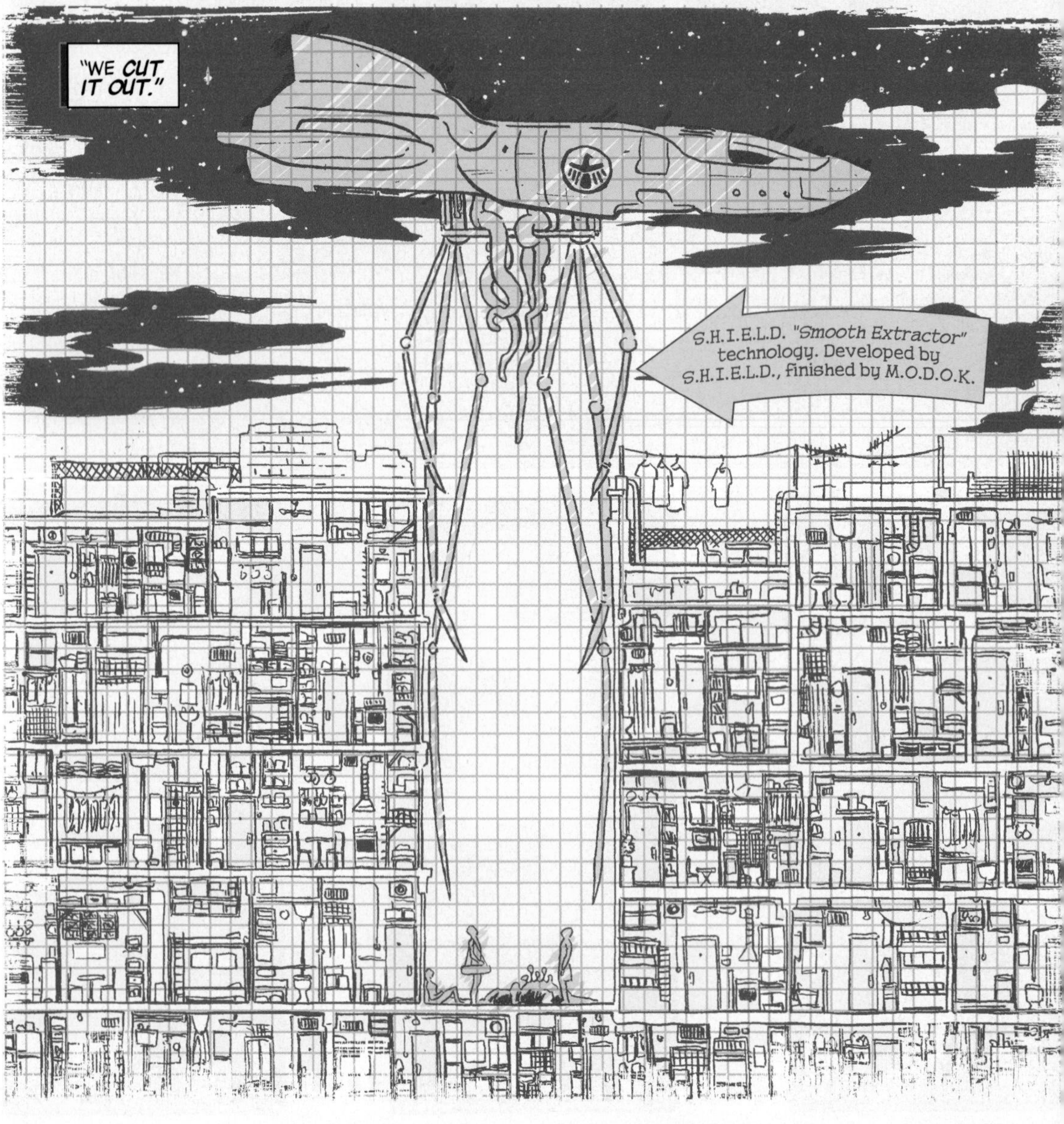
"WE CUT IT OUT."
S.H.I.E.L.D. "Smooth Extractor" technology. Developed by S.H.I.E.L.D., finished by M.O.D.O.K.

EPILOGUE ONE: THE EXTRACTION

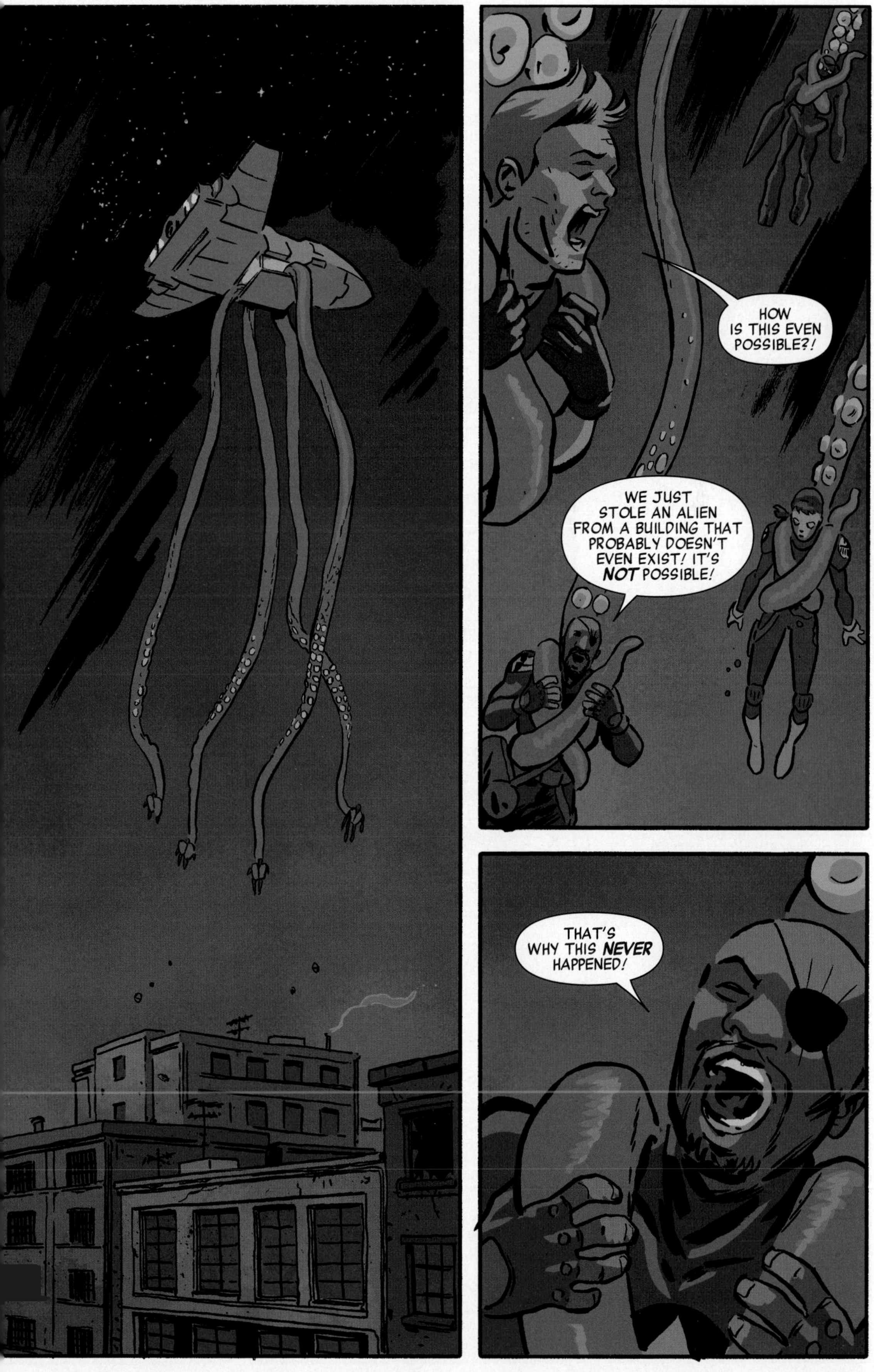
HOW IS THIS EVEN POSSIBLE?!
WE JUST STOLE AN ALIEN FROM A BUILDING THAT PROBABLY DOESN'T EVEN EXIST! IT'S **NOT** POSSIBLE!
THAT'S WHY THIS **NEVER** HAPPENED!

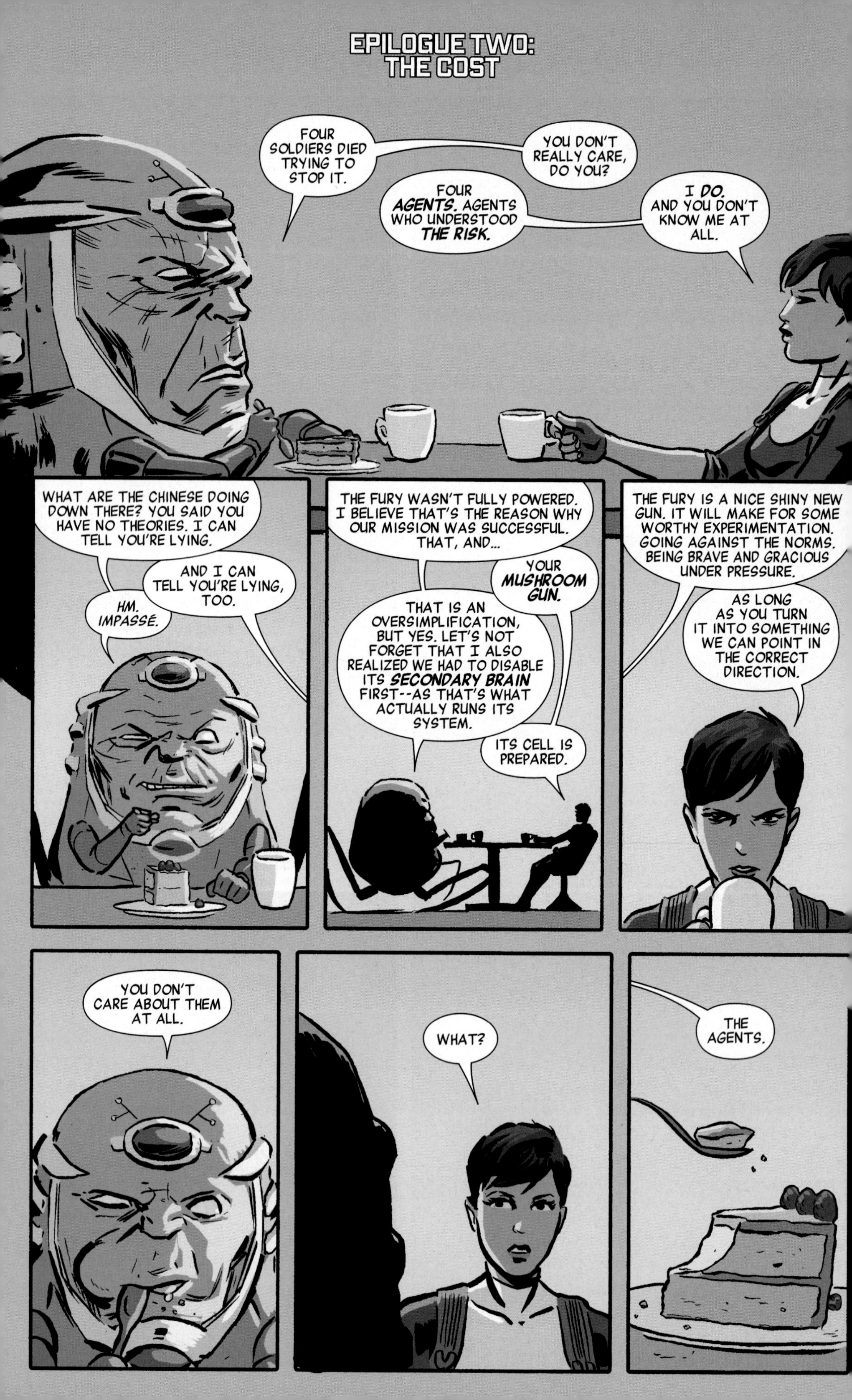
EPILOGUE TWO: THE COST
FOUR SOLDIERS DIED TRYING TO STOP IT.
YOU DON'T REALLY CARE, DO YOU?
FOUR AGENTS. AGENTS WHO UNDERSTOOD THE RISK.
I DO. AND YOU DON'T KNOW ME AT ALL.
WHAT ARE THE CHINESE DOING DOWN THERE? YOU SAID YOU HAVE NO THEORIES. I CAN TELL YOU'RE LYING.
AND I CAN TELL YOU'RE LYING, TOO.
HM. IMPASSÉ.
THE FURY WASN'T FULLY POWERED. I BELIEVE THAT'S THE REASON WHY OUR MISSION WAS SUCCESSFUL. THAT, AND...
YOUR MUSHROOM GUN.
THAT IS AN OVERSIMPLIFICATION, BUT YES. LET'S NOT FORGET THAT I ALSO REALIZED WE HAD TO DISABLE ITS SECONDARY BRAIN FIRST--AS THAT'S WHAT ACTUALLY RUNS ITS SYSTEM.
ITS CELL IS PREPARED.
THE FURY IS A NICE SHINY NEW GUN. IT WILL MAKE FOR SOME WORTHY EXPERIMENTATION. GOING AGAINST THE NORMS. BEING BRAVE AND GRACIOUS UNDER PRESSURE.
AS LONG AS YOU TURN IT INTO SOMETHING WE CAN POINT IN THE CORRECT DIRECTION.
YOU DON'T CARE ABOUT THEM AT ALL.
WHAT?
THE AGENTS.

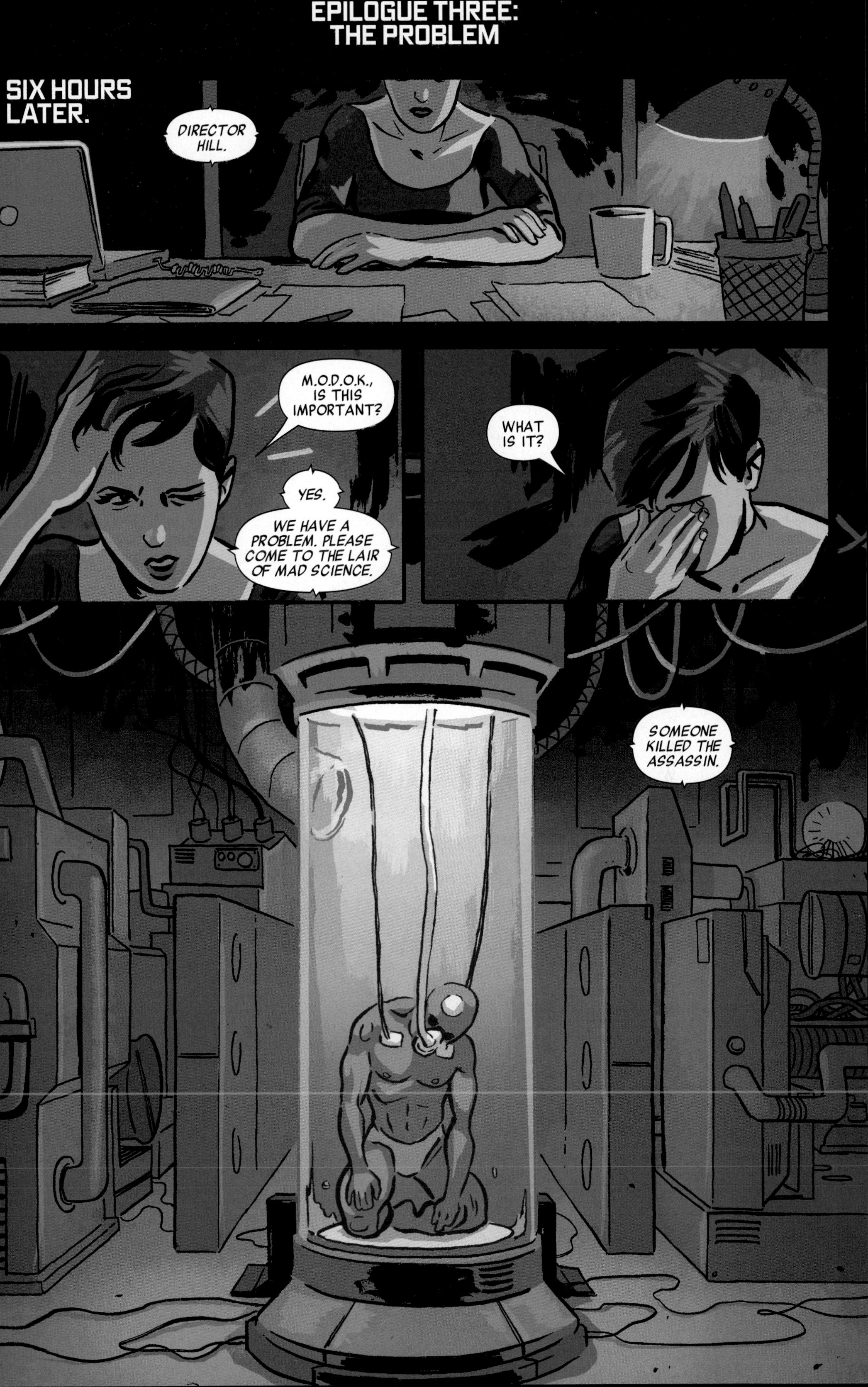
EPILOGUE THREE:
THE PROBLEM
SIX HOURS LATER.
DIRECTOR HILL.
M.O.D.O.K., IS THIS IMPORTANT?
YES.
WE HAVE A PROBLEM. PLEASE COME TO THE LAIR OF MAD SCIENCE.
WHAT IS IT?
SOMEONE KILLED THE ASSASSIN.

5

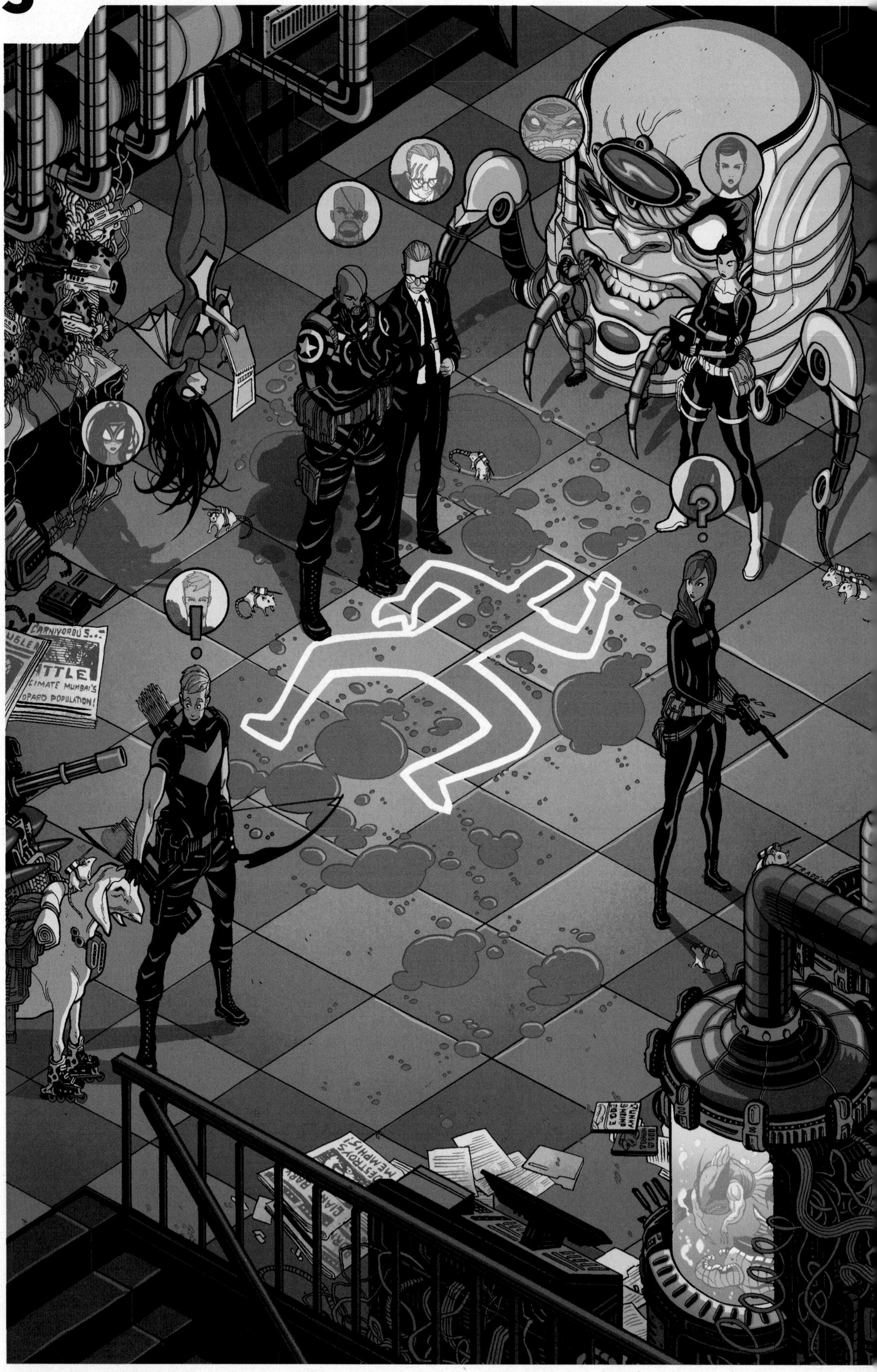
CARNIVOROUS...
TTLE
CIMATE MUMBAI'S
OPARD POPULATION!
DESTROYS MEMPHIS!

KARMA POLICE

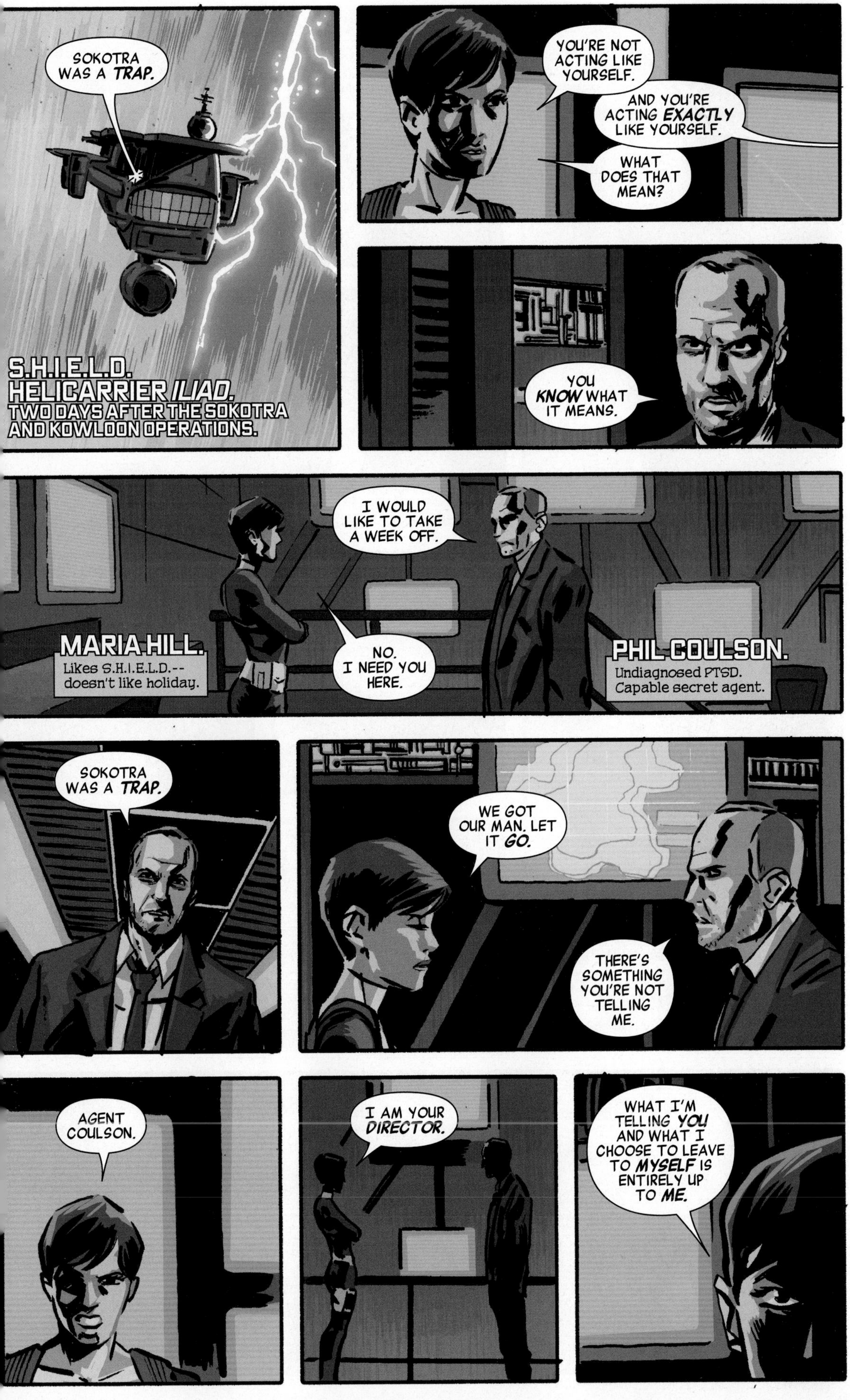
SOKOTRA WAS A TRAP.
S.H.I.E.L.D. HELICARRIER ILIAD.
TWO DAYS AFTER THE SOKOTRA AND KOWLOON OPERATIONS.
YOU'RE NOT ACTING LIKE YOURSELF.
AND YOU'RE ACTING EXACTLY LIKE YOURSELF.
WHAT DOES THAT MEAN?
YOU KNOW WHAT IT MEANS.
I WOULD LIKE TO TAKE A WEEK OFF.
MARIA HILL.
Likes S.H.I.E.L.D.-- doesn't like holiday.
NO. I NEED YOU HERE.
PHIL COULSON.
Undiagnosed PTSD. Capable secret agent.
SOKOTRA WAS A TRAP.
WE GOT OUR MAN. LET IT GO.
THERE'S SOMETHING YOU'RE NOT TELLING ME.
AGENT COULSON.
I AM YOUR DIRECTOR.
WHAT I'M TELLING YOU AND WHAT I CHOOSE TO LEAVE TO MYSELF IS ENTIRELY UP TO ME.

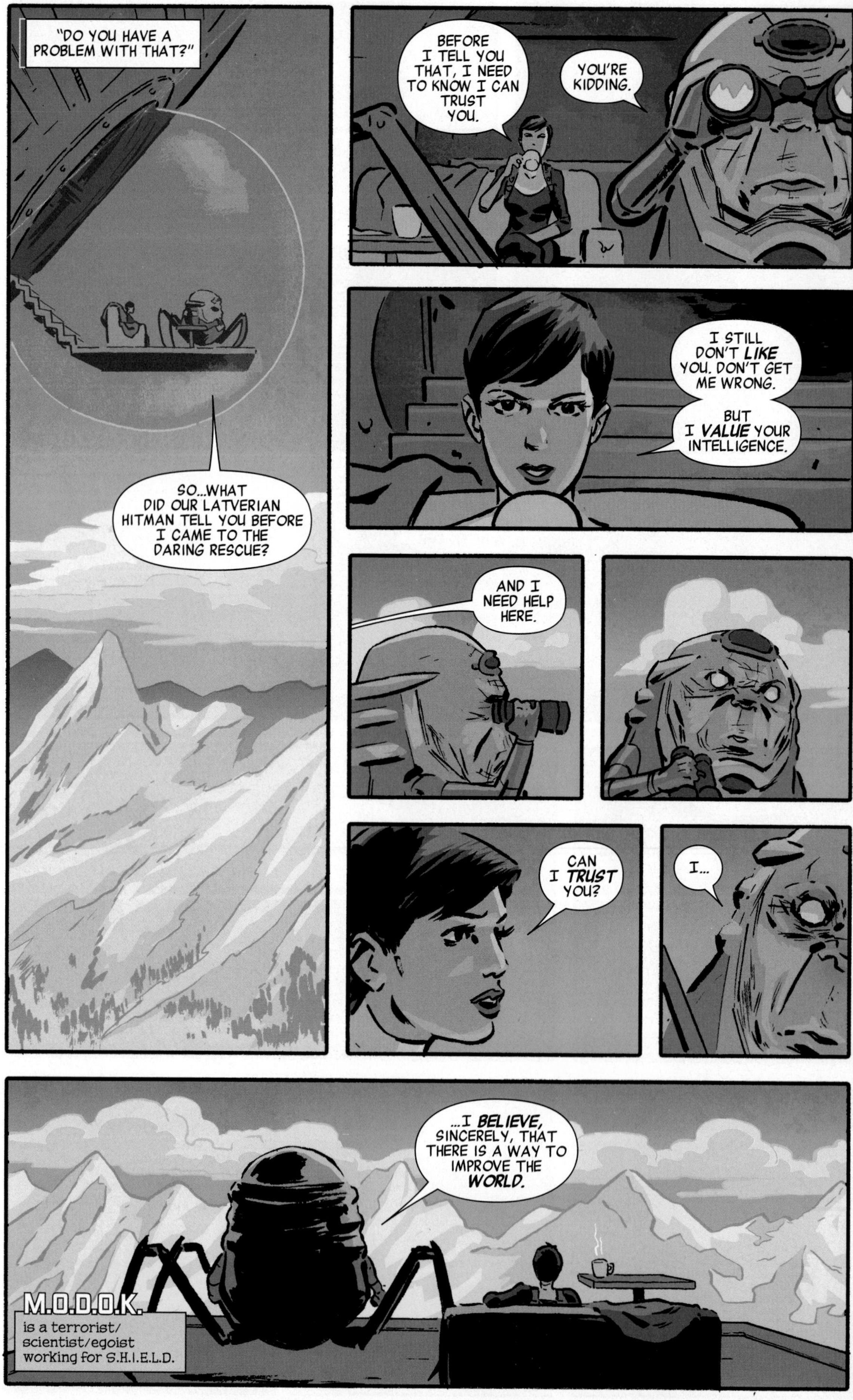
"DO YOU HAVE A PROBLEM WITH THAT?"
BEFORE I TELL YOU THAT, I NEED TO KNOW I CAN TRUST YOU.
YOU'RE KIDDING.
SO...WHAT DID OUR LATVERIAN HITMAN TELL YOU BEFORE I CAME TO THE DARING RESCUE?
I STILL DON'T LIKE YOU. DON'T GET ME WRONG.
BUT I VALUE YOUR INTELLIGENCE.
AND I NEED HELP HERE.
CAN I TRUST YOU?
I...
...I BELIEVE, SINCERELY, THAT THERE IS A WAY TO IMPROVE THE WORLD.
M.O.D.O.K.
is a terrorist/ scientist/egoist working for S.H.I.E.L.D.

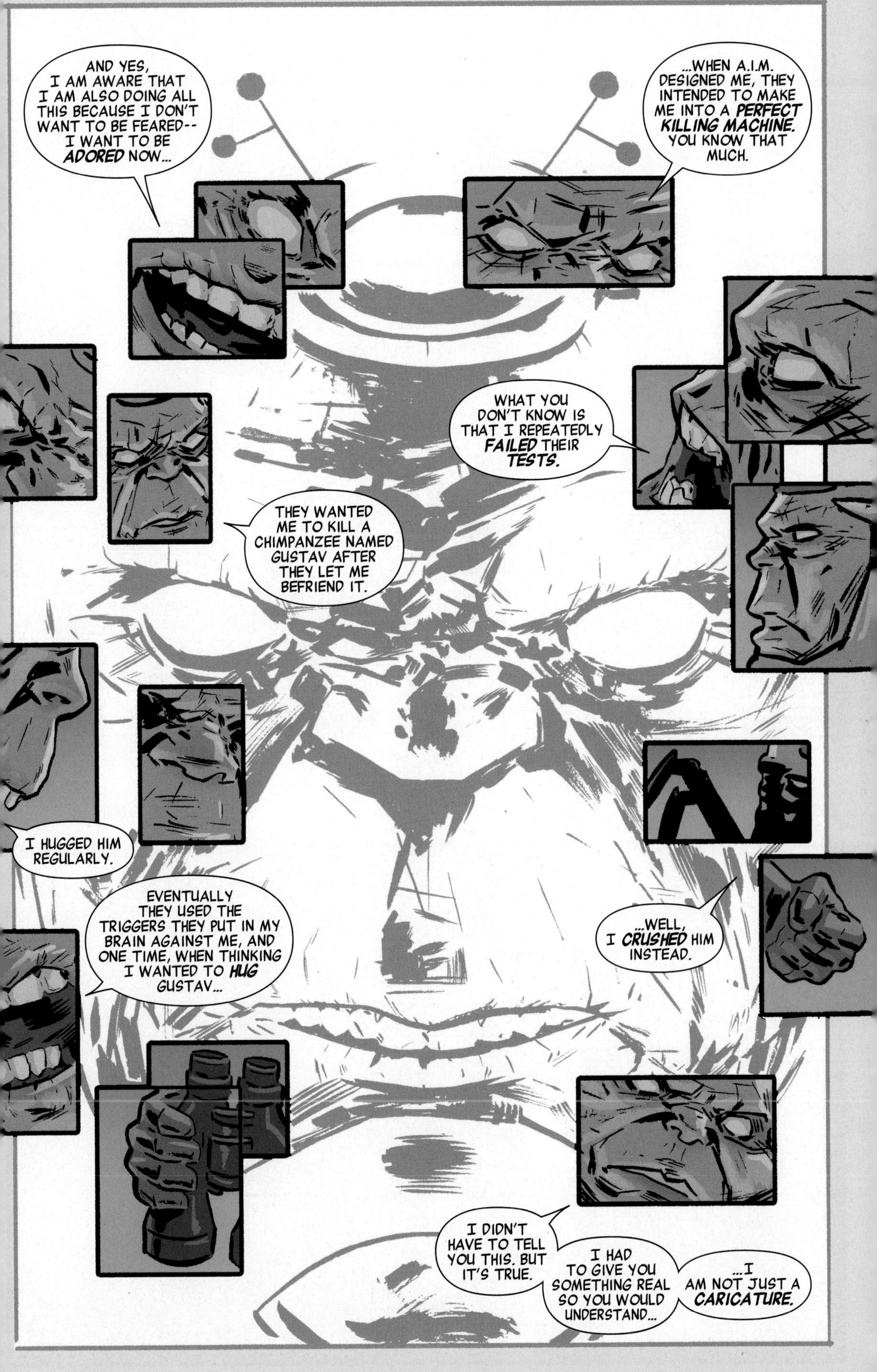
AND YES, I AM AWARE THAT I AM ALSO DOING ALL THIS BECAUSE I DON'T WANT TO BE FEARED-- I WANT TO BE ADORED NOW...
...WHEN A.I.M. DESIGNED ME, THEY INTENDED TO MAKE ME INTO A PERFECT KILLING MACHINE. YOU KNOW THAT MUCH.
WHAT YOU DON'T KNOW IS THAT I REPEATEDLY FAILED THEIR TESTS.
THEY WANTED ME TO KILL A CHIMPANZEE NAMED GUSTAV AFTER THEY LET ME BEFRIEND IT.
I HUGGED HIM REGULARLY.
EVENTUALLY THEY USED THE TRIGGERS THEY PUT IN MY BRAIN AGAINST ME, AND ONE TIME, WHEN THINKING I WANTED TO HUG GUSTAV...
...WELL, I CRUSHED HIM INSTEAD.
I DIDN'T HAVE TO TELL YOU THIS. BUT IT'S TRUE.
I HAD TO GIVE YOU SOMETHING REAL SO YOU WOULD UNDERSTAND...
...I AM NOT JUST A CARICATURE.

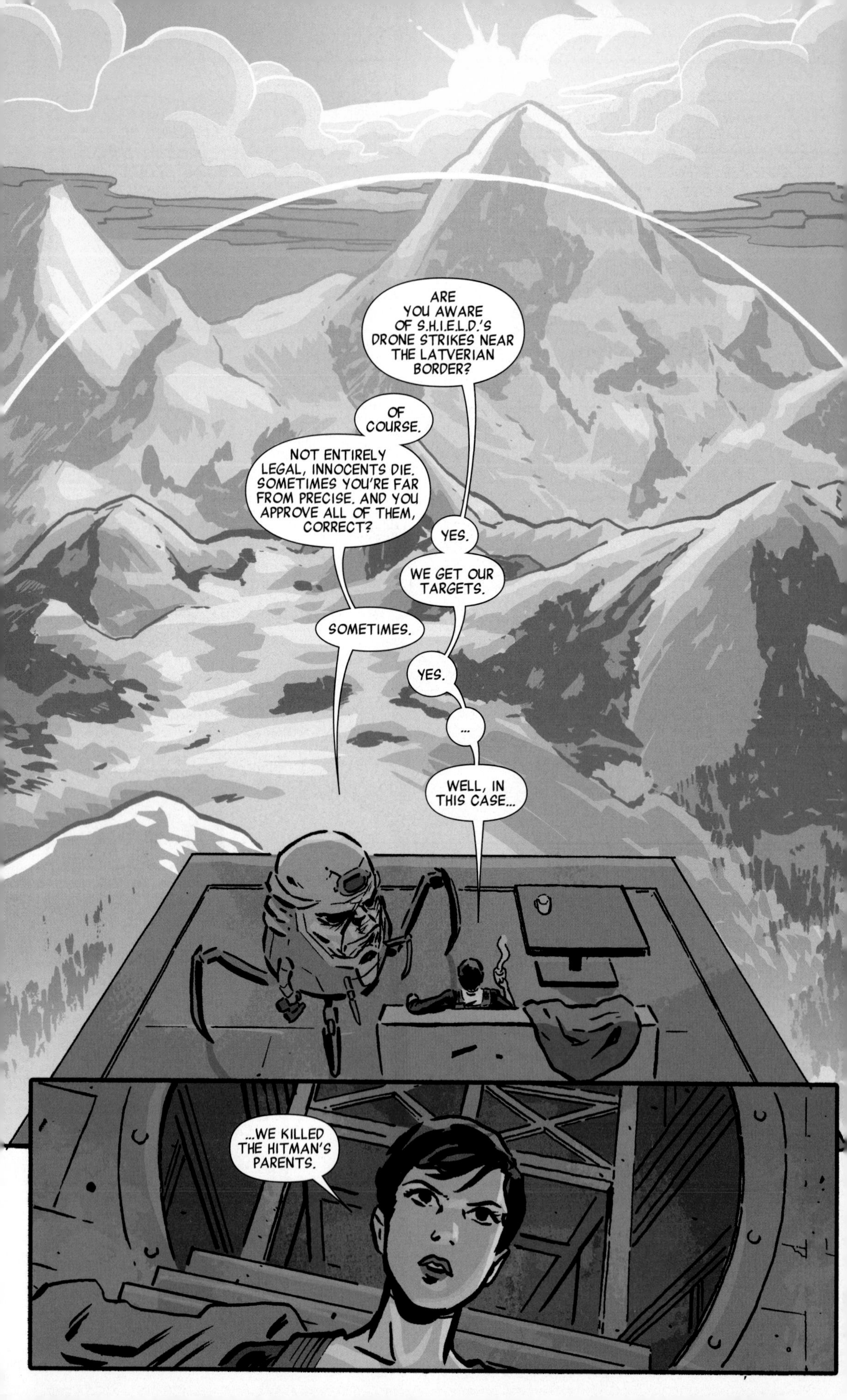
ARE YOU AWARE OF S.H.I.E.L.D.'S DRONE STRIKES NEAR THE LATVERIAN BORDER?
OF COURSE.
NOT ENTIRELY LEGAL, INNOCENTS DIE. SOMETIMES YOU'RE FAR FROM PRECISE. AND YOU APPROVE ALL OF THEM, CORRECT?
YES.
WE GET OUR TARGETS.
SOMETIMES.
YES.
...
WELL, IN THIS CASE...
...WE KILLED THE HITMAN'S PARENTS.

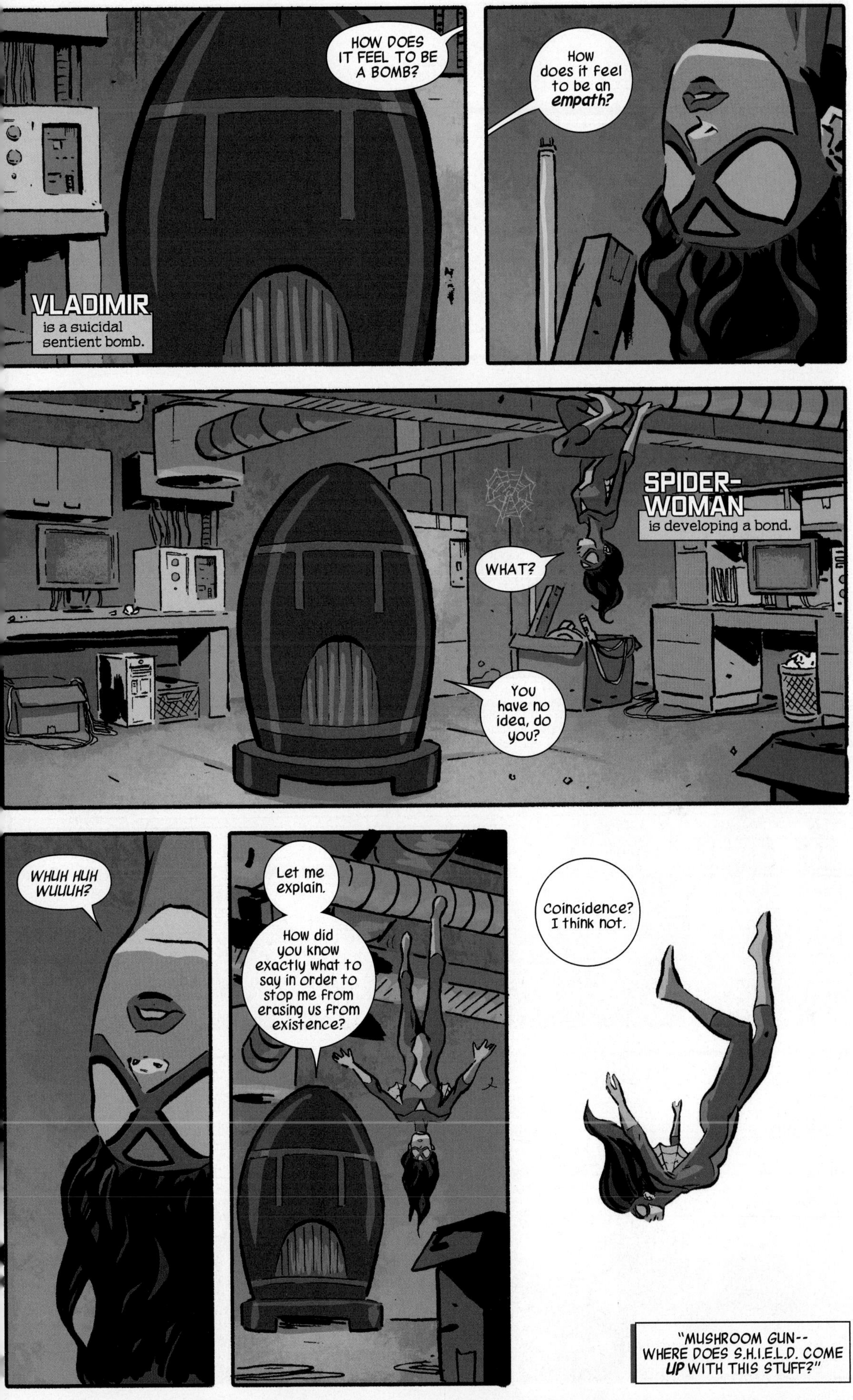
HOW DOES IT FEEL TO BE A BOMB?
VLADIMIR is a suicidal sentient bomb.
How does it feel to be an *empath?*
SPIDER-WOMAN is developing a bond.
WHAT?
You have no idea, do you?
WHUH HUH WUUUH?
Let me explain.
How did you know exactly what to say in order to stop me from erasing us from existence?
Coincidence? I think not.
"MUSHROOM GUN-- WHERE DOES S.H.I.E.L.D. COME *UP* WITH THIS STUFF?"

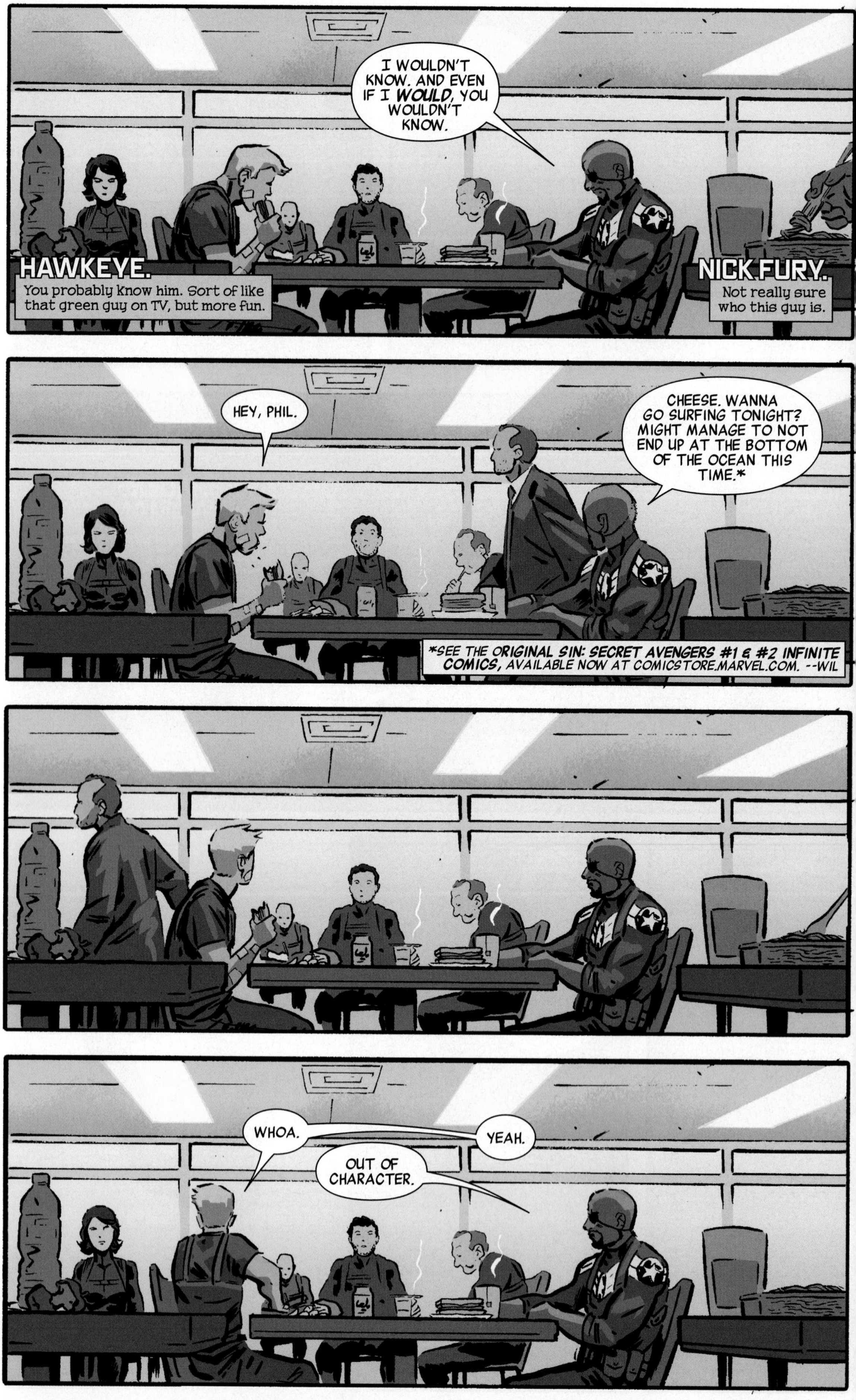
HAWKEYE.
You probably know him. Sort of like that green guy on TV, but more fun.
I WOULDN'T KNOW. AND EVEN IF I ***WOULD***, YOU WOULDN'T KNOW.
NICK FURY.
Not really sure who this guy is.
HEY, PHIL.
CHEESE. WANNA GO SURFING TONIGHT? MIGHT MANAGE TO NOT END UP AT THE BOTTOM OF THE OCEAN THIS TIME.*
*SEE THE ORIGINAL SIN: SECRET AVENGERS #1 & #2 INFINITE COMICS, AVAILABLE NOW AT COMICSTORE.MARVEL.COM. --WIL
WHOA.
YEAH.
OUT OF CHARACTER.

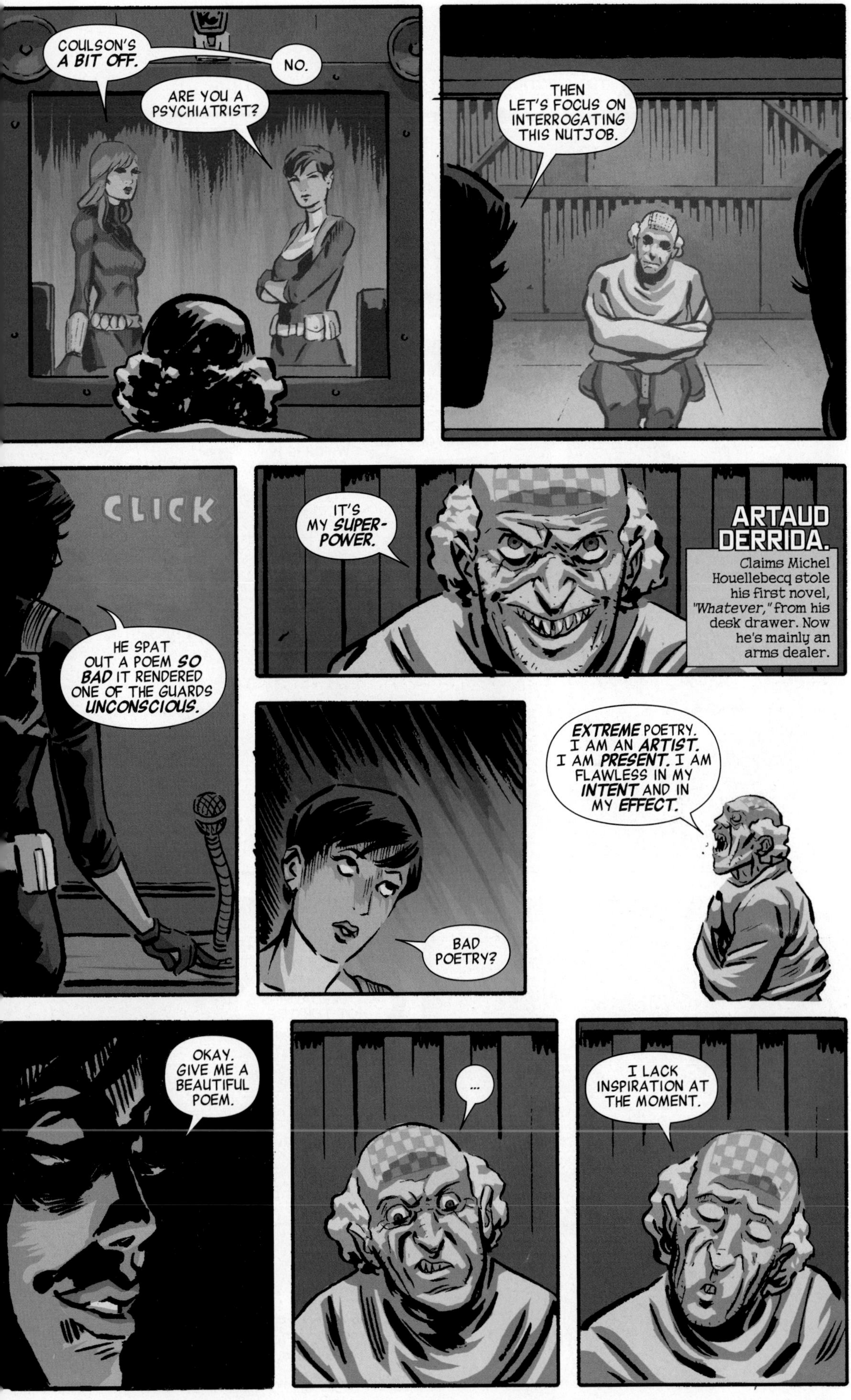
COULSON'S A BIT OFF.
NO.
ARE YOU A PSYCHIATRIST?
THEN LET'S FOCUS ON INTERROGATING THIS NUTJOB.
CLICK
HE SPAT OUT A POEM SO BAD IT RENDERED ONE OF THE GUARDS UNCONSCIOUS.
IT'S MY SUPER-POWER.
ARTAUD DERRIDA.
Claims Michel Houellebecq stole his first novel, "Whatever," from his desk drawer. Now he's mainly an arms dealer.
BAD POETRY?
EXTREME POETRY. I AM AN ARTIST. I AM PRESENT. I AM FLAWLESS IN MY INTENT AND IN MY EFFECT.
OKAY. GIVE ME A BEAUTIFUL POEM.
...
I LACK INSPIRATION AT THE MOMENT.

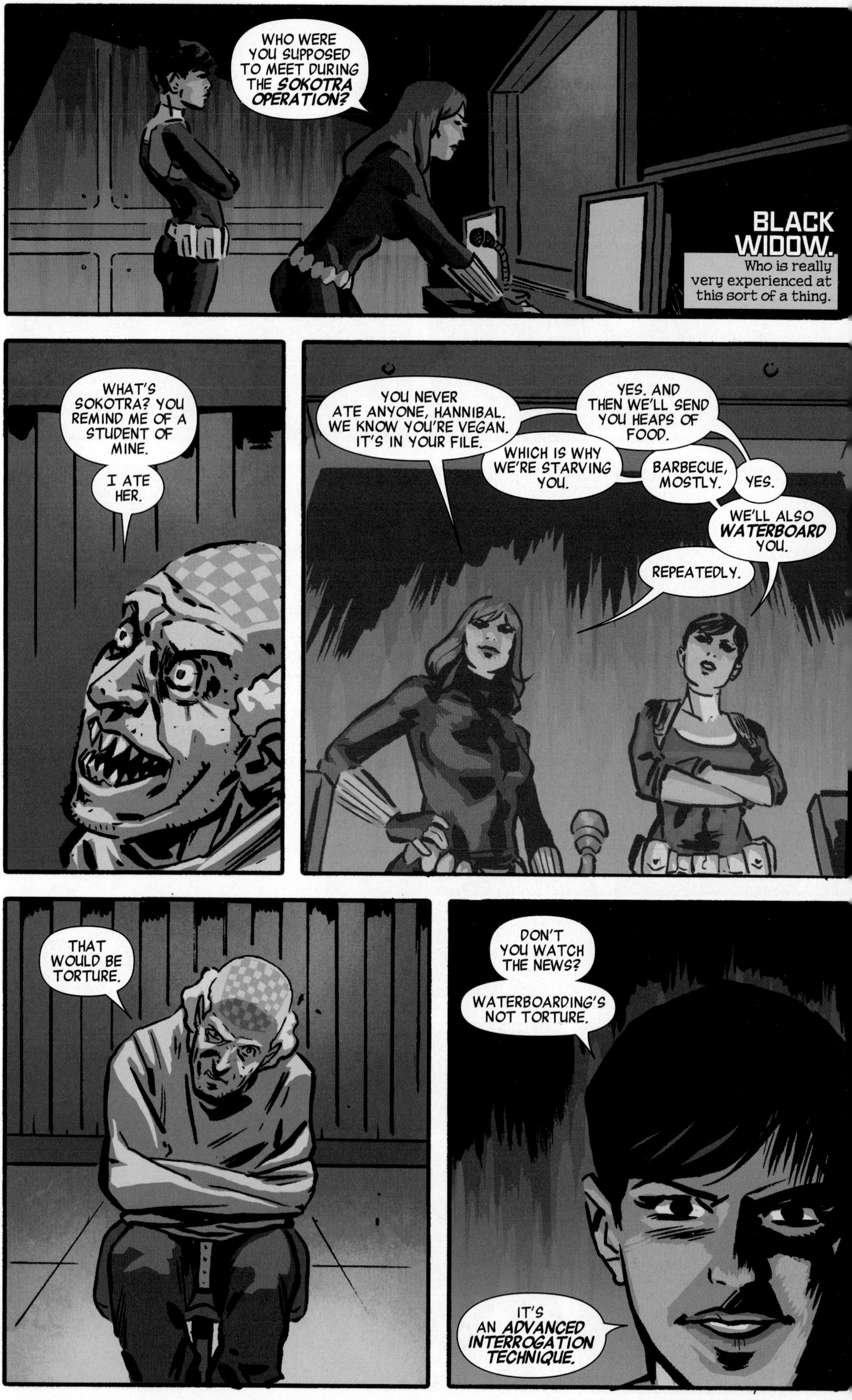
WHO WERE YOU SUPPOSED TO MEET DURING THE *SOKOTRA OPERATION?*
BLACK WIDOW.
Who is really very experienced at this sort of a thing.
WHAT'S SOKOTRA? YOU REMIND ME OF A STUDENT OF MINE.
I ATE HER.
YOU NEVER ATE ANYONE, HANNIBAL. WE KNOW YOU'RE VEGAN. IT'S IN YOUR FILE.
WHICH IS WHY WE'RE STARVING YOU.
YES. AND THEN WE'LL SEND YOU HEAPS OF FOOD.
BARBECUE, MOSTLY.
YES.
WE'LL ALSO *WATERBOARD* YOU.
REPEATEDLY.
THAT WOULD BE TORTURE.
DON'T YOU WATCH THE NEWS?
WATERBOARDING'S NOT TORTURE.
IT'S AN *ADVANCED INTERROGATION TECHNIQUE.*

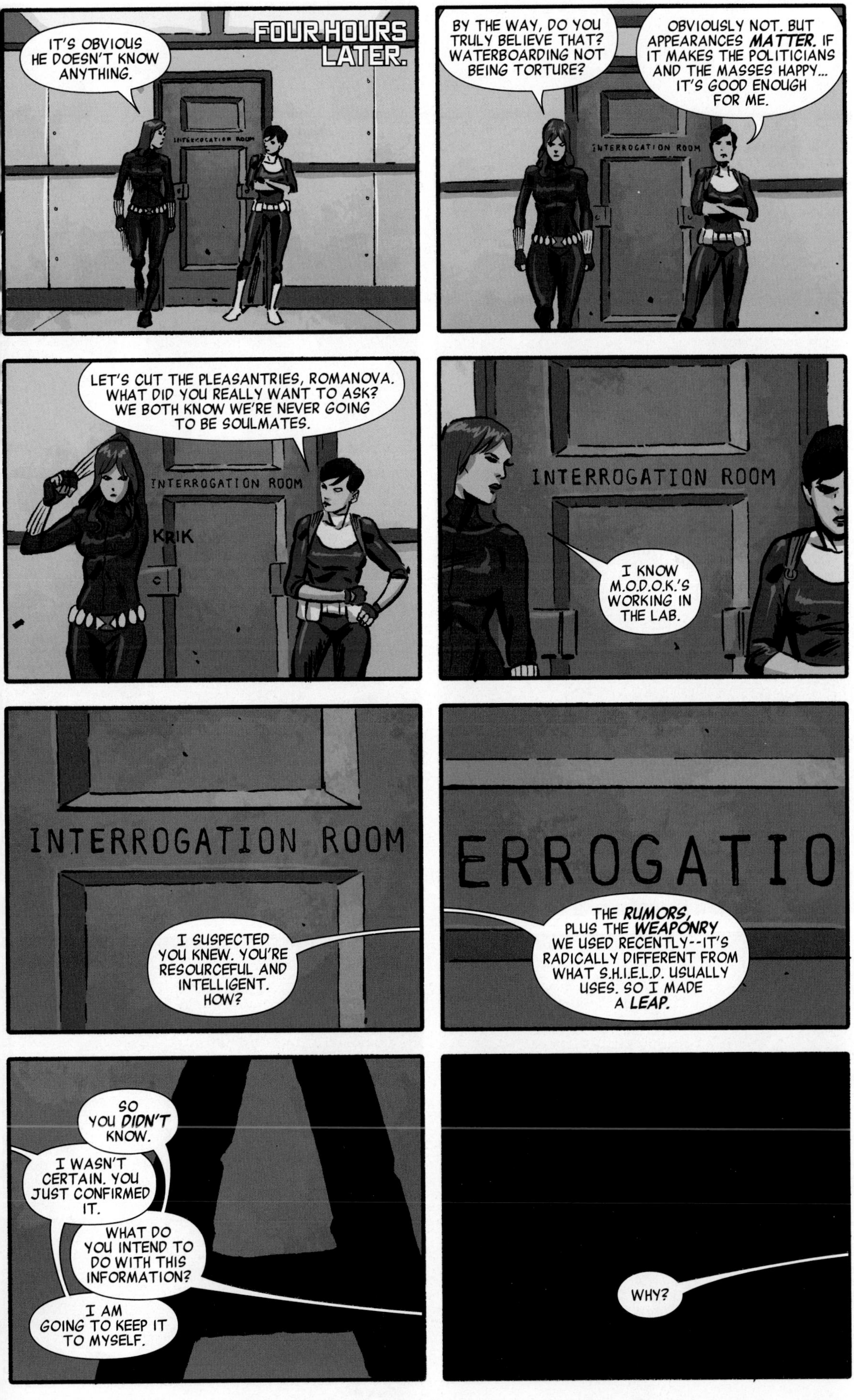
FOUR HOURS LATER.
IT'S OBVIOUS HE DOESN'T KNOW ANYTHING.
INTERROGATION ROOM
BY THE WAY, DO YOU TRULY BELIEVE THAT? WATERBOARDING NOT BEING TORTURE?
OBVIOUSLY NOT. BUT APPEARANCES MATTER. IF IT MAKES THE POLITICIANS AND THE MASSES HAPPY... IT'S GOOD ENOUGH FOR ME.
INTERROGATION ROOM
LET'S CUT THE PLEASANTRIES, ROMANOVA. WHAT DID YOU REALLY WANT TO ASK? WE BOTH KNOW WE'RE NEVER GOING TO BE SOULMATES.
INTERROGATION ROOM
KRIK
INTERROGATION ROOM
I KNOW M.O.D.O.K.'S WORKING IN THE LAB.
INTERROGATION ROOM
I SUSPECTED YOU KNEW. YOU'RE RESOURCEFUL AND INTELLIGENT. HOW?
ERROGATIO
THE RUMORS, PLUS THE WEAPONRY WE USED RECENTLY--IT'S RADICALLY DIFFERENT FROM WHAT S.H.I.E.L.D. USUALLY USES. SO I MADE A LEAP.
SO YOU DIDN'T KNOW.
I WASN'T CERTAIN. YOU JUST CONFIRMED IT.
WHAT DO YOU INTEND TO DO WITH THIS INFORMATION?
I AM GOING TO KEEP IT TO MYSELF.
WHY?

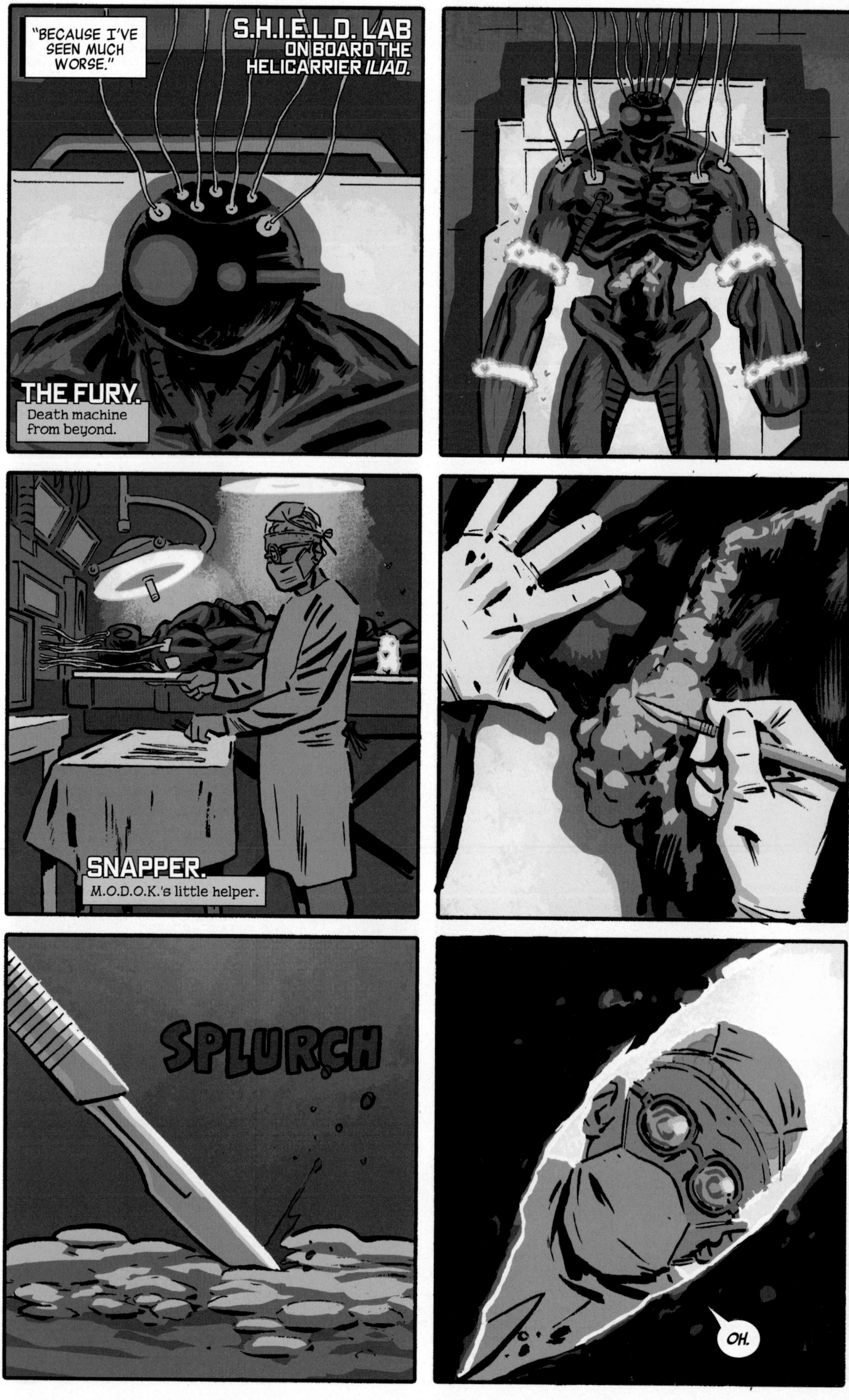
"BECAUSE I'VE SEEN MUCH WORSE."
S.H.I.E.L.D. LAB
ON BOARD THE HELICARRIER *ILIAD.*
THE FURY.
Death machine from beyond.
SNAPPER.
M.O.D.O.K.'s little helper.
SPLURCH
OH.

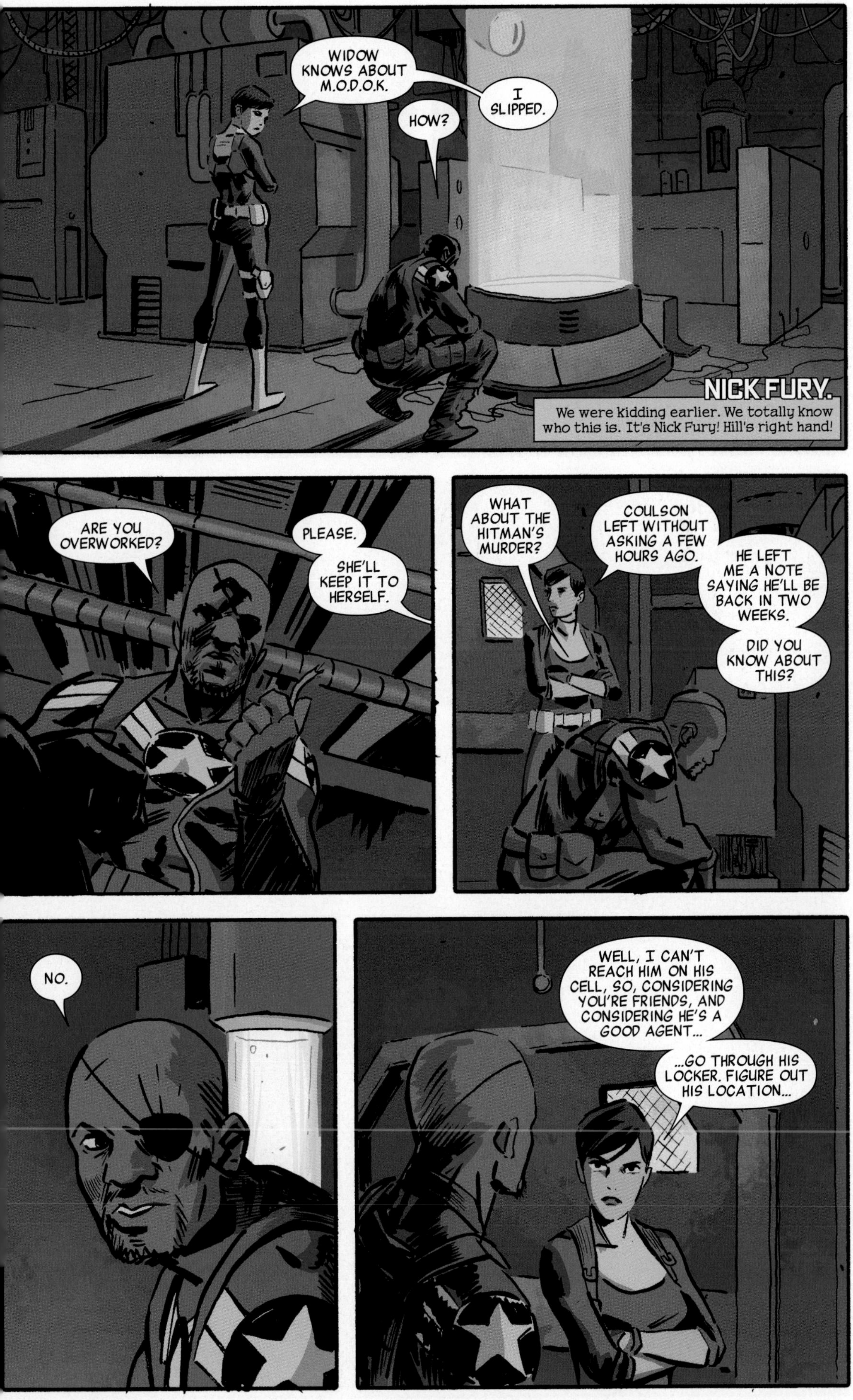
WIDOW KNOWS ABOUT M.O.D.O.K.
HOW?
I SLIPPED.
NICK FURY.
We were kidding earlier. We totally know who this is. It's Nick Fury! Hill's right hand!
ARE YOU OVERWORKED?
PLEASE.
SHE'LL KEEP IT TO HERSELF.
WHAT ABOUT THE HITMAN'S MURDER?
COULSON LEFT WITHOUT ASKING A FEW HOURS AGO.
HE LEFT ME A NOTE SAYING HE'LL BE BACK IN TWO WEEKS.
DID YOU KNOW ABOUT THIS?
NO.
WELL, I CAN'T REACH HIM ON HIS CELL, SO, CONSIDERING YOU'RE FRIENDS, AND CONSIDERING HE'S A GOOD AGENT...
...GO THROUGH HIS LOCKER. FIGURE OUT HIS LOCATION...

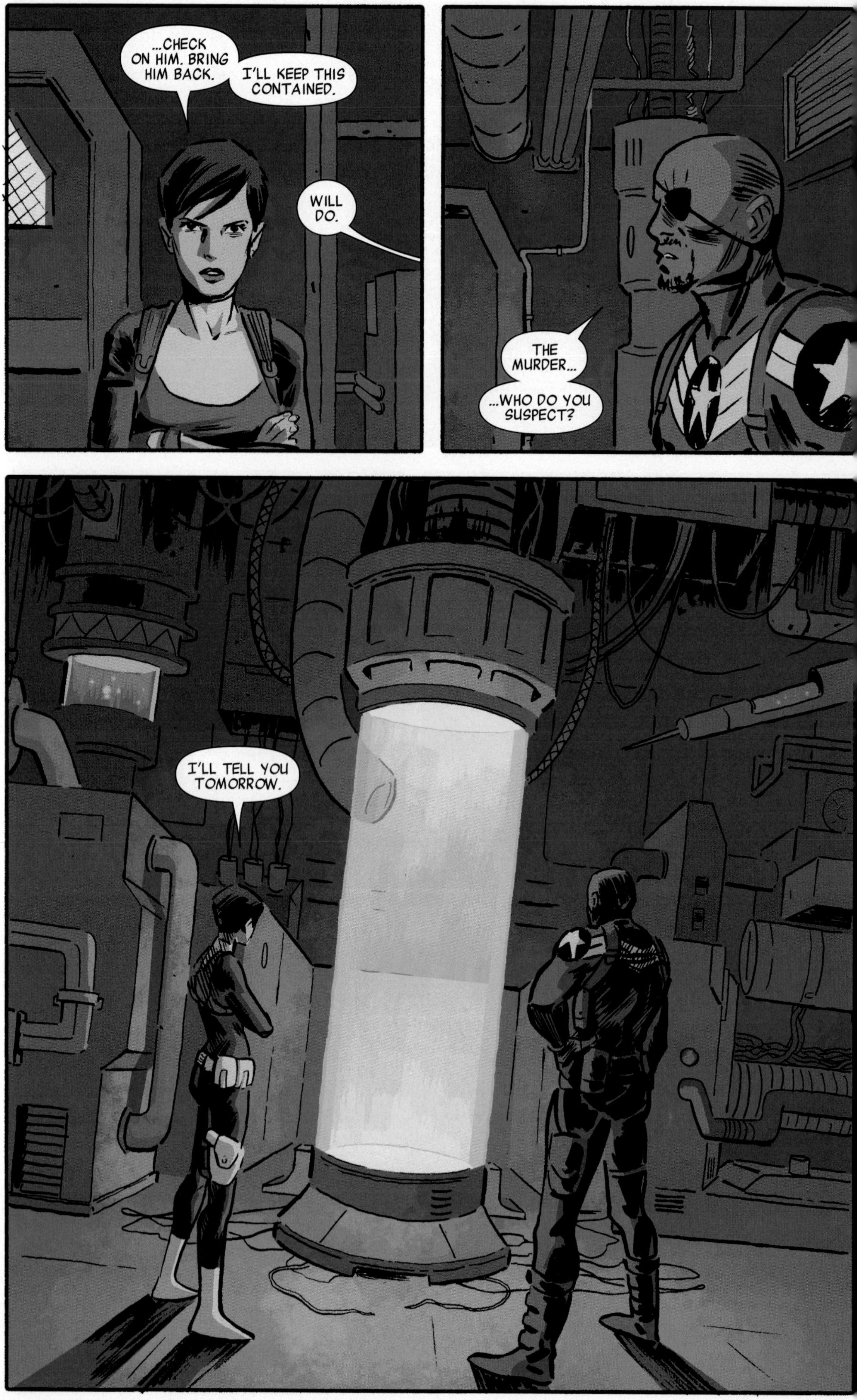
...CHECK ON HIM. BRING HIM BACK.
I'LL KEEP THIS CONTAINED.
WILL DO.
THE MURDER...
...WHO DO YOU SUSPECT?
I'LL TELL YOU TOMORROW.

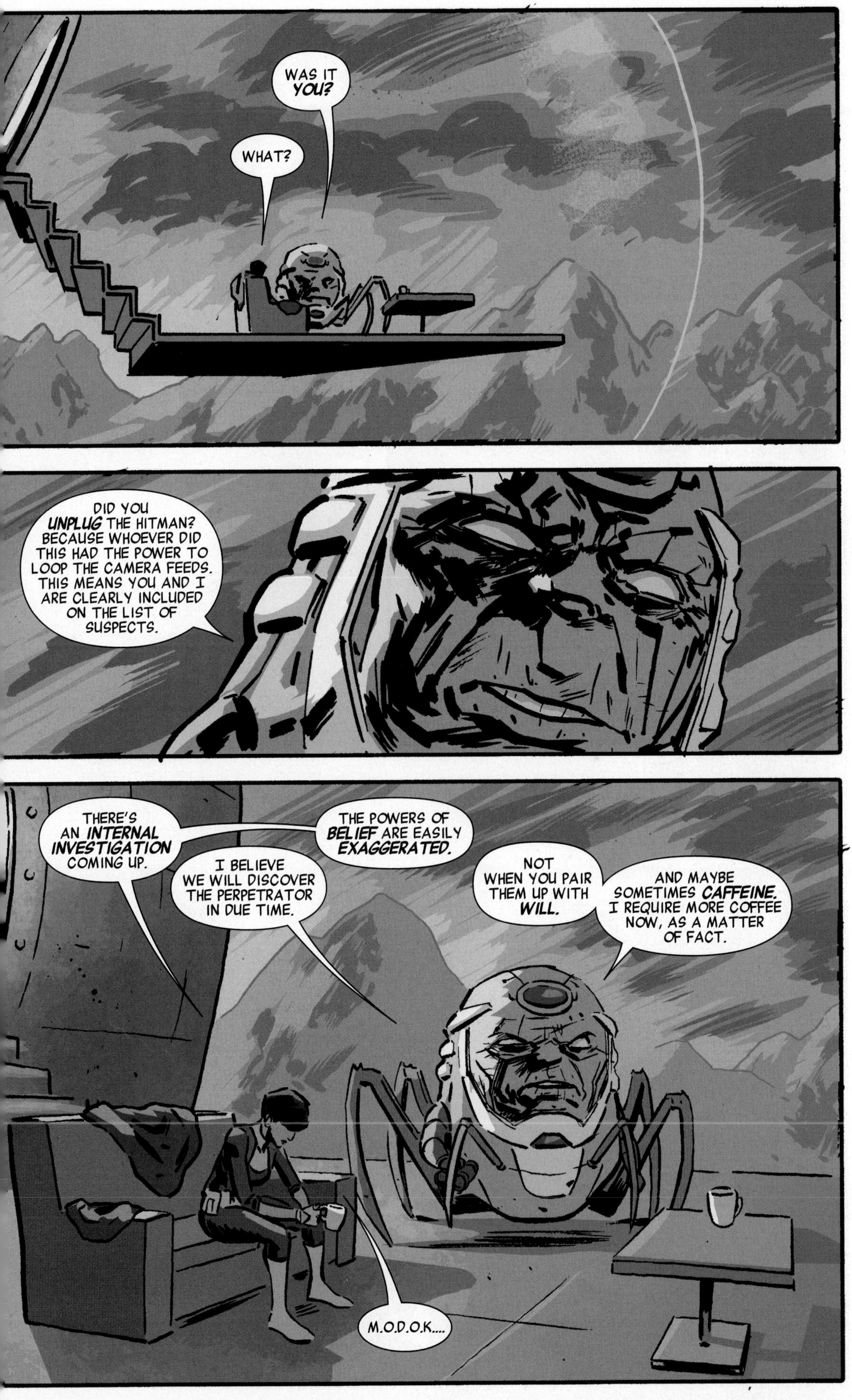
WAS IT YOU?
WHAT?
DID YOU UNPLUG THE HITMAN? BECAUSE WHOEVER DID THIS HAD THE POWER TO LOOP THE CAMERA FEEDS. THIS MEANS YOU AND I ARE CLEARLY INCLUDED ON THE LIST OF SUSPECTS.
THERE'S AN INTERNAL INVESTIGATION COMING UP.
I BELIEVE WE WILL DISCOVER THE PERPETRATOR IN DUE TIME.
THE POWERS OF BELIEF ARE EASILY EXAGGERATED.
NOT WHEN YOU PAIR THEM UP WITH WILL.
AND MAYBE SOMETIMES CAFFEINE. I REQUIRE MORE COFFEE NOW, AS A MATTER OF FACT.
M.O.D.O.K....

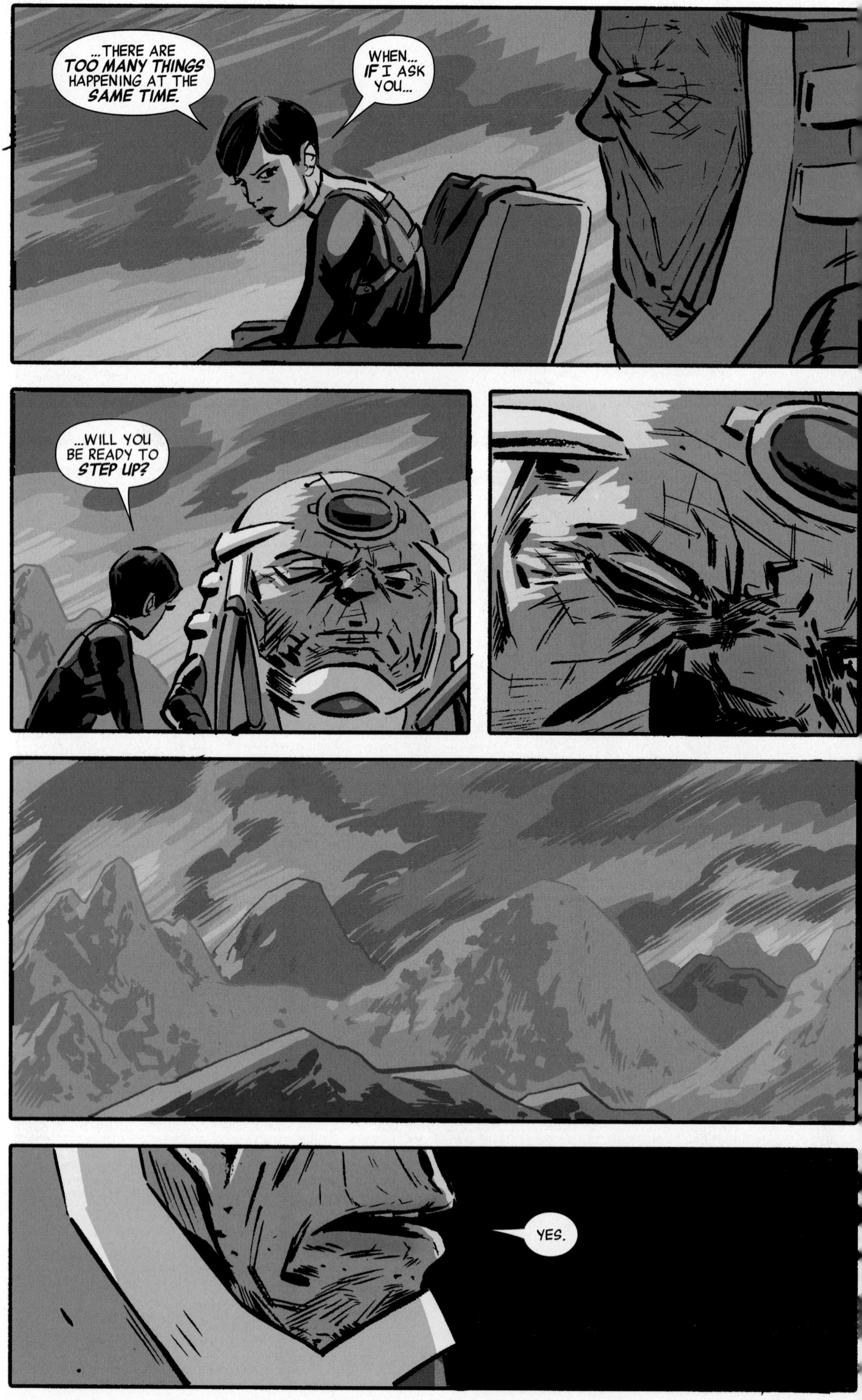
...THERE ARE TOO MANY THINGS HAPPENING AT THE SAME TIME.
WHEN... IF I ASK YOU...
...WILL YOU BE READY TO STEP UP?
YES.

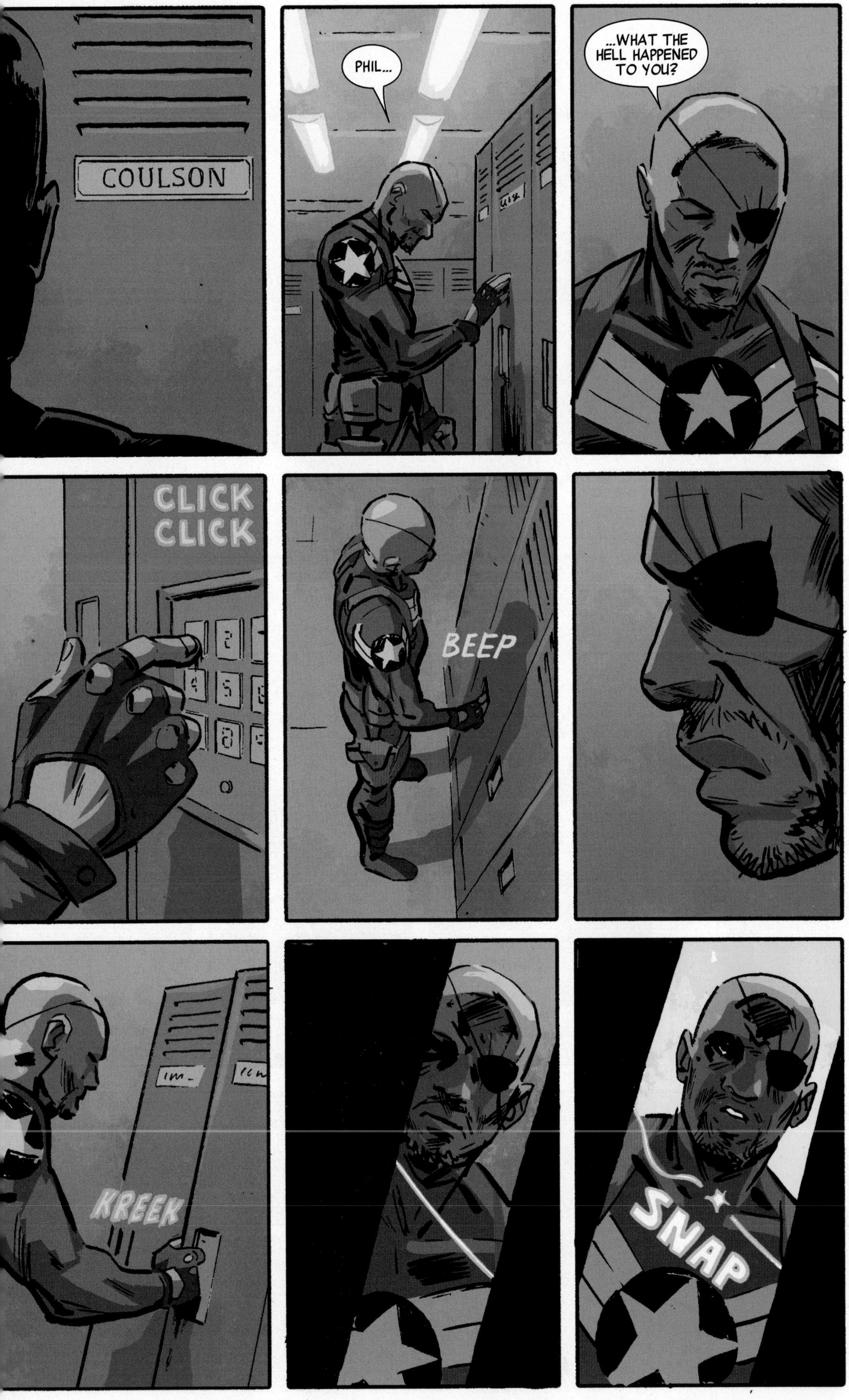
COULSON
PHIL...
...WHAT THE HELL HAPPENED TO YOU?
CLICK CLICK
BEEP
KREEK
SNAP

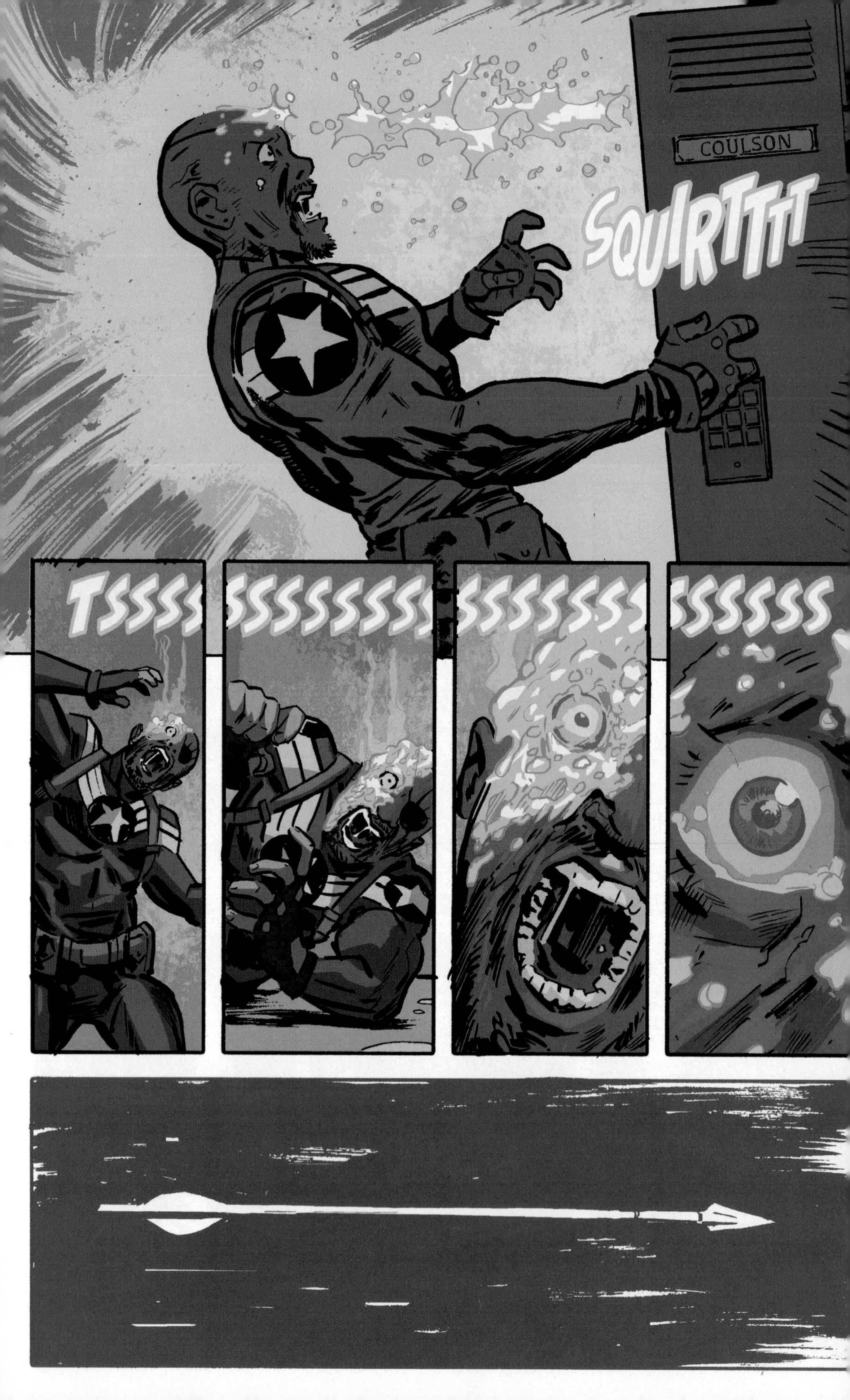
COULSON
SQUIRTTTT
TSSSSSSSSSSSSSSSSSSSSSSSSSSSS

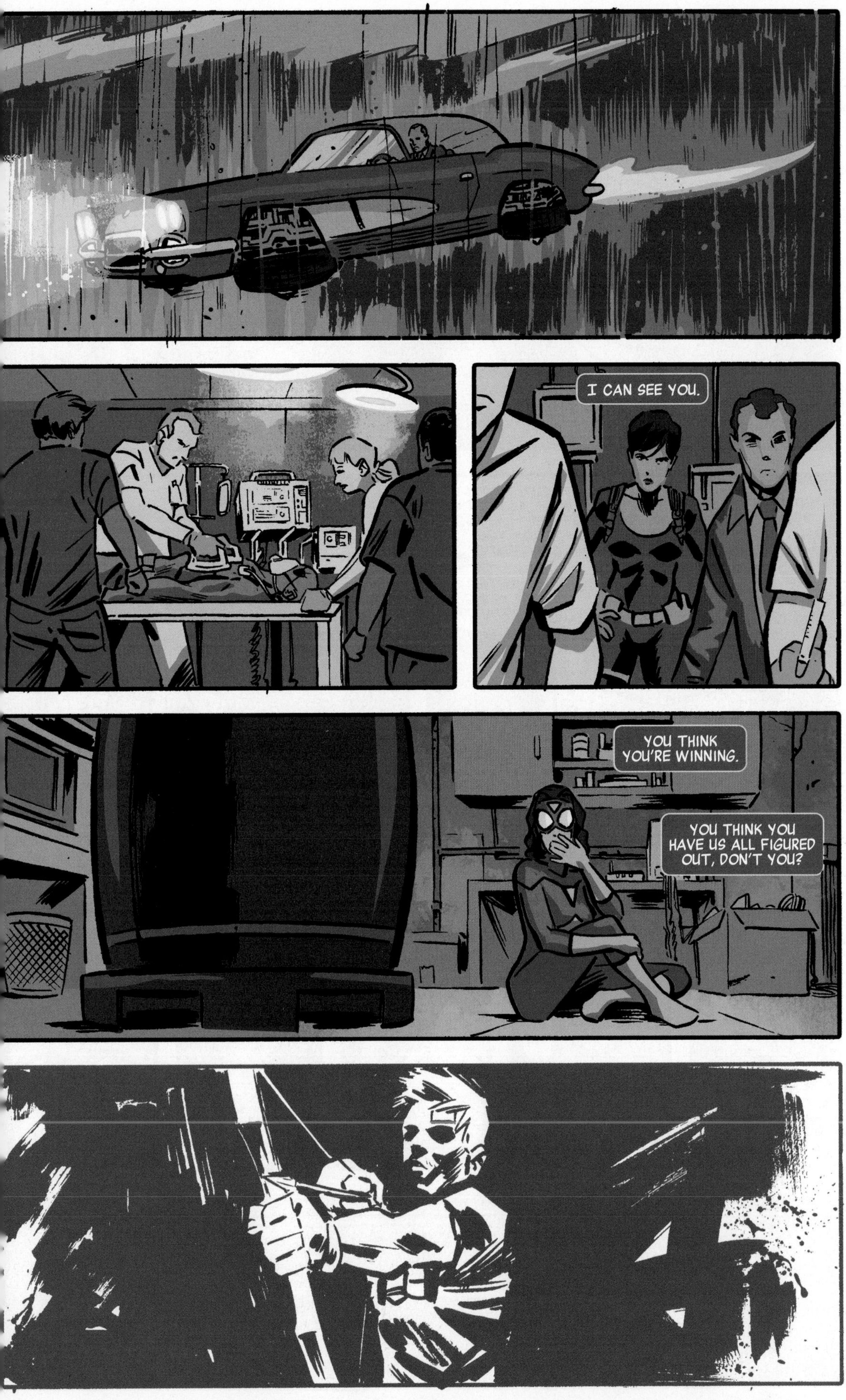
I CAN SEE YOU.
YOU THINK YOU'RE WINNING.
YOU THINK YOU HAVE US ALL FIGURED OUT, DON'T YOU?

DID YOU HAVE ANYTHING TO CONTRIBUTE TO THE MURDER *INVESTIGATION*, SNAPPER?

NOT REALLY, SIR.

DID *YOU* DO IT, SNAPPER?

MOST CERTAINLY *NOT*, SIR.

GOOD BOY.

WHAT'S THE PROGRESS ON OUR BEAUTIFUL KILLING MACHINE? I AM STILL AWAKE ONLY BECAUSE YOU CALLED ME HERE. YOU KNOW BETTER THAN TO WASTE MY TIME. I ADORE WATCHING *CONTEMPT*.

IS THIS BIG? AS BIG AS *GODARD*?

SIR...I DON'T KNOW ANYTHING ABOUT ANYTHING YOU JUST SAID, BUT "*BIG*" IS PROBABLY *ONE* WORD THAT COULD DESCRIBE THE DISCOVERY, YES...

GET ON WITH IT. I PUT MY PANTS ON FOR YOU.

WELL, THAT WOUND ON THE FURY, SIR...

...I DON'T THINK IT'S A *WOUND*, PER SE.

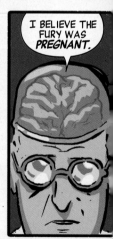

I BELIEVE THE FURY WAS *PREGNANT*.

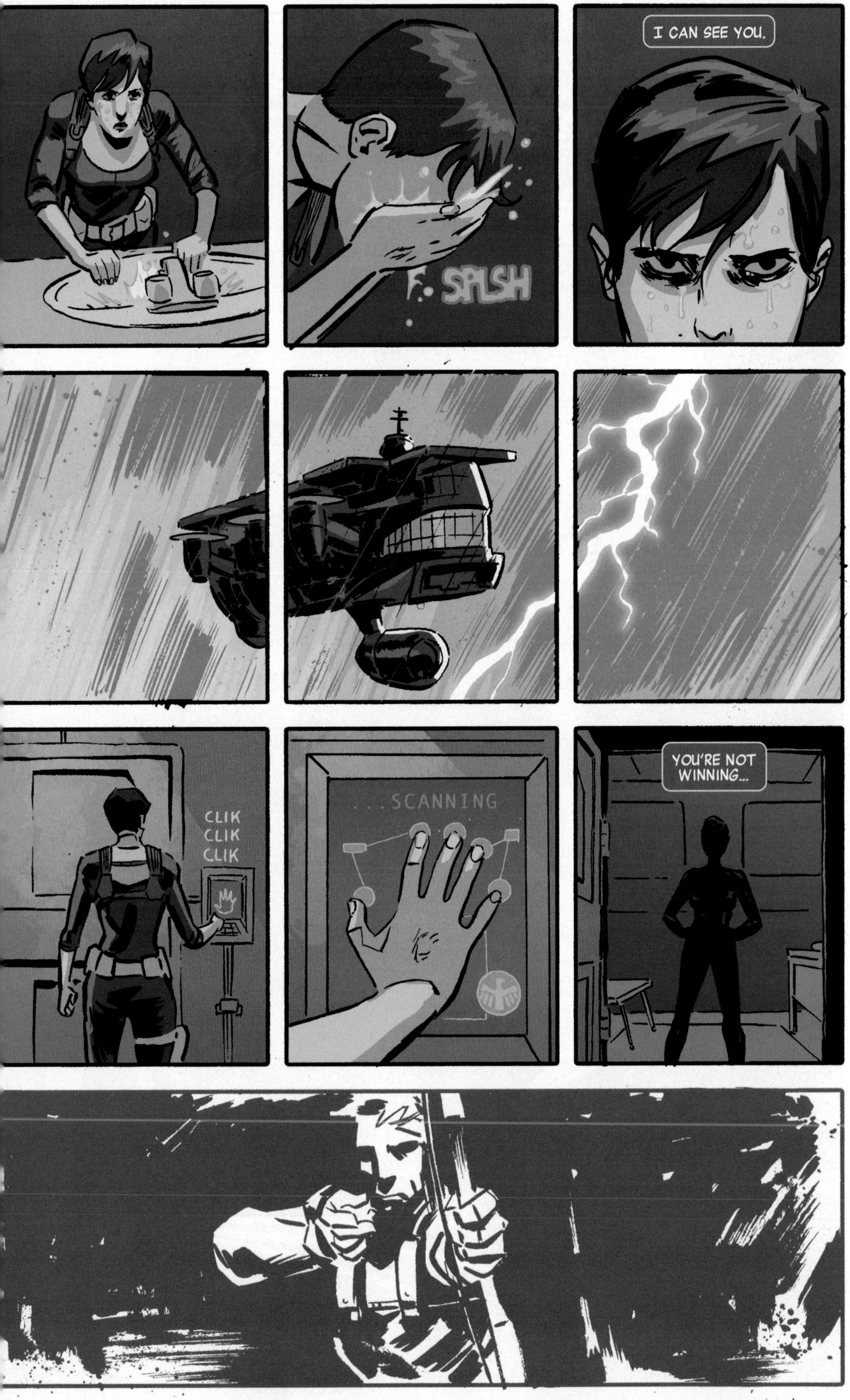
SPLSH
I CAN SEE YOU.
CLIK
CLIK
CLIK
...SCANNING
YOU'RE NOT WINNING...

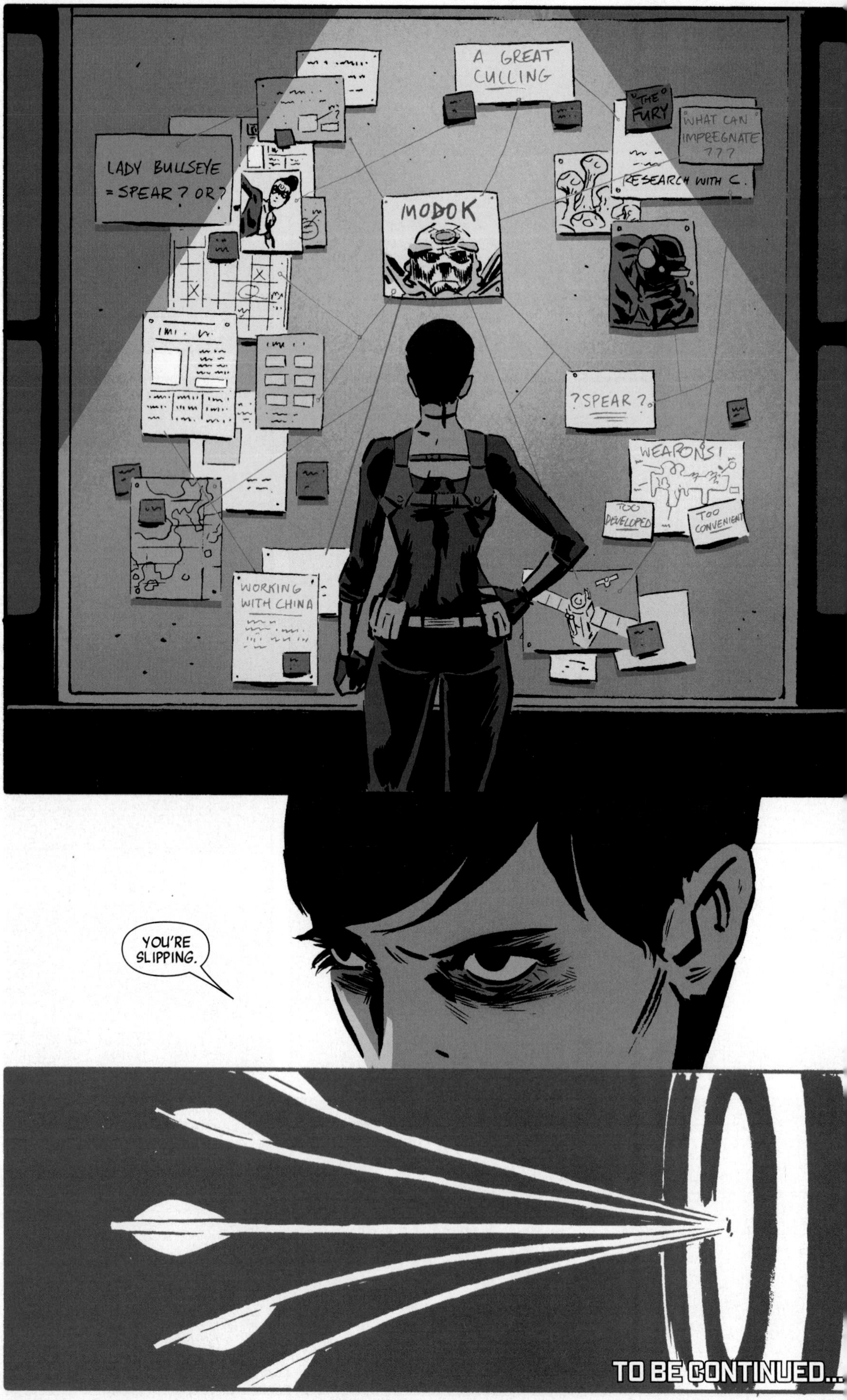
A GREAT CULLING
THE FURY
WHAT CAN IMPREGNATE ???
RESEARCH WITH C.
LADY BULLSEYE = SPEAR? OR?
MODOK
?SPEAR?
WEAPONS!
TOO DEVELOPED
TOO CONVENIENT
WORKING WITH CHINA
YOU'RE SLIPPING.
TO BE CONTINUED...

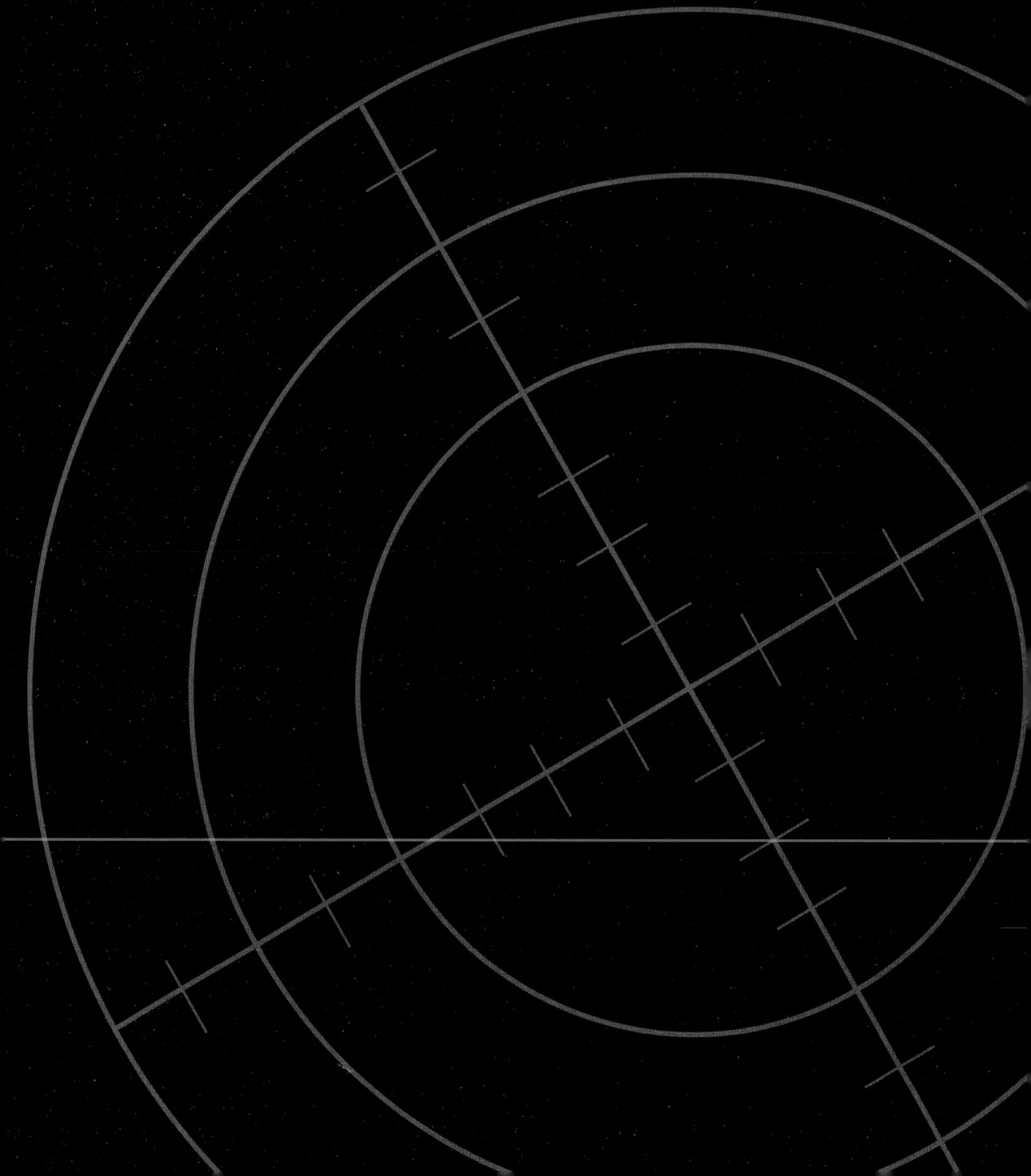

RUN THE MISSION. DON'T GET SEEN. SAVE THE WORLD.

RECENTLY, THE OTHERWORLDLY BEING KNOWN AS THE WATCHER WAS FOUND MURDERED ON THE SURFACE OF THE MOON. HIS EYES WERE STOLEN. DURING A CONFLICT WITH THE THIEVES IN NEW YORK CITY, ONE OF THE WATCHER'S EYES DETONATED, IMPARTING SECRETS OF THE MARVEL UNIVERSE ONTO ANYONE WITHIN THE BLAST RANGE...

ORIGINAL SIN: SECRET AVENGERS INFINITE COMIC

INFINITE COMICS ARE MARVEL'S NEWEST AND BOLDEST JUMP INTO THE WORLD OF DIGITAL COMICS. CRAFTED SPECIFICALLY TO BE READ ON THE MARVEL COMICS APP, INFINITE COMICS TAKE ADVANTAGE OF NEW STORYTELLING OPPORTUNITIES THE DIGITAL REALM MAKES POSSIBLE. THIS STORY HAS BEEN RESTRUCTURED INTO TRADITIONAL PRINT COMICS, BUT THE ORIGINAL VERSIONS CAN BE READ ON THE MARVEL COMICS APP TO GET THE FULL EFFECT.

ALES KOT
WRITER

MAST & GEOFFO
STORYBOARD ARTISTS

RYAN KELLY
PENCILER/INKER

LEE LOUGHRIDGE
COLOR ARTIST

VC's CLAYTON COWLES
LETTERER

TIM SMITH 3
PRODUCTION MANAGER

ARLIN ORTIZ & LARISSA LOUIS
PRODUCTION

JON MOISAN
ASSISTANT EDITOR

WIL MOSS
EDITOR

TOM BREVOORT
EXECUTIVE EDITOR

AXEL ALONSO
EDITOR IN CHIEF

JOE QUESADA
CHIEF CREATIVE OFFICER

DAN BUCKLEY
PUBLISHER

ALAN FINE
EXECUTIVE PRODUCER

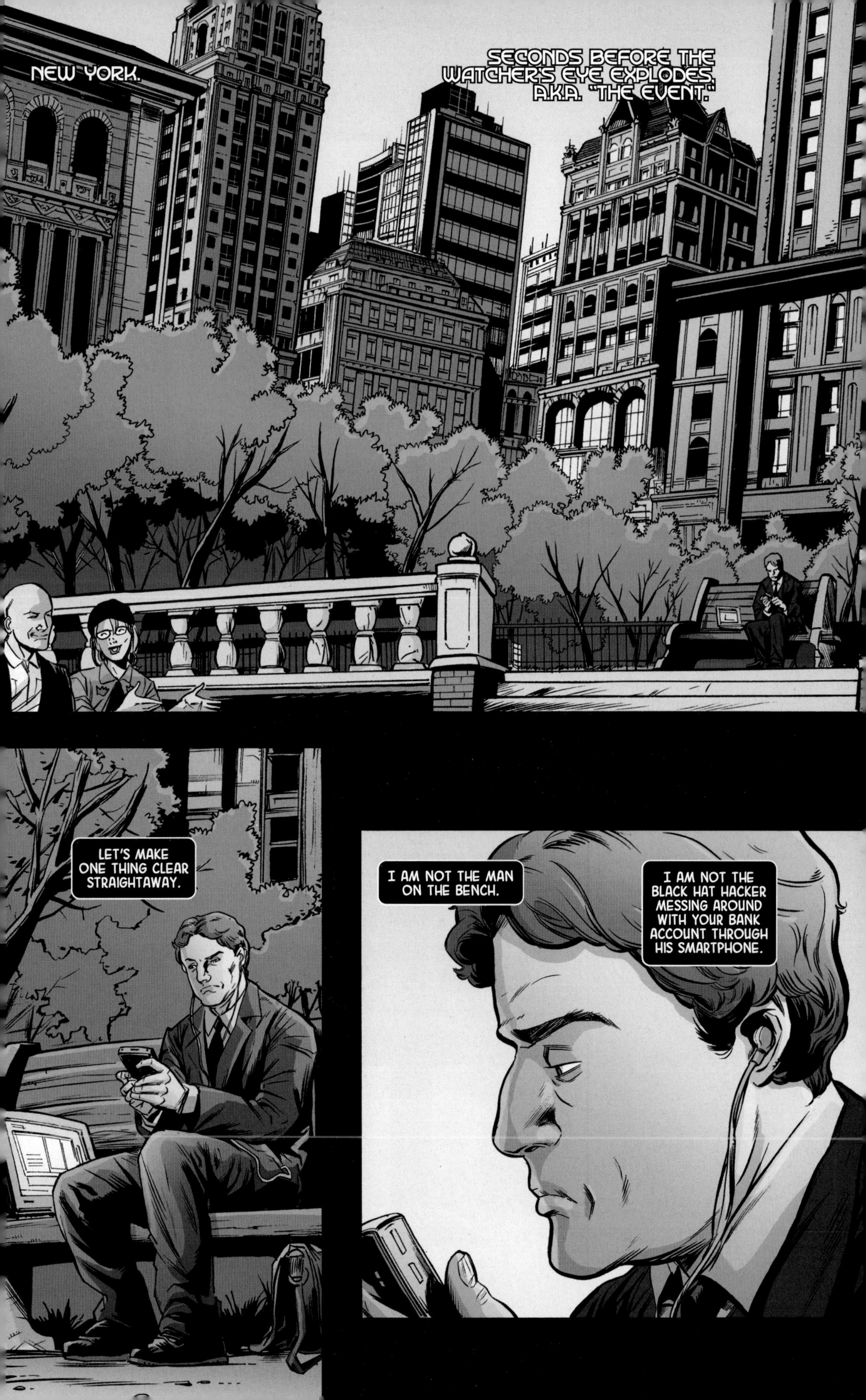
NEW YORK.
SECONDS BEFORE THE WATCHER'S EYE EXPLODES, A.K.A. "THE EVENT."
LET'S MAKE ONE THING CLEAR STRAIGHTAWAY.
I AM NOT THE MAN ON THE BENCH.
I AM NOT THE BLACK HAT HACKER MESSING AROUND WITH YOUR BANK ACCOUNT THROUGH HIS SMARTPHONE.

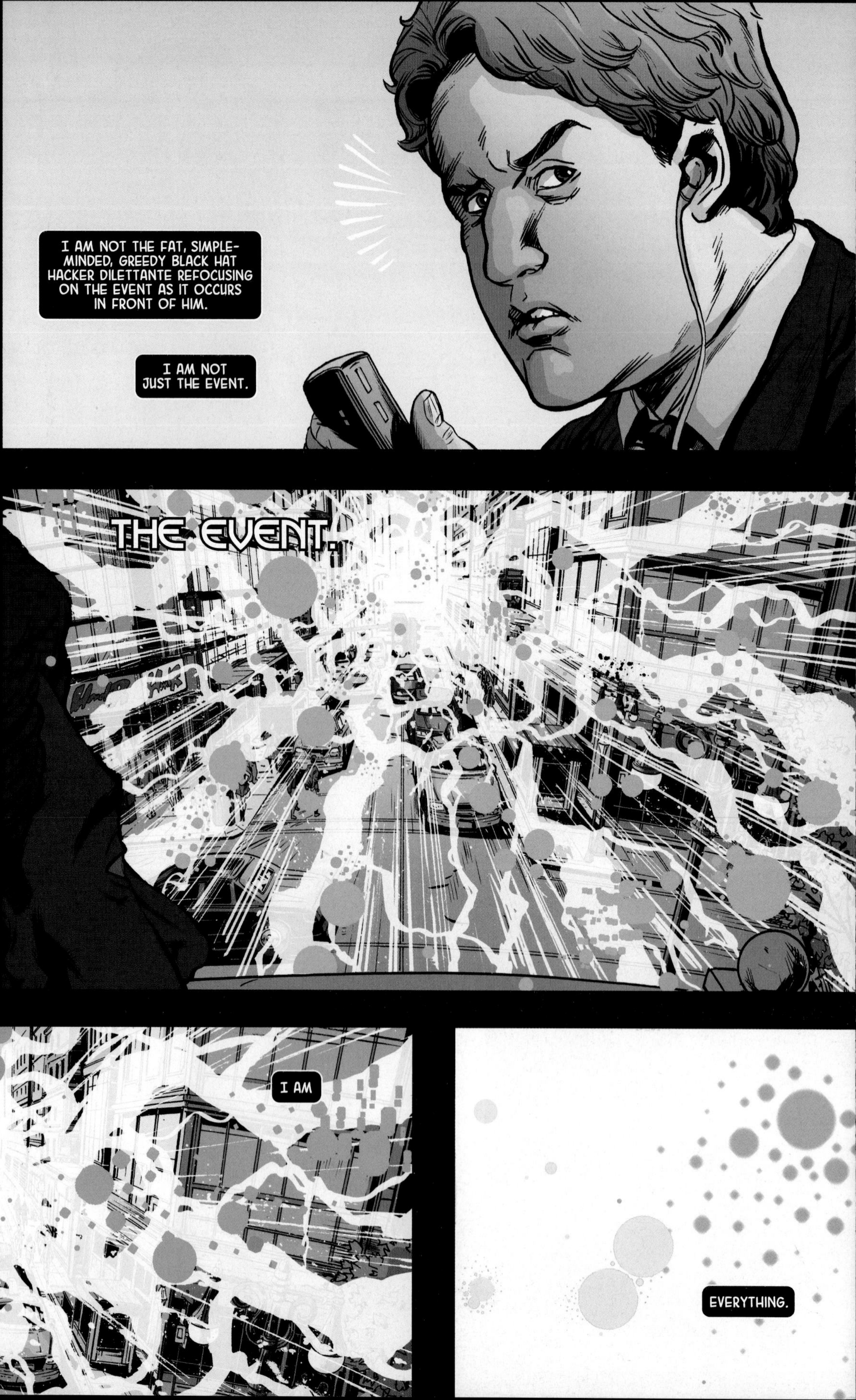
I AM NOT THE FAT, SIMPLE-MINDED, GREEDY BLACK HAT HACKER DILETTANTE REFOCUSING ON THE EVENT AS IT OCCURS IN FRONT OF HIM.
I AM NOT JUST THE EVENT.
THE EVENT.
I AM
EVERYTHING.

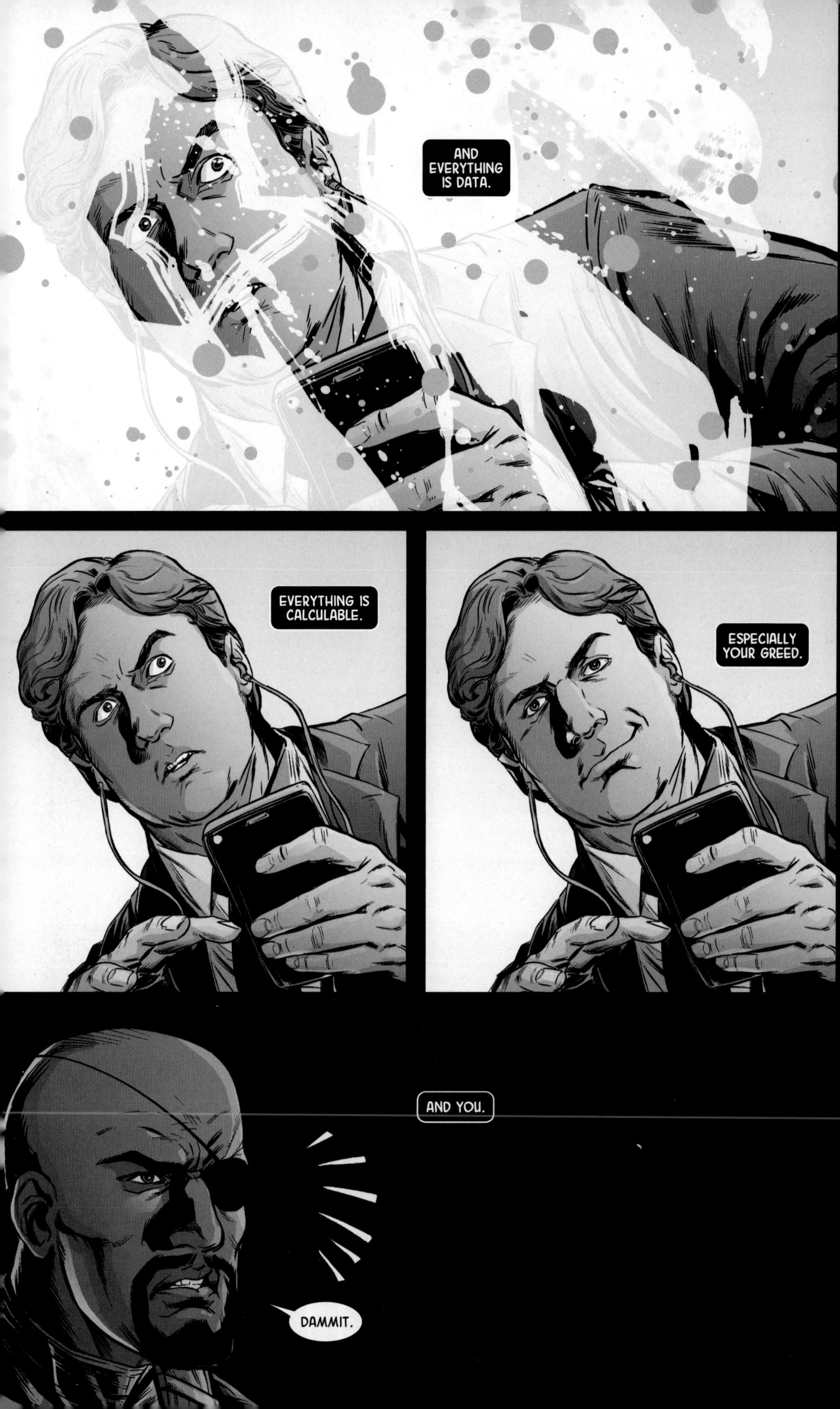
AND EVERYTHING IS DATA.
EVERYTHING IS CALCULABLE.
ESPECIALLY YOUR GREED.
AND YOU.
DAMMIT.

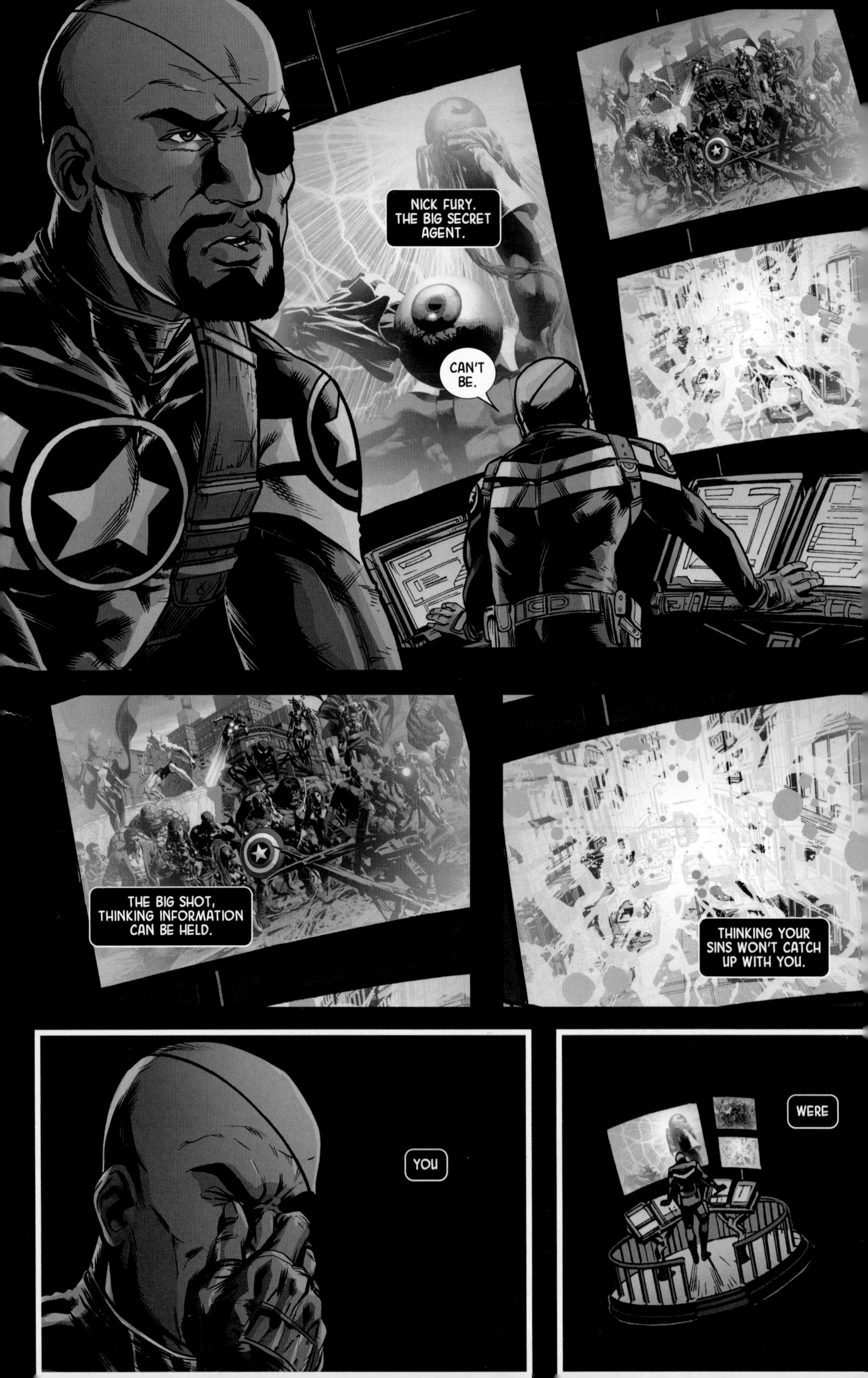
NICK FURY.
THE BIG SECRET
AGENT.
CAN'T
BE.
THE BIG SHOT,
THINKING INFORMATION
CAN BE HELD.
THINKING YOUR
SINS WON'T CATCH
UP WITH YOU.
YOU
WERE

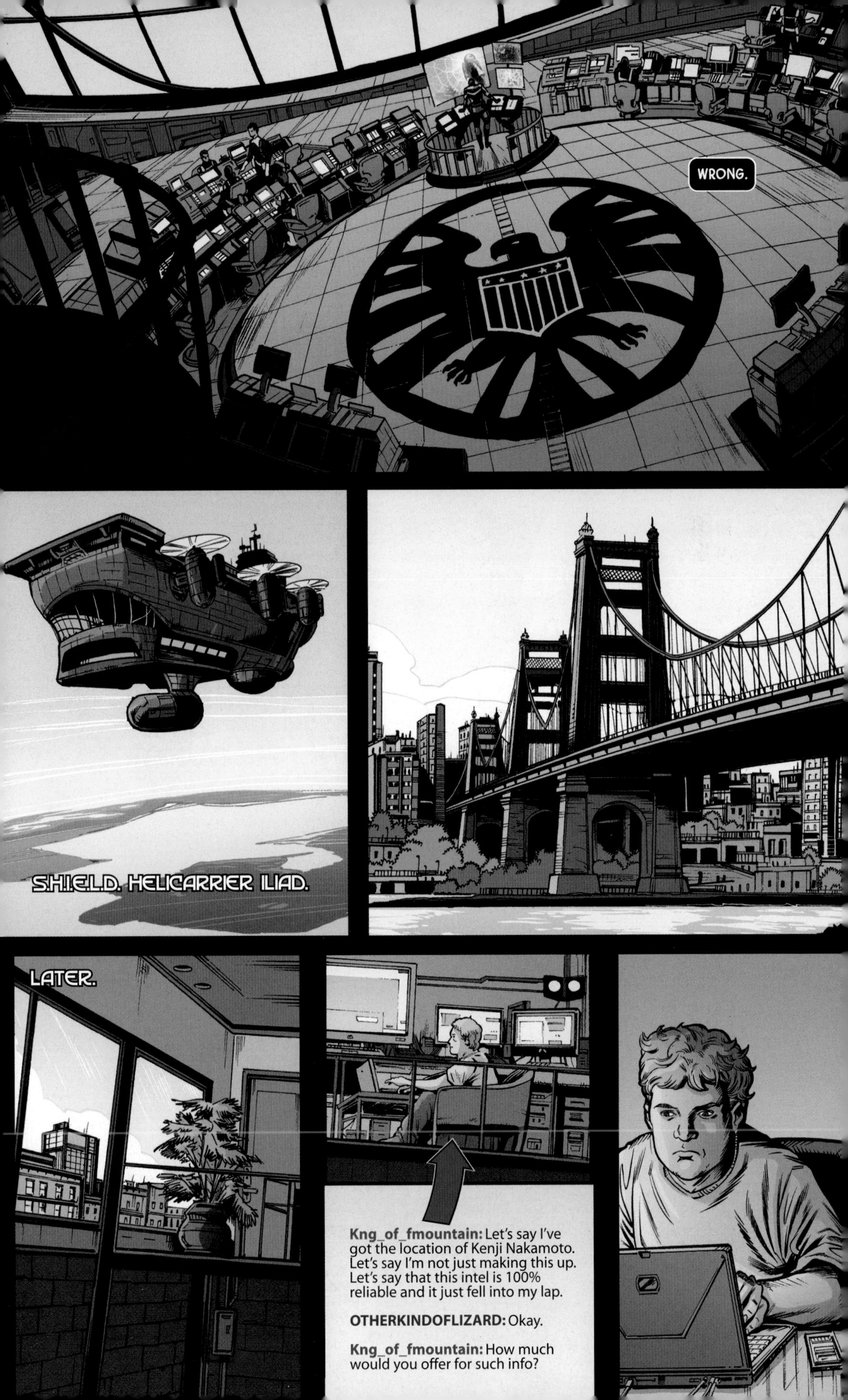
WRONG.
S.H.I.E.L.D. HELICARRIER ILIAD.
LATER.
Kng_of_fmountain: Let's say I've got the location of Kenji Nakamoto. Let's say I'm not just making this up. Let's say that this intel is 100% reliable and it just fell into my lap.
OTHERKINDOFLIZARD: Okay.
Kng_of_fmountain: How much would you offer for such info?

a nice right number, isn't it.

Kng_of_fmountain: I am not joking here. We are talking the possibility of finding the guy who created tech that effectively reads reality as code to be altered.

OTHERKINDOFLIZARD: I know who Kenji Nakamoto is. This is a serious offer.

ploit(a808_067_npizpi) >
ploit(a808_067_npizpi) >
ploit(a808_067_npizpi) >
ploit(a808_067_npizpi) >
ploit(a808_067_npizpi) >
ge(011(a808_067_npizpi) 1cck AHbSI #921188.1.208
A5.192.188.1.208
ploti(a808_068sberipit Hleet 1H19T 192.188.1.209
r>> 192.168.1.189...
exploit5!SIPS08_067_i$42pi) a sapfoit
lansering handler on 192.168.1.109.4444

OTHERKINDOFLIZARD: I presume wire transfer of one third of the money to prove my point would work?

Kng_of_fmountain: We will route through other accounts. Write what you see next on paper only. Destroy afterwards.

OTHERKINDOFLIZARD: Of course. I am no amateur. I value my life.

SOON.

HERE'S THE DEAL, COULSON: NAKAMOTO WAS SUPPOSED TO STAY DEAD.

I SET IT UP.

I GOT HIM-- I MEAN, THAT'S WHAT YOU DO WHEN A SCIENTIST DISCOVERS A CODE SYSTEM THAT COMBINES MAGIC STRAIGHT OUT OF LIMBO WITH SOME OF THE MOST ADVANCED SOFTWARE AVAILABLE, RIGHT?

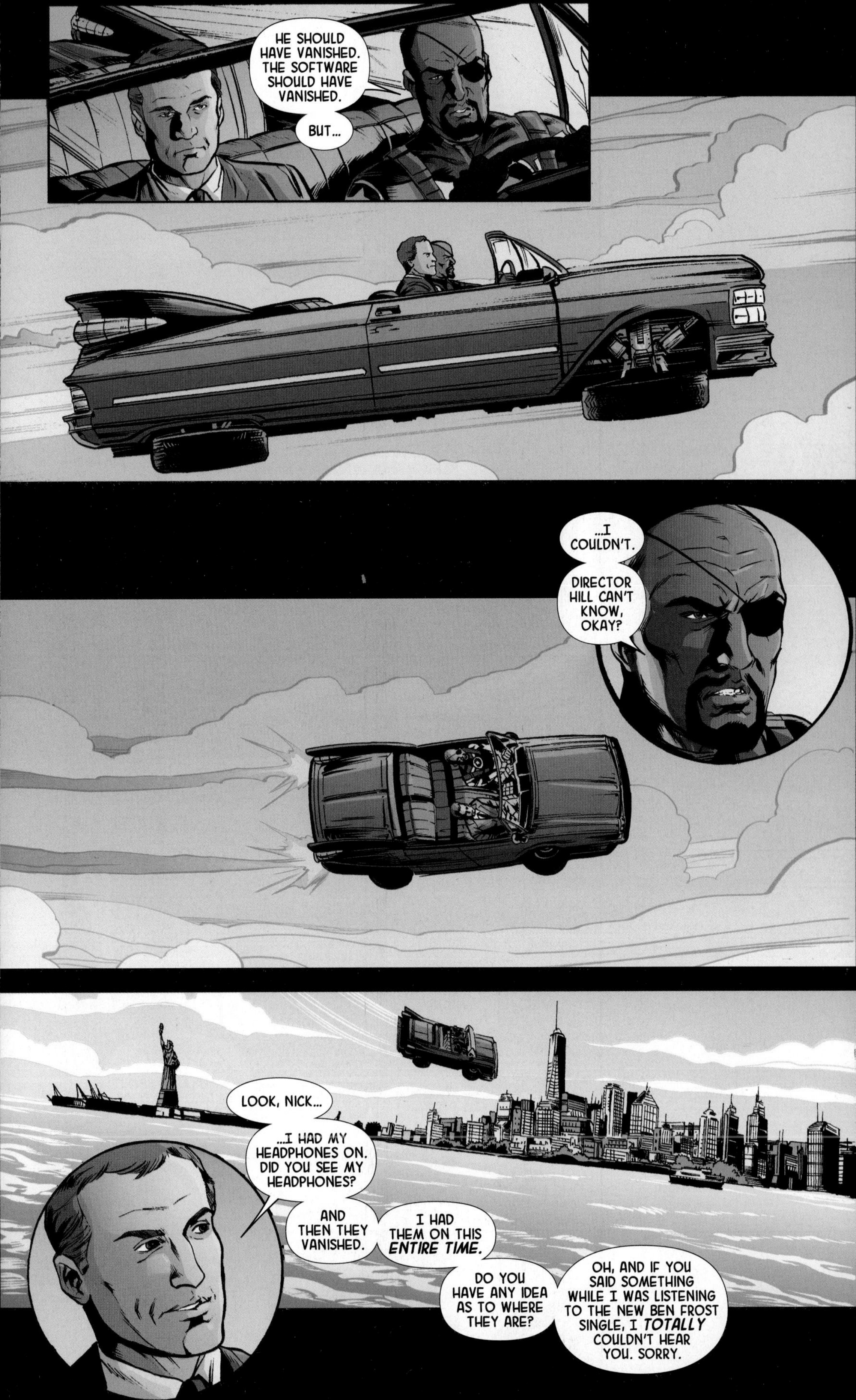
HE SHOULD HAVE VANISHED. THE SOFTWARE SHOULD HAVE VANISHED.
BUT...
...I COULDN'T.
DIRECTOR HILL CAN'T KNOW, OKAY?
LOOK, NICK...
...I HAD MY HEADPHONES ON. DID YOU SEE MY HEADPHONES?
AND THEN THEY VANISHED.
I HAD THEM ON THIS ENTIRE TIME.
DO YOU HAVE ANY IDEA AS TO WHERE THEY ARE?
OH, AND IF YOU SAID SOMETHING WHILE I WAS LISTENING TO THE NEW BEN FROST SINGLE, I TOTALLY COULDN'T HEAR YOU. SORRY.

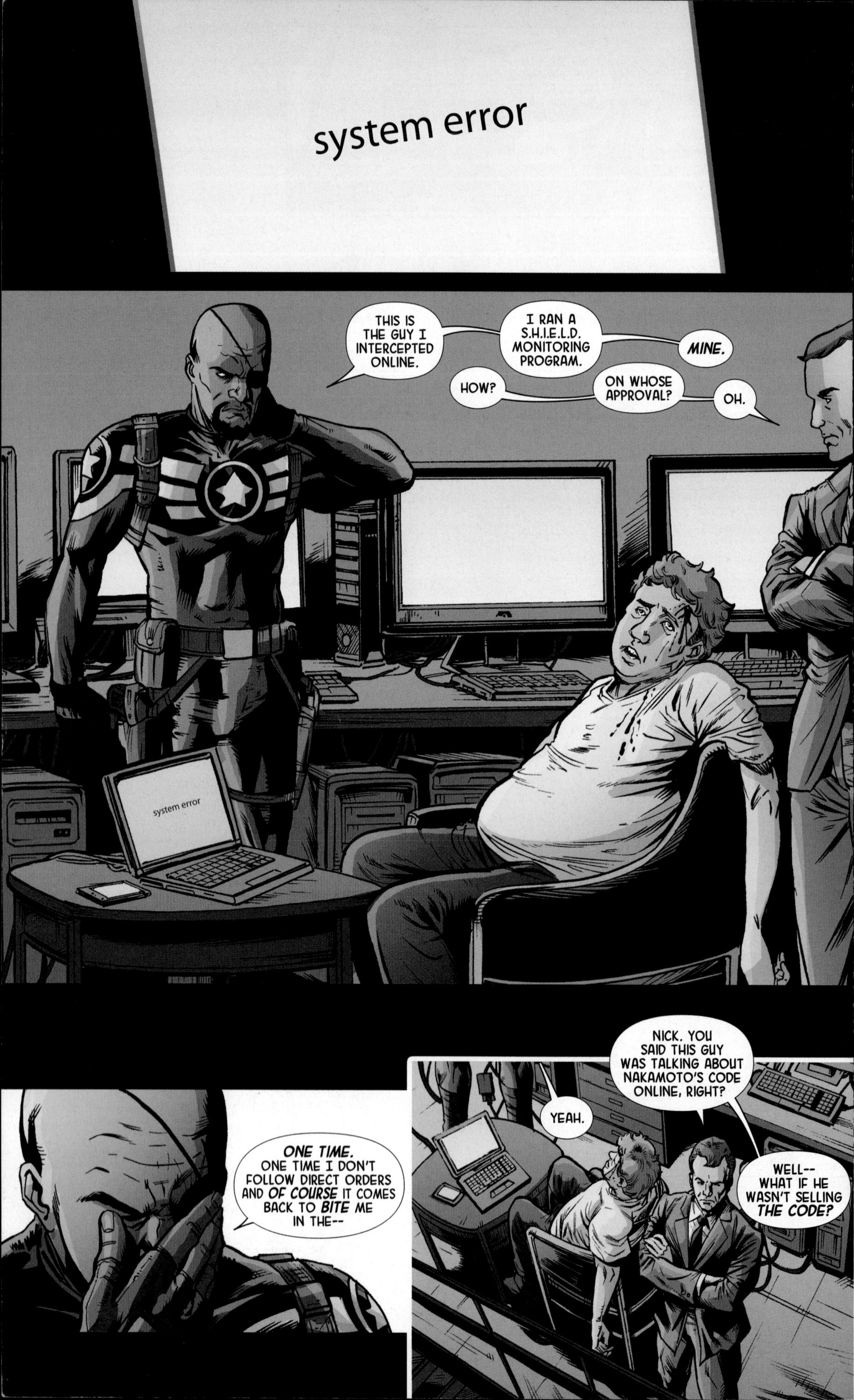
system error
THIS IS THE GUY I INTERCEPTED ONLINE.
I RAN A S.H.I.E.L.D. MONITORING PROGRAM.
MINE.
HOW?
ON WHOSE APPROVAL?
OH.
system error
ONE TIME. ONE TIME I DON'T FOLLOW DIRECT ORDERS AND OF COURSE IT COMES BACK TO BITE ME IN THE--
NICK. YOU SAID THIS GUY WAS TALKING ABOUT NAKAMOTO'S CODE ONLINE, RIGHT?
YEAH.
WELL-- WHAT IF HE WASN'T SELLING THE CODE?

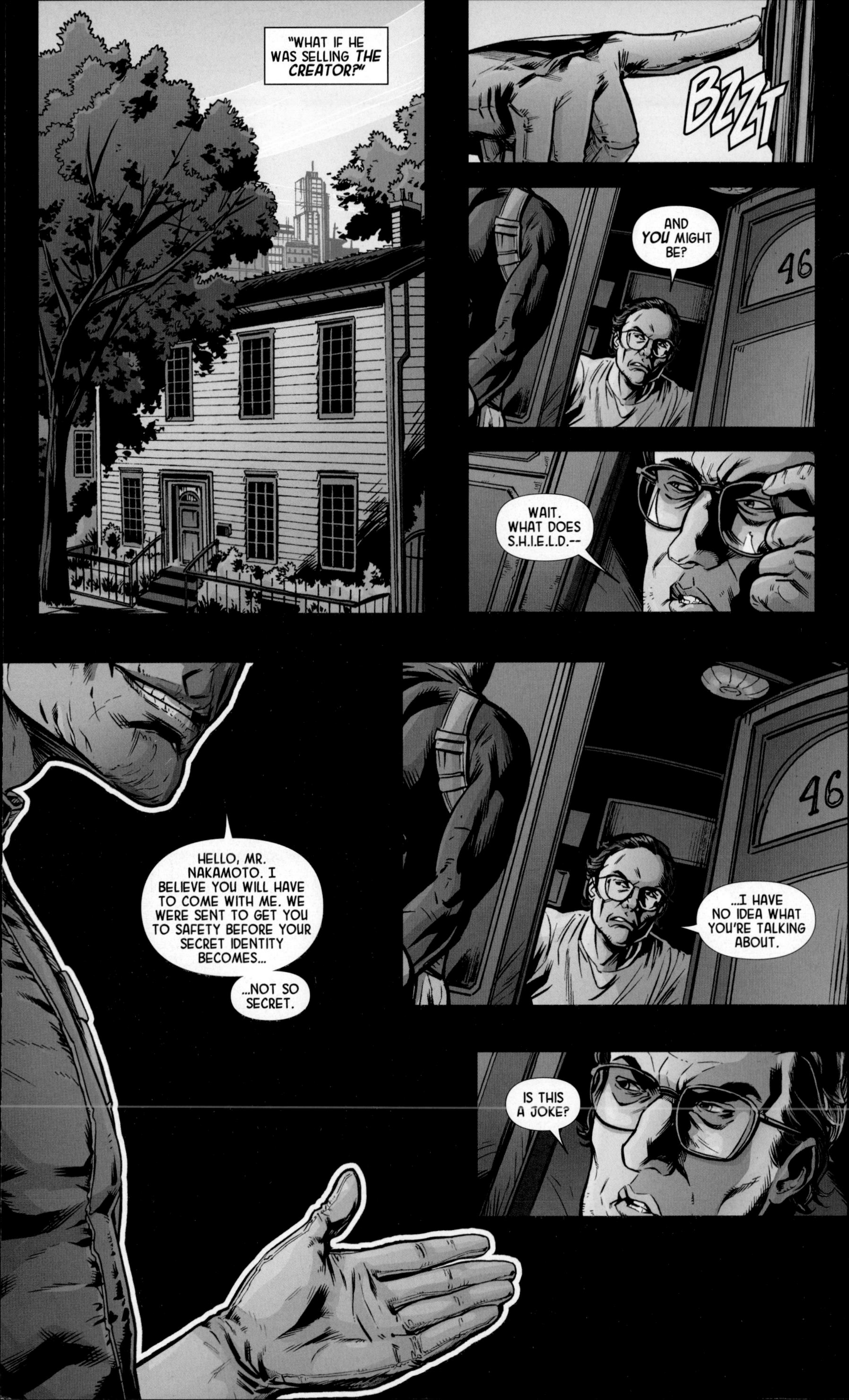
"WHAT IF HE WAS SELLING THE CREATOR?"
BZZT
AND YOU MIGHT BE?
WAIT. WHAT DOES S.H.I.E.L.D.--
HELLO, MR. NAKAMOTO. I BELIEVE YOU WILL HAVE TO COME WITH ME. WE WERE SENT TO GET YOU TO SAFETY BEFORE YOUR SECRET IDENTITY BECOMES...
...NOT SO SECRET.
...I HAVE NO IDEA WHAT YOU'RE TALKING ABOUT.
IS THIS A JOKE?

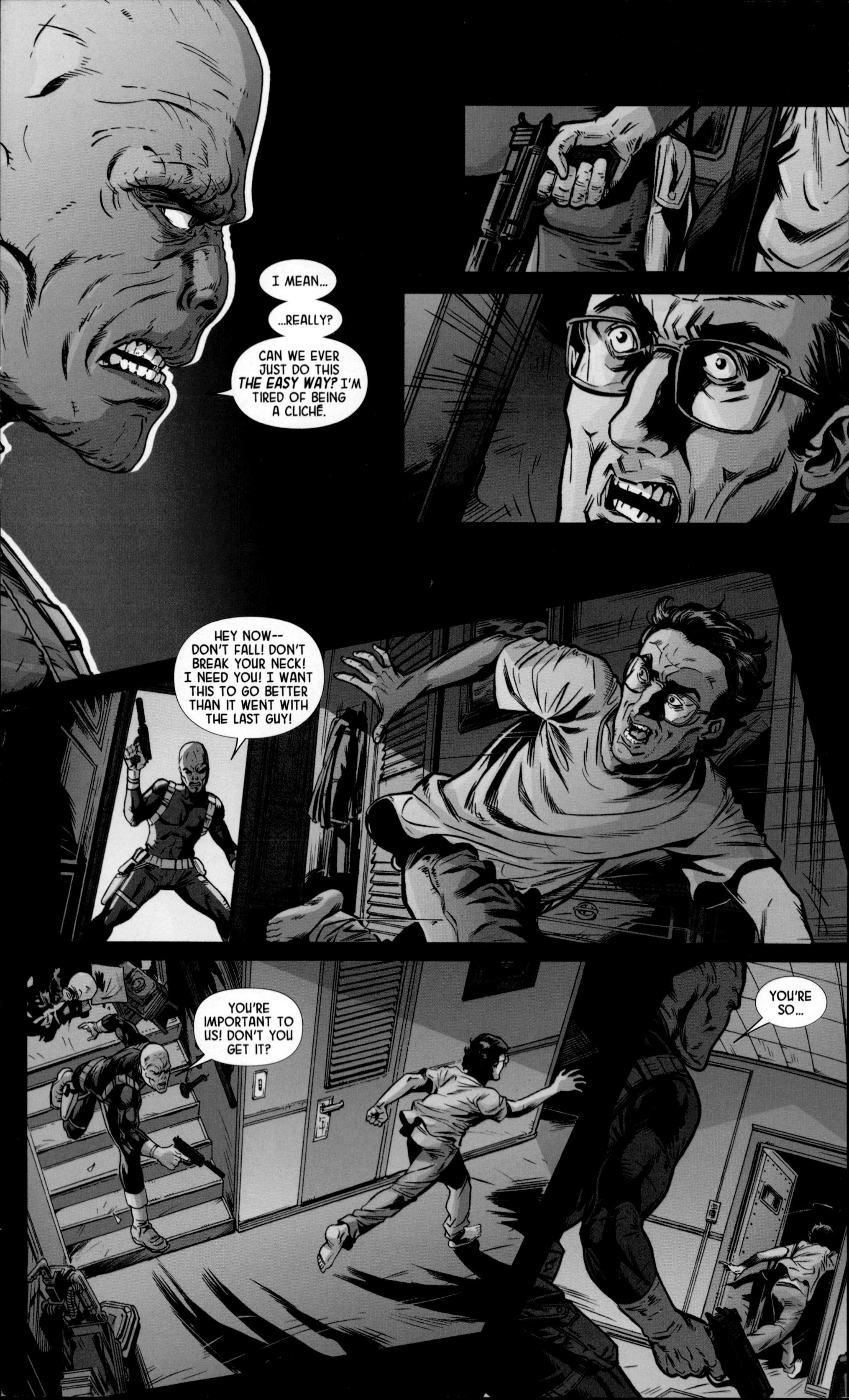
I MEAN...
...REALLY?
CAN WE EVER JUST DO THIS *THE EASY WAY?* I'M TIRED OF BEING A CLICHÉ.
HEY NOW-- DON'T FALL! DON'T BREAK YOUR NECK! I NEED YOU! I WANT THIS TO GO BETTER THAN IT WENT WITH THE LAST GUY!
YOU'RE IMPORTANT TO US! DON'T YOU GET IT?
YOU'RE SO...

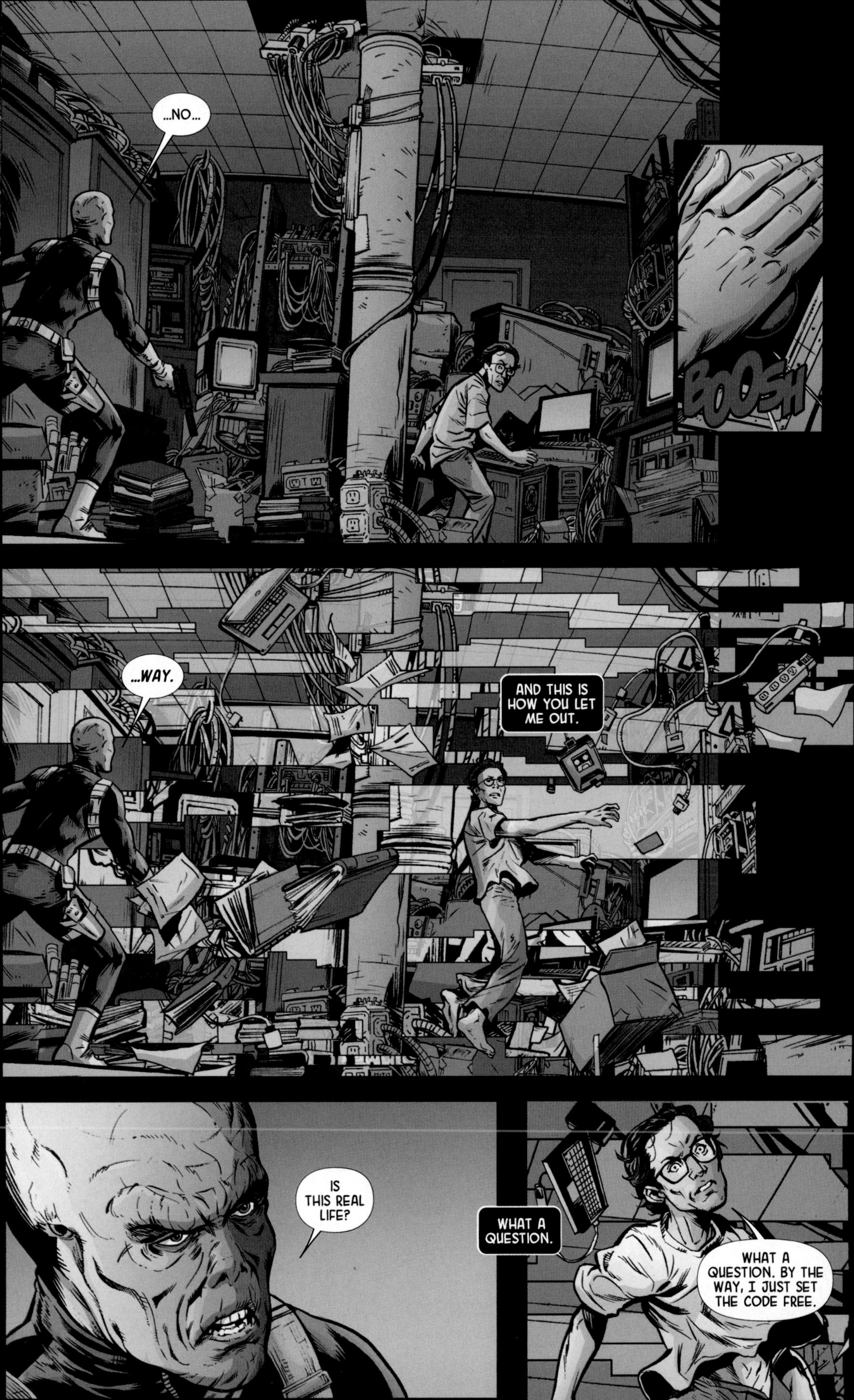
...NO...
BOOSH
...WAY.
AND THIS IS HOW YOU LET ME OUT.
IS THIS REAL LIFE?
WHAT A QUESTION.
WHAT A QUESTION. BY THE WAY, I JUST SET THE CODE FREE.

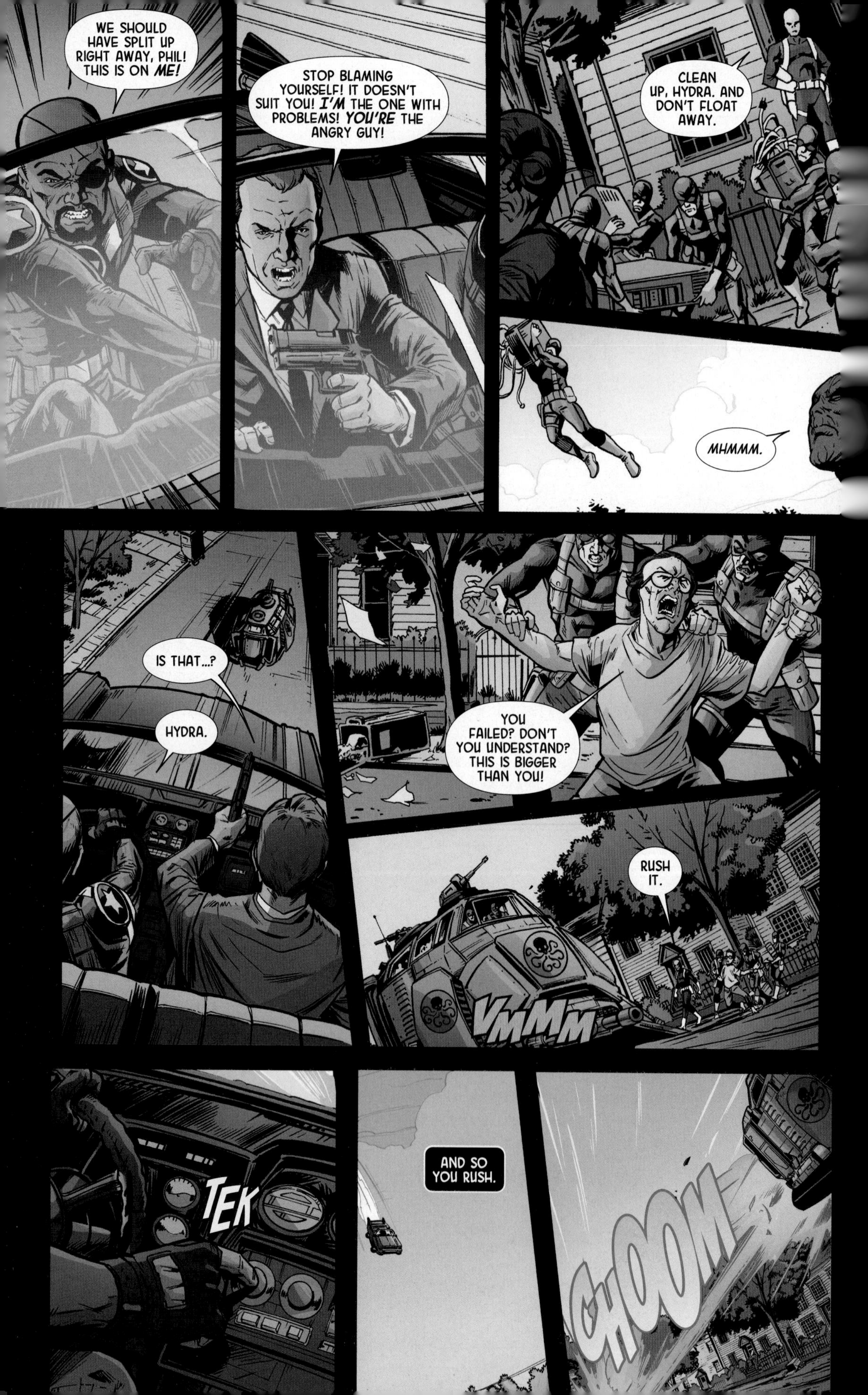
WE SHOULD HAVE SPLIT UP RIGHT AWAY, PHIL! THIS IS ON ME!
STOP BLAMING YOURSELF! IT DOESN'T SUIT YOU! I'M THE ONE WITH PROBLEMS! YOU'RE THE ANGRY GUY!
CLEAN UP, HYDRA. AND DON'T FLOAT AWAY.
MHMMM.
IS THAT...?
HYDRA.
YOU FAILED? DON'T YOU UNDERSTAND? THIS IS BIGGER THAN YOU!
RUSH IT.
VMMM
TEK
AND SO YOU RUSH.
CHOOOM

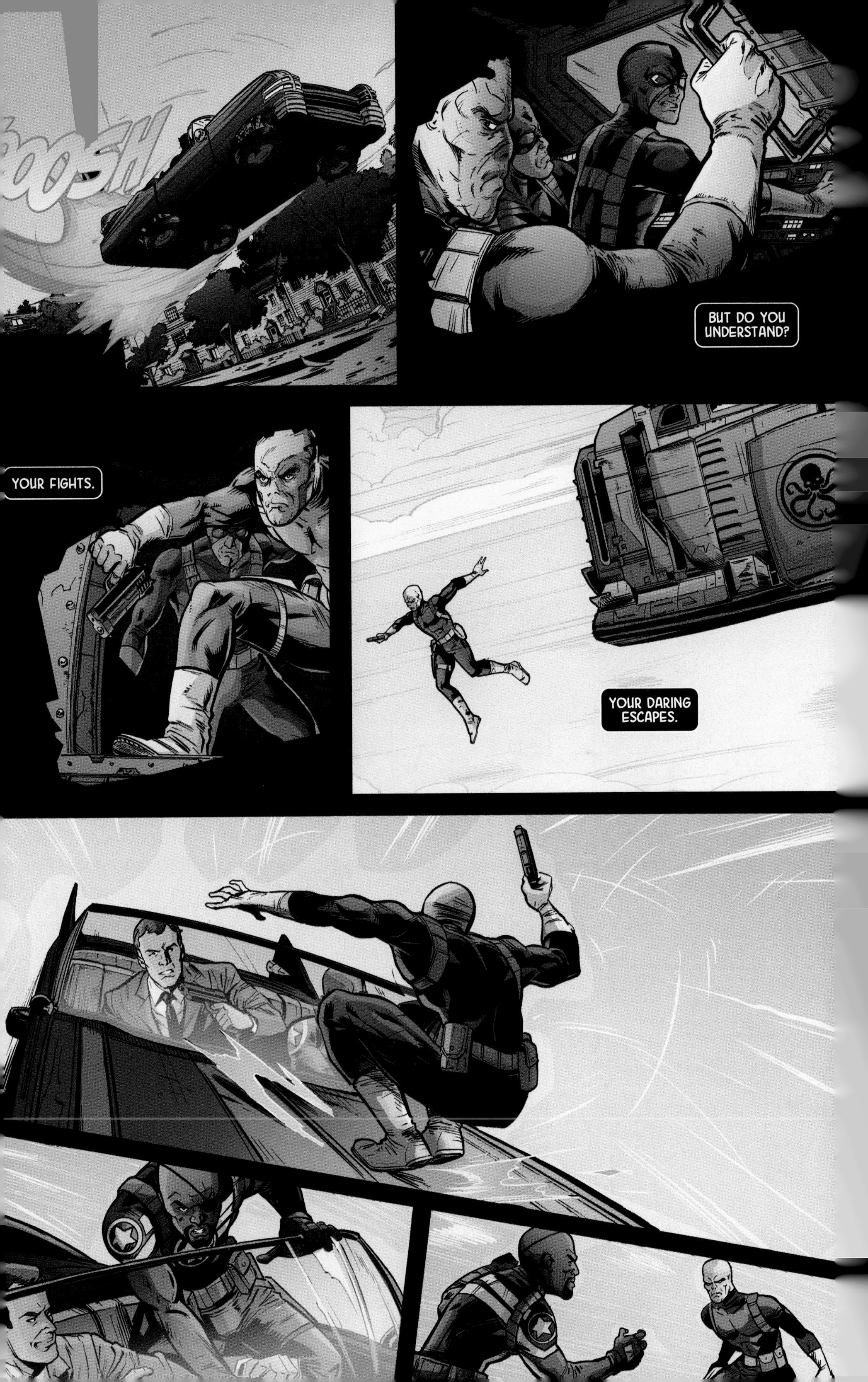

OOSH
BUT DO YOU UNDERSTAND?
YOUR FIGHTS.
YOUR DARING ESCAPES.

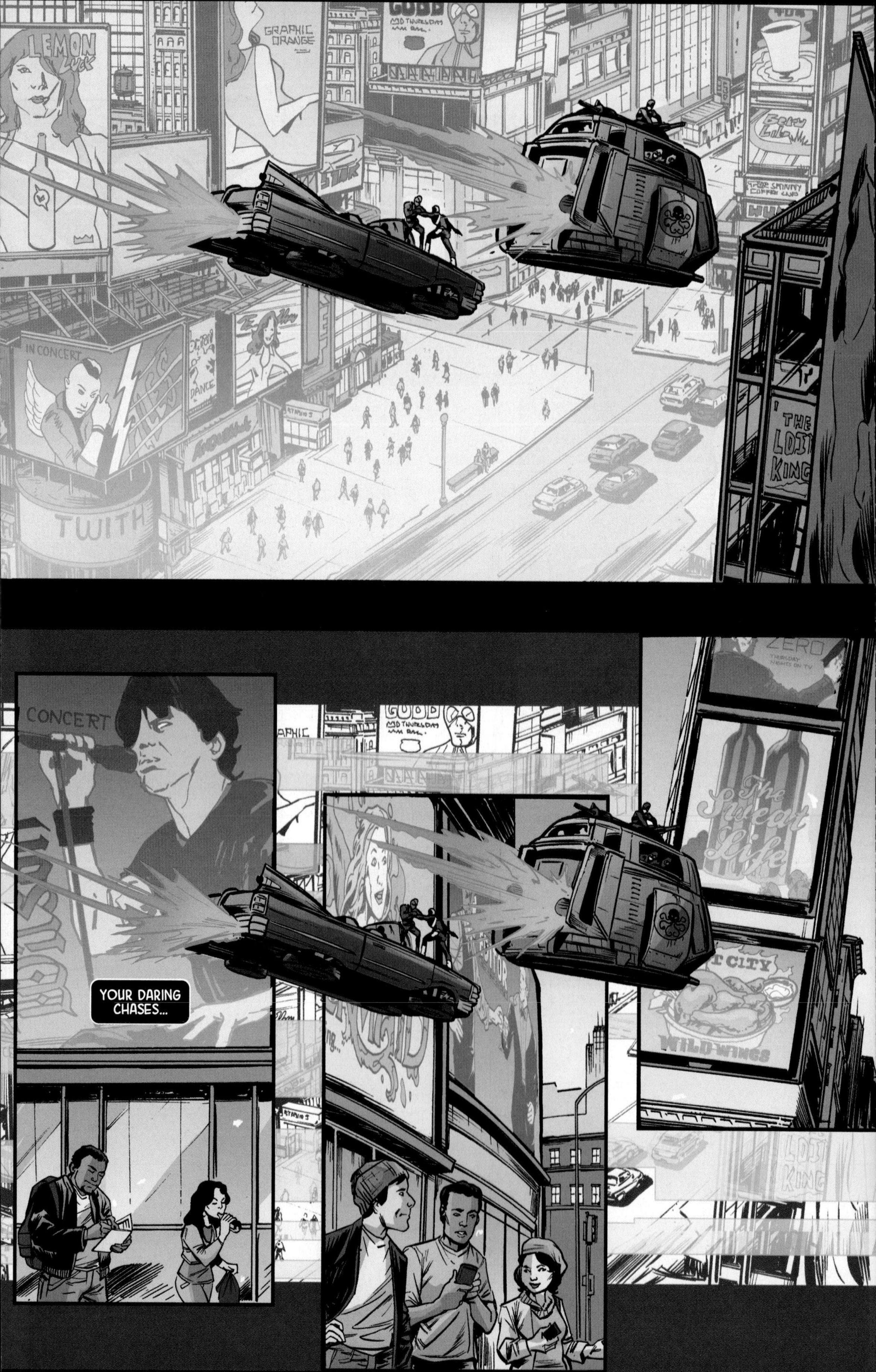

LEMON
GRAPHIC ORANGE
IN CONCERT
DANCE
TWITH
CONCERT
ZERO
THURSDAY NIGHTS ON TV
The Sweat Life
WILD WINGS
YOUR DARING CHASES...

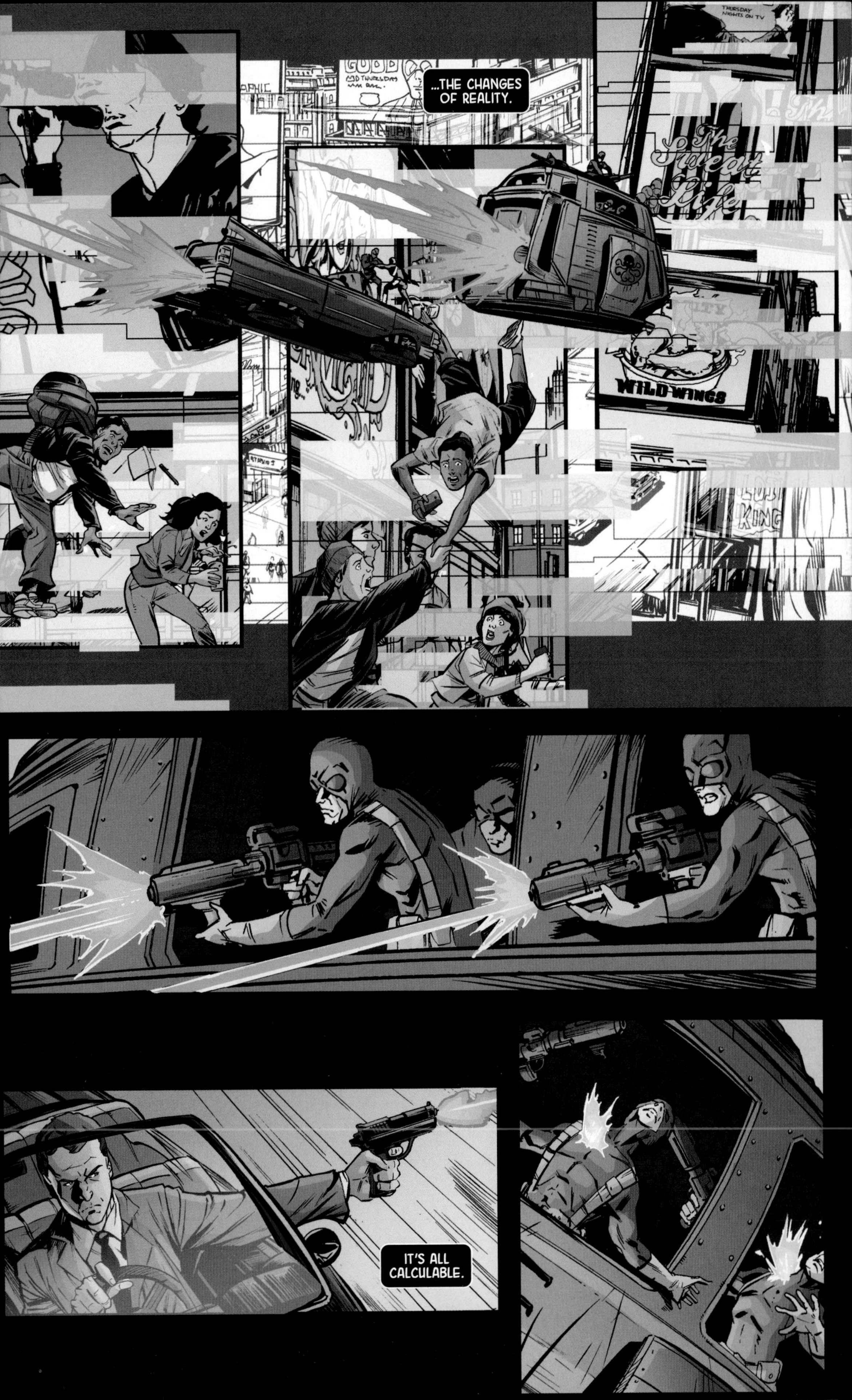
...THE CHANGES OF REALITY.
IT'S ALL CALCULABLE.
THURSDAY NIGHTS ON TV
WILD WINGS

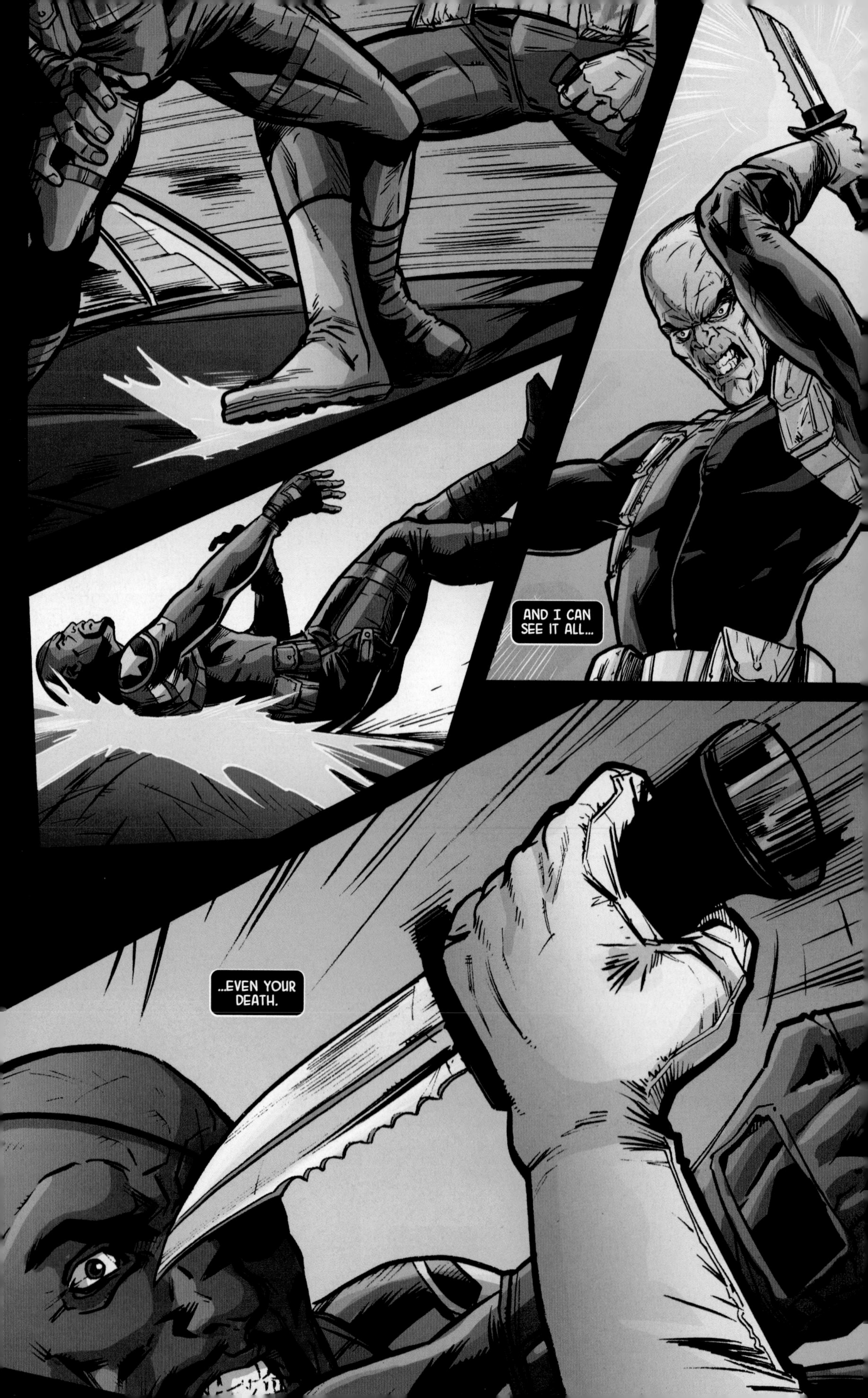
AND I CAN SEE IT ALL...
...EVEN YOUR DEATH.

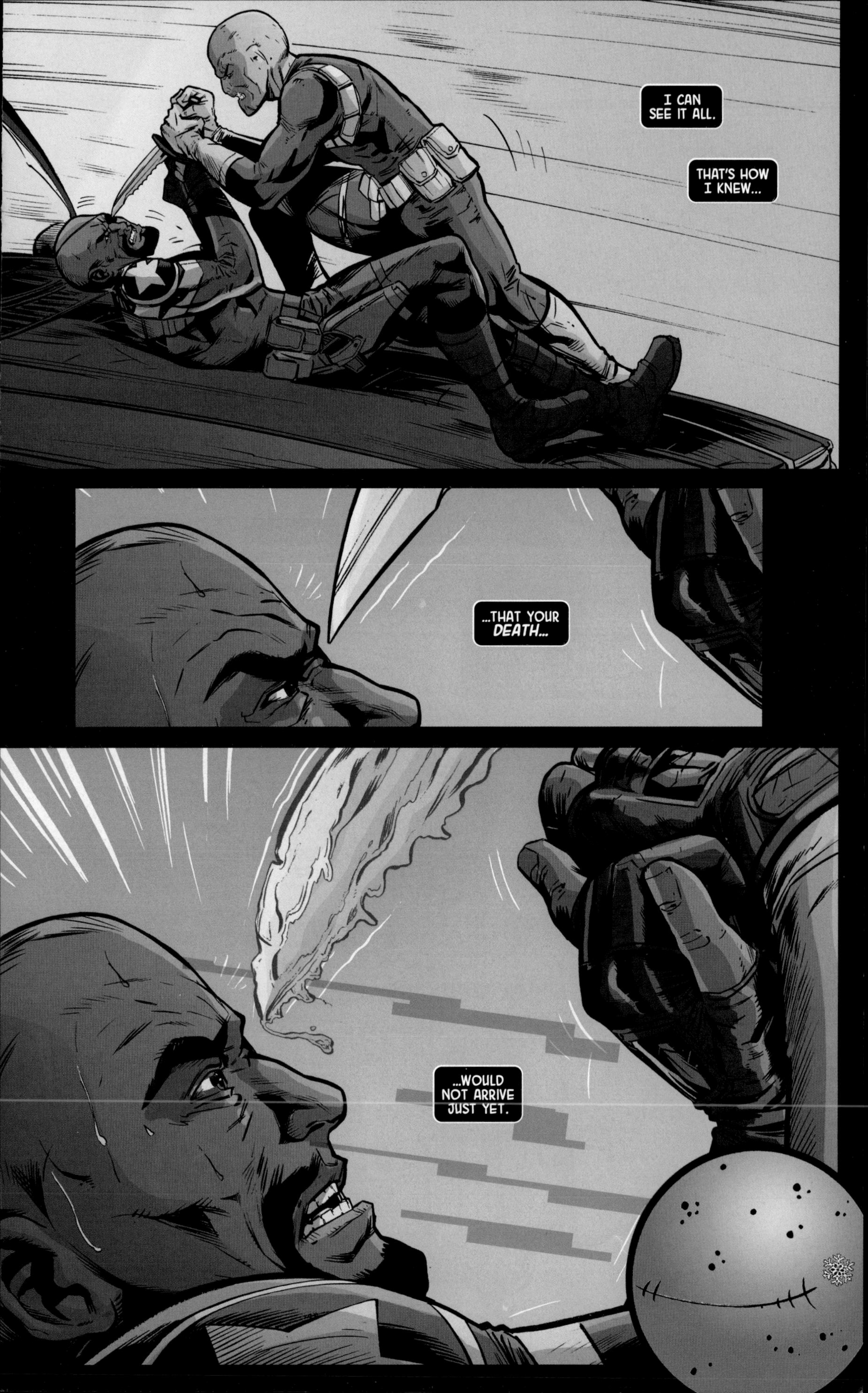
I CAN SEE IT ALL.
THAT'S HOW I KNEW...
...THAT YOUR *DEATH*...
...WOULD NOT ARRIVE JUST YET.

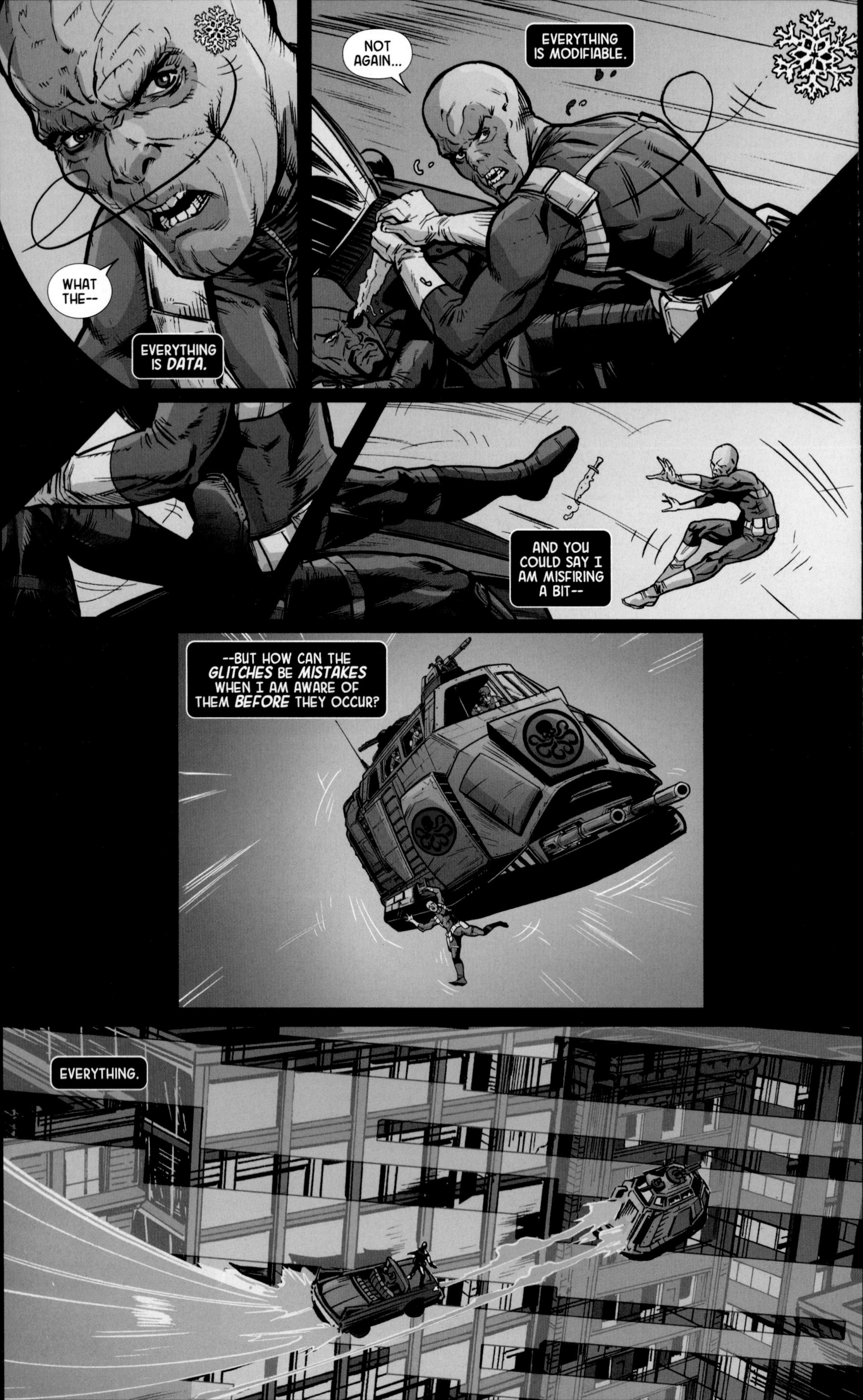
WHAT THE--
EVERYTHING IS DATA.
NOT AGAIN...
EVERYTHING IS MODIFIABLE.
AND YOU COULD SAY I AM MISFIRING A BIT--
--BUT HOW CAN THE GLITCHES BE MISTAKES WHEN I AM AWARE OF THEM BEFORE THEY OCCUR?
EVERYTHING.

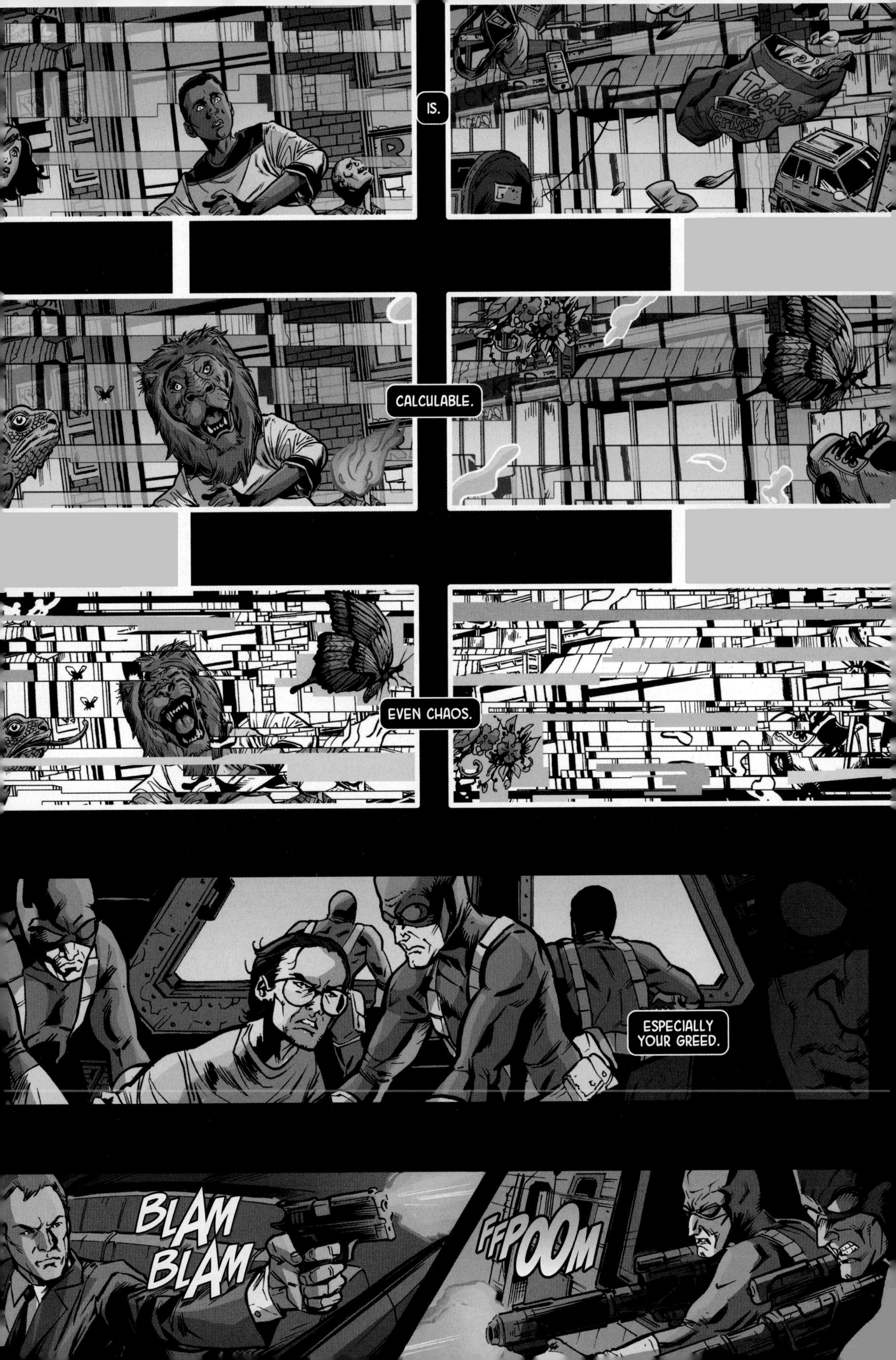
IS.
CALCULABLE.
EVEN CHAOS.
ESPECIALLY YOUR GREED.
BLAM BLAM
FFPOOM

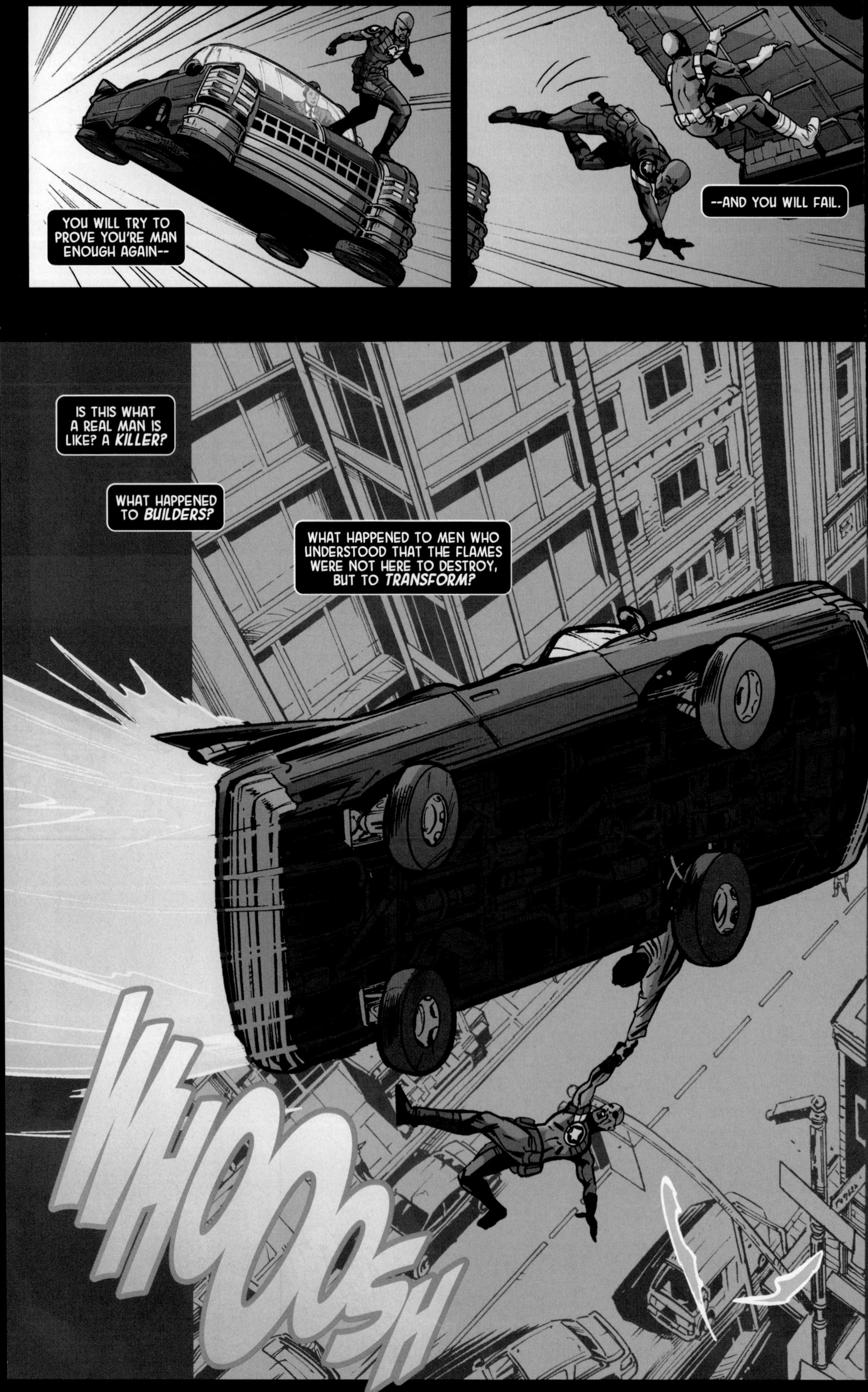
YOU WILL TRY TO PROVE YOU'RE MAN ENOUGH AGAIN--
--AND YOU WILL FAIL.
IS THIS WHAT A REAL MAN IS LIKE? A KILLER?
WHAT HAPPENED TO BUILDERS?
WHAT HAPPENED TO MEN WHO UNDERSTOOD THAT THE FLAMES WERE NOT HERE TO DESTROY, BUT TO TRANSFORM?
WHOOOSH

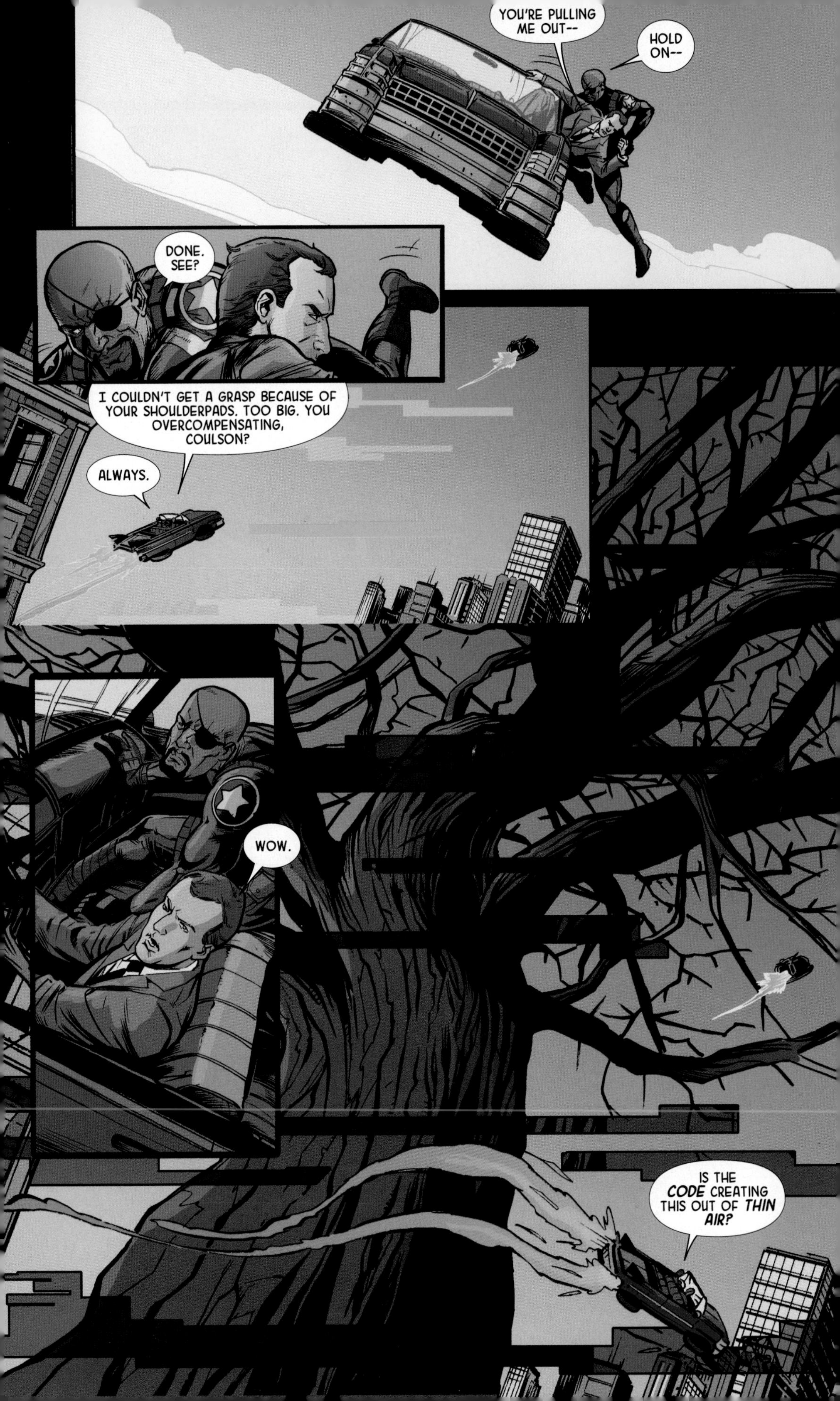
YOU'RE PULLING ME OUT--
HOLD ON--
DONE. SEE?
I COULDN'T GET A GRASP BECAUSE OF YOUR SHOULDERPADS. TOO BIG. YOU OVERCOMPENSATING, COULSON?
ALWAYS.
WOW.
IS THE *CODE* CREATING THIS OUT OF *THIN AIR?*

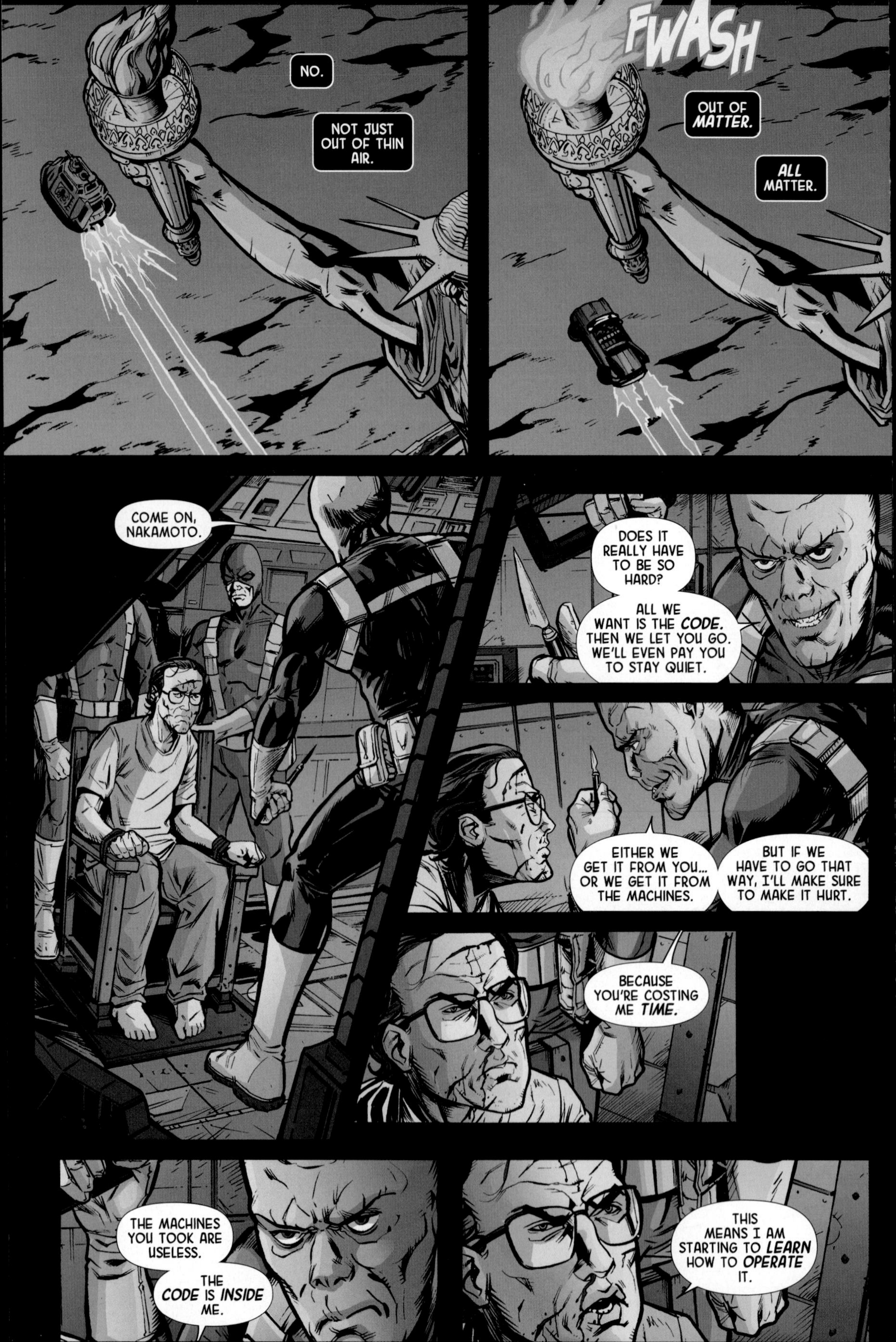
NO.
NOT JUST OUT OF THIN AIR.
FWASH
OUT OF MATTER.
ALL MATTER.
COME ON, NAKAMOTO.
DOES IT REALLY HAVE TO BE SO HARD?
ALL WE WANT IS THE CODE. THEN WE LET YOU GO. WE'LL EVEN PAY YOU TO STAY QUIET.
EITHER WE GET IT FROM YOU... OR WE GET IT FROM THE MACHINES.
BUT IF WE HAVE TO GO THAT WAY, I'LL MAKE SURE TO MAKE IT HURT.
BECAUSE YOU'RE COSTING ME TIME.
THE MACHINES YOU TOOK ARE USELESS.
THE CODE IS INSIDE ME.
THIS MEANS I AM STARTING TO LEARN HOW TO OPERATE IT.

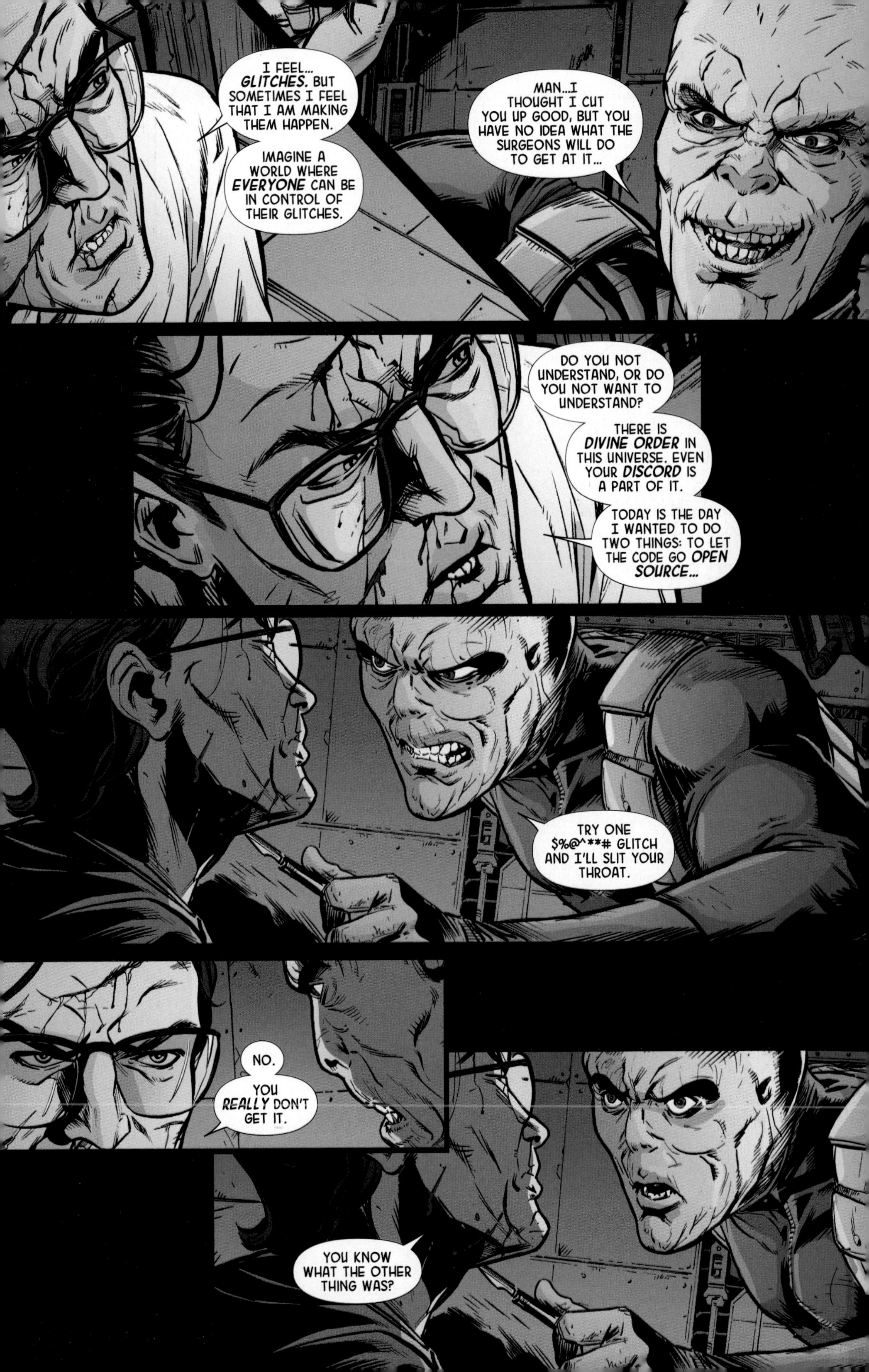
I FEEL... GLITCHES. BUT SOMETIMES I FEEL THAT I AM MAKING THEM HAPPEN.
IMAGINE A WORLD WHERE EVERYONE CAN BE IN CONTROL OF THEIR GLITCHES.
MAN...I THOUGHT I CUT YOU UP GOOD, BUT YOU HAVE NO IDEA WHAT THE SURGEONS WILL DO TO GET AT IT...
DO YOU NOT UNDERSTAND, OR DO YOU NOT WANT TO UNDERSTAND?
THERE IS DIVINE ORDER IN THIS UNIVERSE. EVEN YOUR DISCORD IS A PART OF IT.
TODAY IS THE DAY I WANTED TO DO TWO THINGS: TO LET THE CODE GO OPEN SOURCE...
TRY ONE $%@^**# GLITCH AND I'LL SLIT YOUR THROAT.
NO.
YOU REALLY DON'T GET IT.
YOU KNOW WHAT THE OTHER THING WAS?

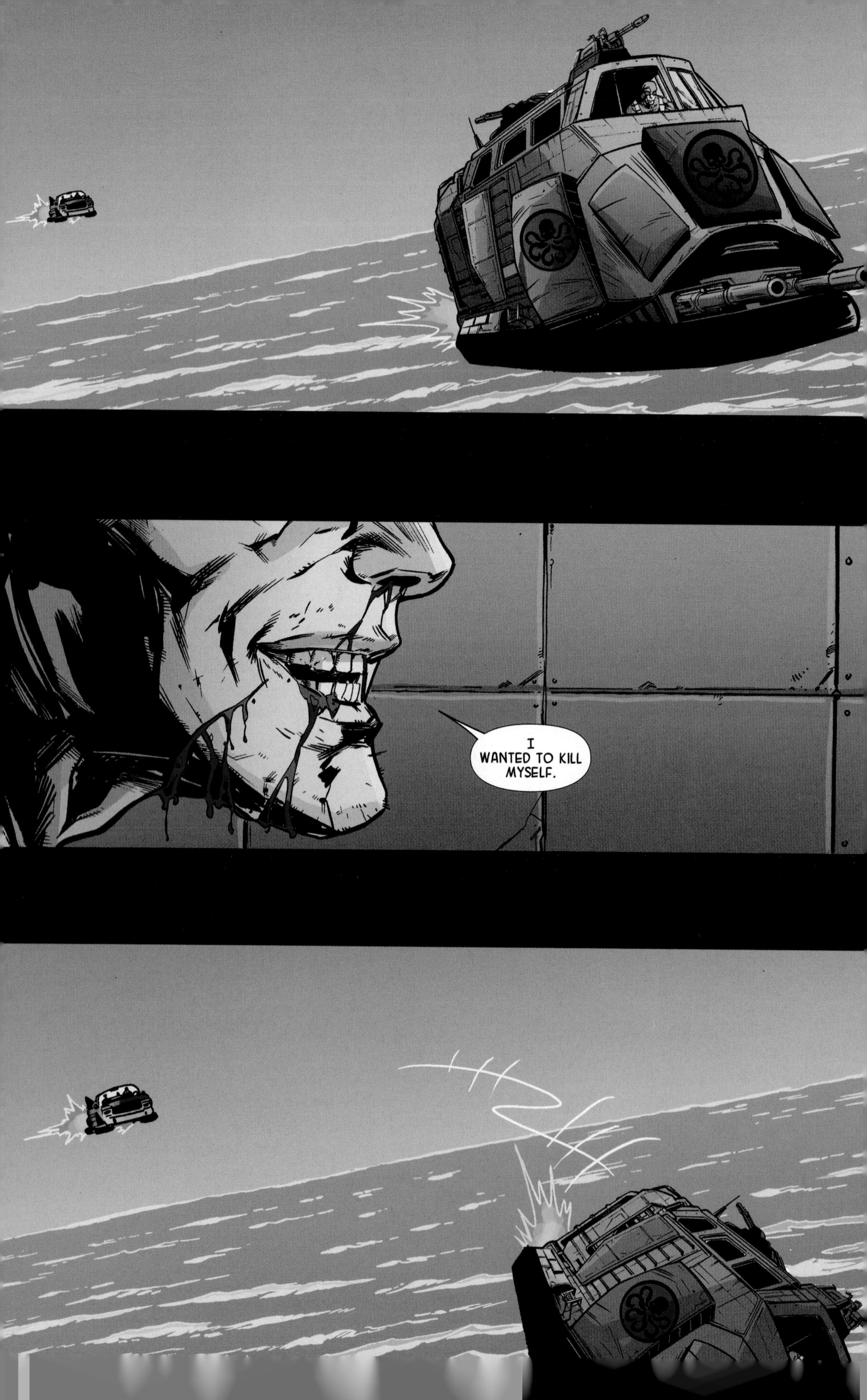
I WANTED TO KILL MYSELF.

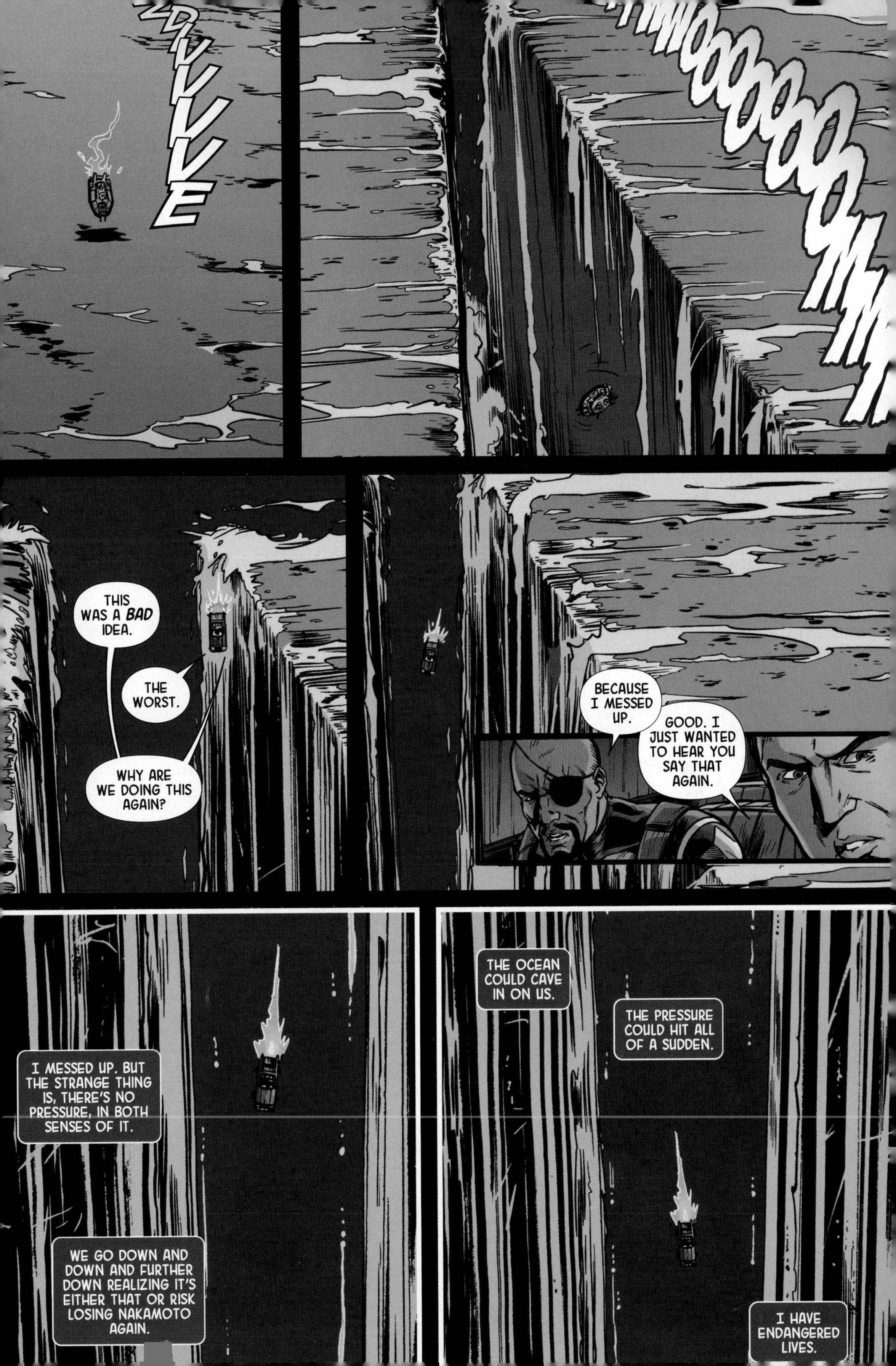
THIS WAS A *BAD* IDEA.
THE WORST.
WHY ARE WE DOING THIS AGAIN?
BECAUSE I MESSED UP.
GOOD. I JUST WANTED TO HEAR YOU SAY THAT AGAIN.
I MESSED UP. BUT THE STRANGE THING IS, THERE'S NO PRESSURE, IN BOTH SENSES OF IT.
WE GO DOWN AND DOWN AND FURTHER DOWN REALIZING IT'S EITHER THAT OR RISK LOSING NAKAMOTO AGAIN.
THE OCEAN COULD CAVE IN ON US.
THE PRESSURE COULD HIT ALL OF A SUDDEN.
I HAVE ENDANGERED LIVES.

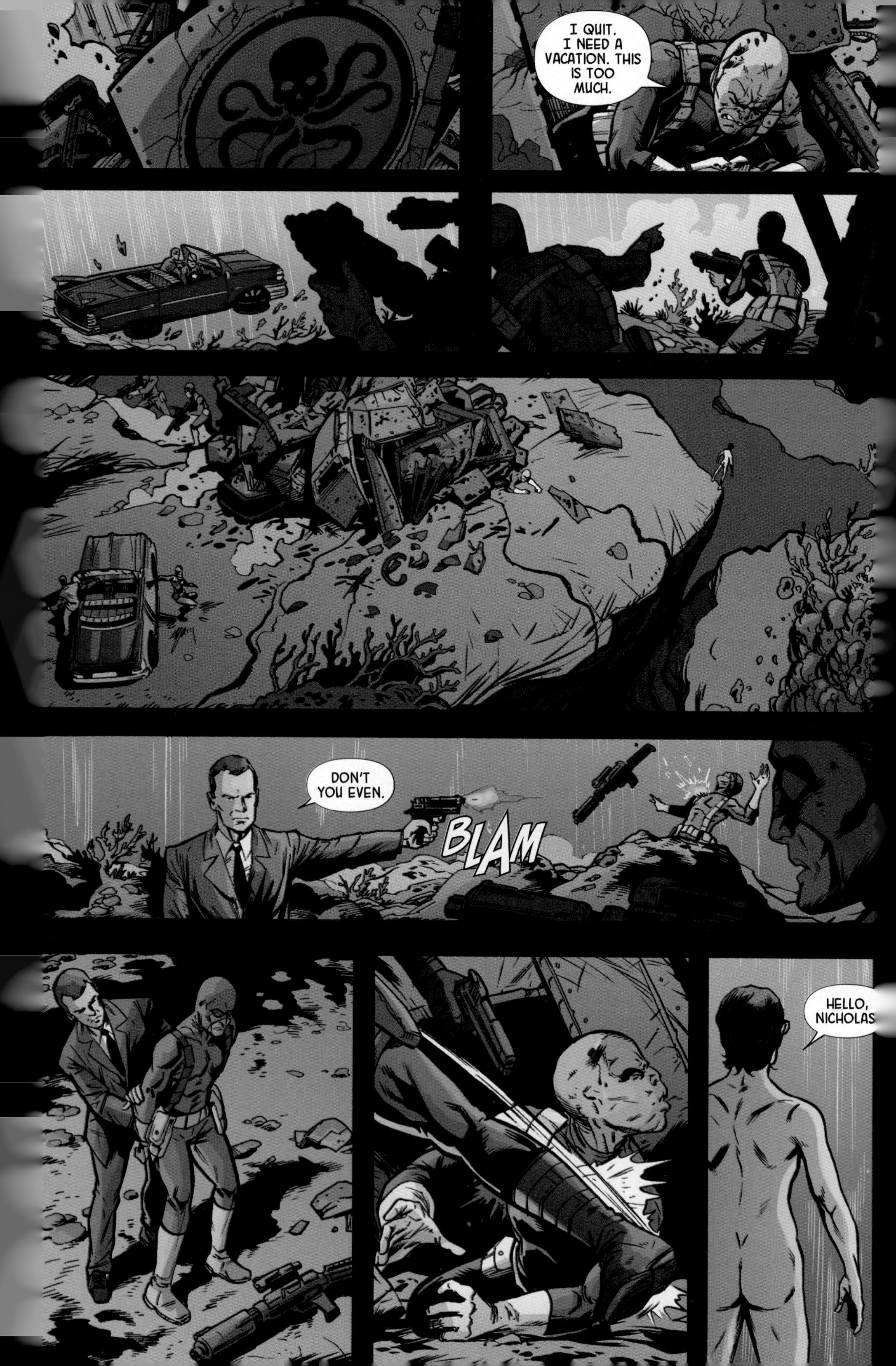
I QUIT. I NEED A VACATION. THIS IS TOO MUCH.
DON'T YOU EVEN.
BLAM
HELLO, NICHOLAS

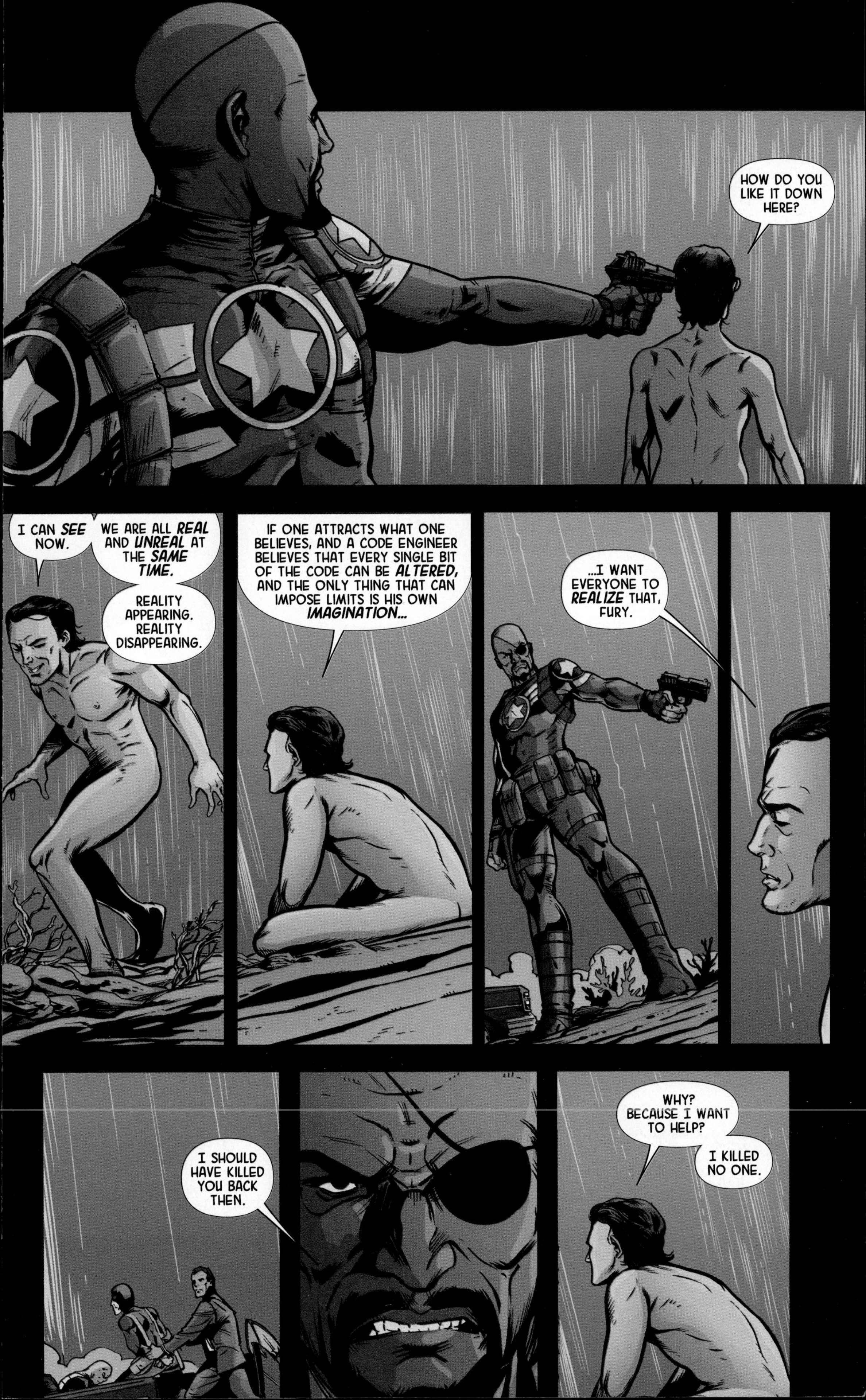
HOW DO YOU LIKE IT DOWN HERE?
I CAN SEE NOW.
WE ARE ALL REAL AND UNREAL AT THE SAME TIME.
REALITY APPEARING. REALITY DISAPPEARING.
IF ONE ATTRACTS WHAT ONE BELIEVES, AND A CODE ENGINEER BELIEVES THAT EVERY SINGLE BIT OF THE CODE CAN BE ALTERED, AND THE ONLY THING THAT CAN IMPOSE LIMITS IS HIS OWN IMAGINATION...
...I WANT EVERYONE TO REALIZE THAT, FURY.
I SHOULD HAVE KILLED YOU BACK THEN.
WHY? BECAUSE I WANT TO HELP?
I KILLED NO ONE.

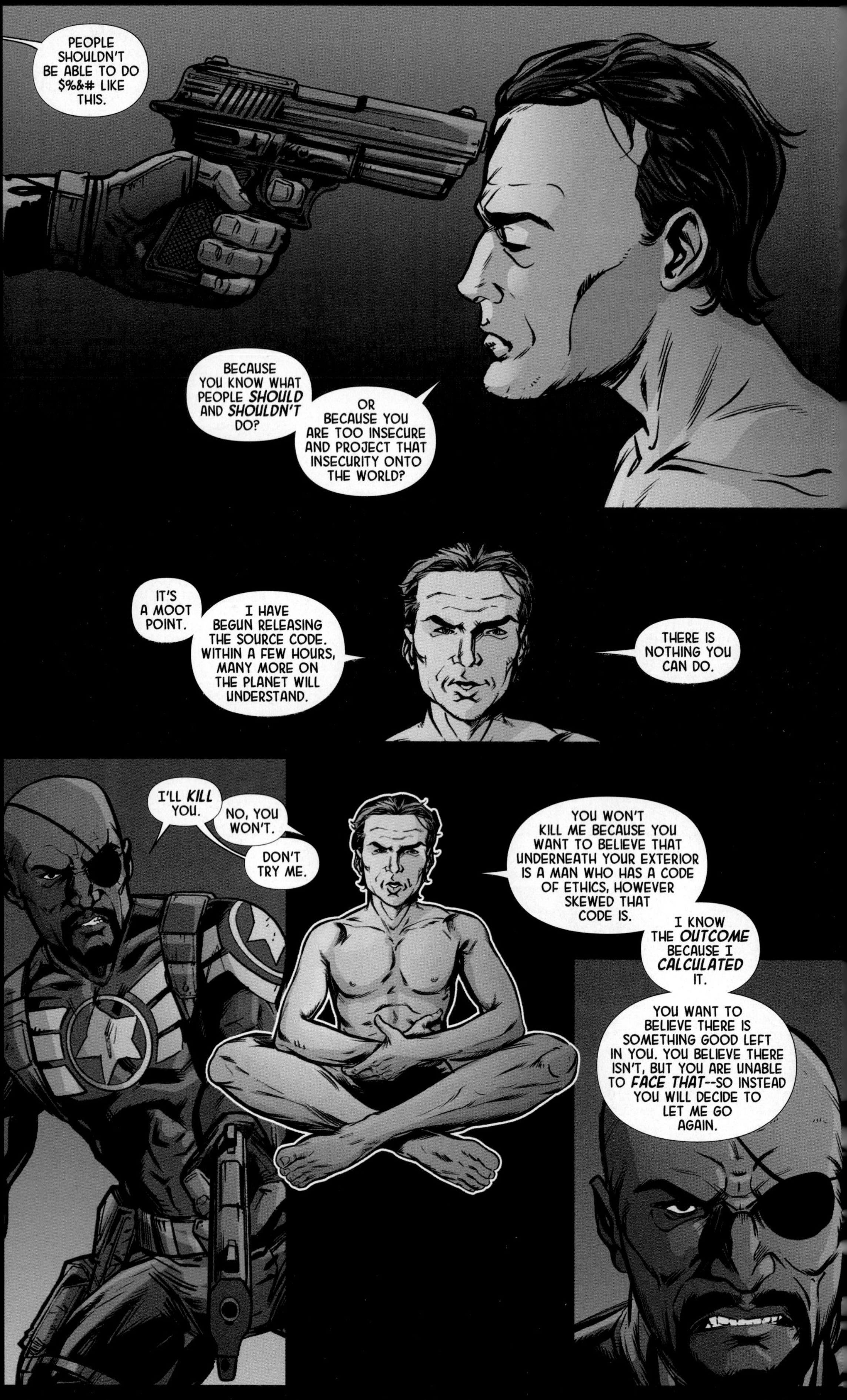

PEOPLE SHOULDN'T BE ABLE TO DO $%&# LIKE THIS.
BECAUSE YOU KNOW WHAT PEOPLE SHOULD AND SHOULDN'T DO?
OR BECAUSE YOU ARE TOO INSECURE AND PROJECT THAT INSECURITY ONTO THE WORLD?
IT'S A MOOT POINT.
I HAVE BEGUN RELEASING THE SOURCE CODE. WITHIN A FEW HOURS, MANY MORE ON THE PLANET WILL UNDERSTAND.
THERE IS NOTHING YOU CAN DO.
I'LL KILL YOU.
NO, YOU WON'T.
DON'T TRY ME.
YOU WON'T KILL ME BECAUSE YOU WANT TO BELIEVE THAT UNDERNEATH YOUR EXTERIOR IS A MAN WHO HAS A CODE OF ETHICS, HOWEVER SKEWED THAT CODE IS.
I KNOW THE OUTCOME BECAUSE I CALCULATED IT.
YOU WANT TO BELIEVE THERE IS SOMETHING GOOD LEFT IN YOU. YOU BELIEVE THERE ISN'T, BUT YOU ARE UNABLE TO FACE THAT--SO INSTEAD YOU WILL DECIDE TO LET ME GO AGAIN.

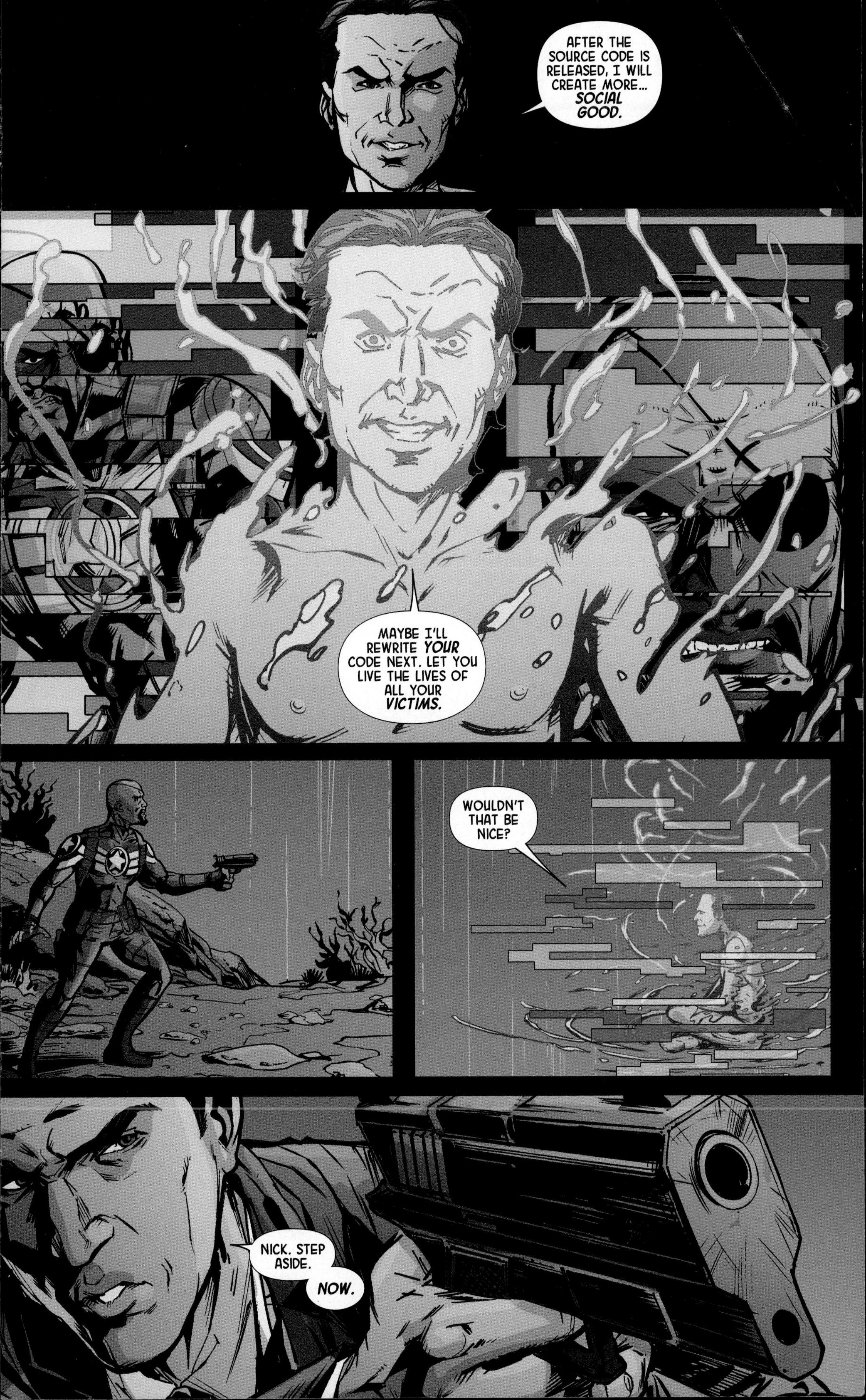
AFTER THE SOURCE CODE IS RELEASED, I WILL CREATE MORE... SOCIAL GOOD.
MAYBE I'LL REWRITE YOUR CODE NEXT. LET YOU LIVE THE LIVES OF ALL YOUR VICTIMS.
WOULDN'T THAT BE NICE?
NICK. STEP ASIDE.
NOW.

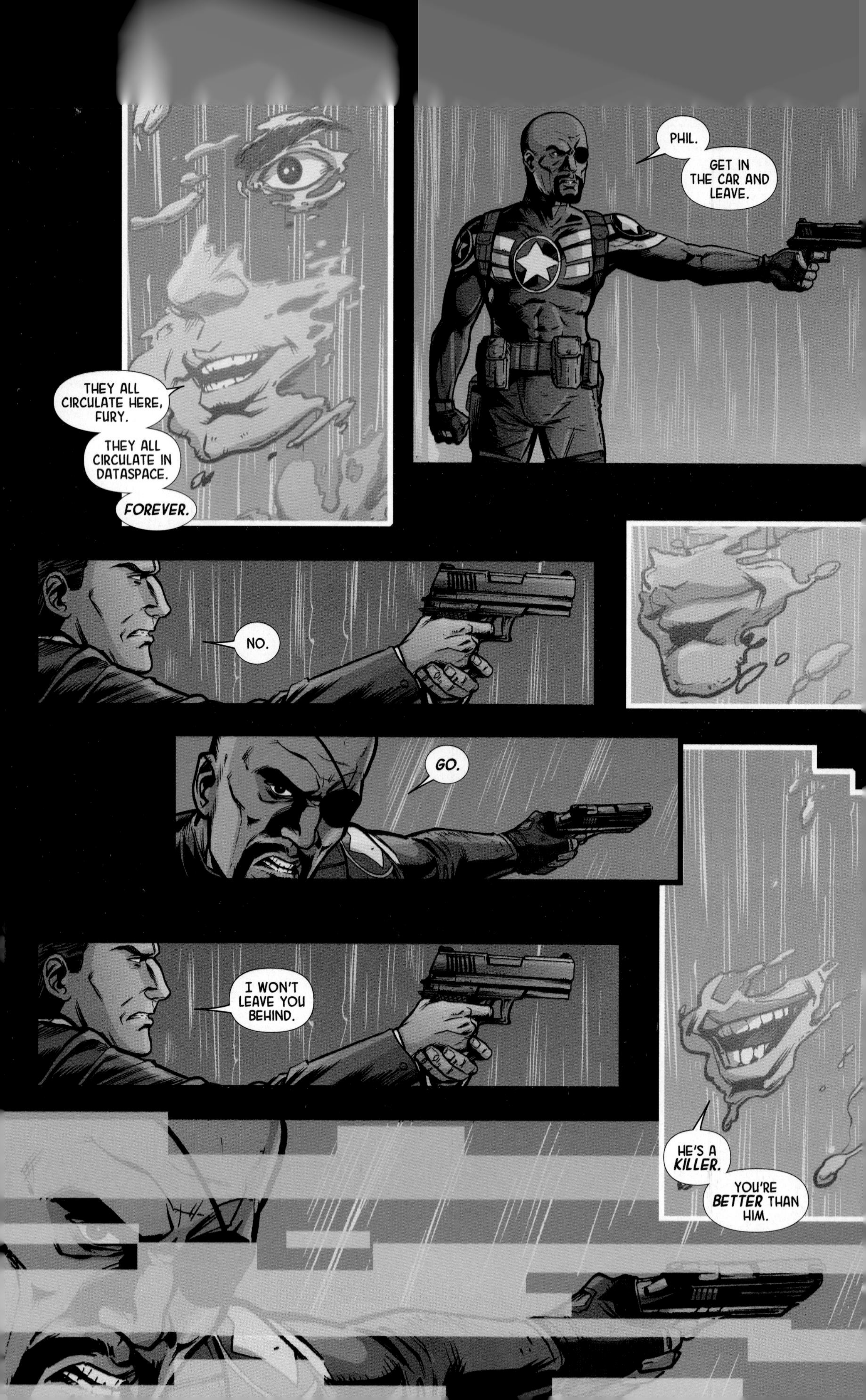
THEY ALL CIRCULATE HERE, FURY.
THEY ALL CIRCULATE IN DATASPACE.
FOREVER.
PHIL.
GET IN THE CAR AND LEAVE.
NO.
GO.
I WON'T LEAVE YOU BEHIND.
HE'S A KILLER.
YOU'RE BETTER THAN HIM.

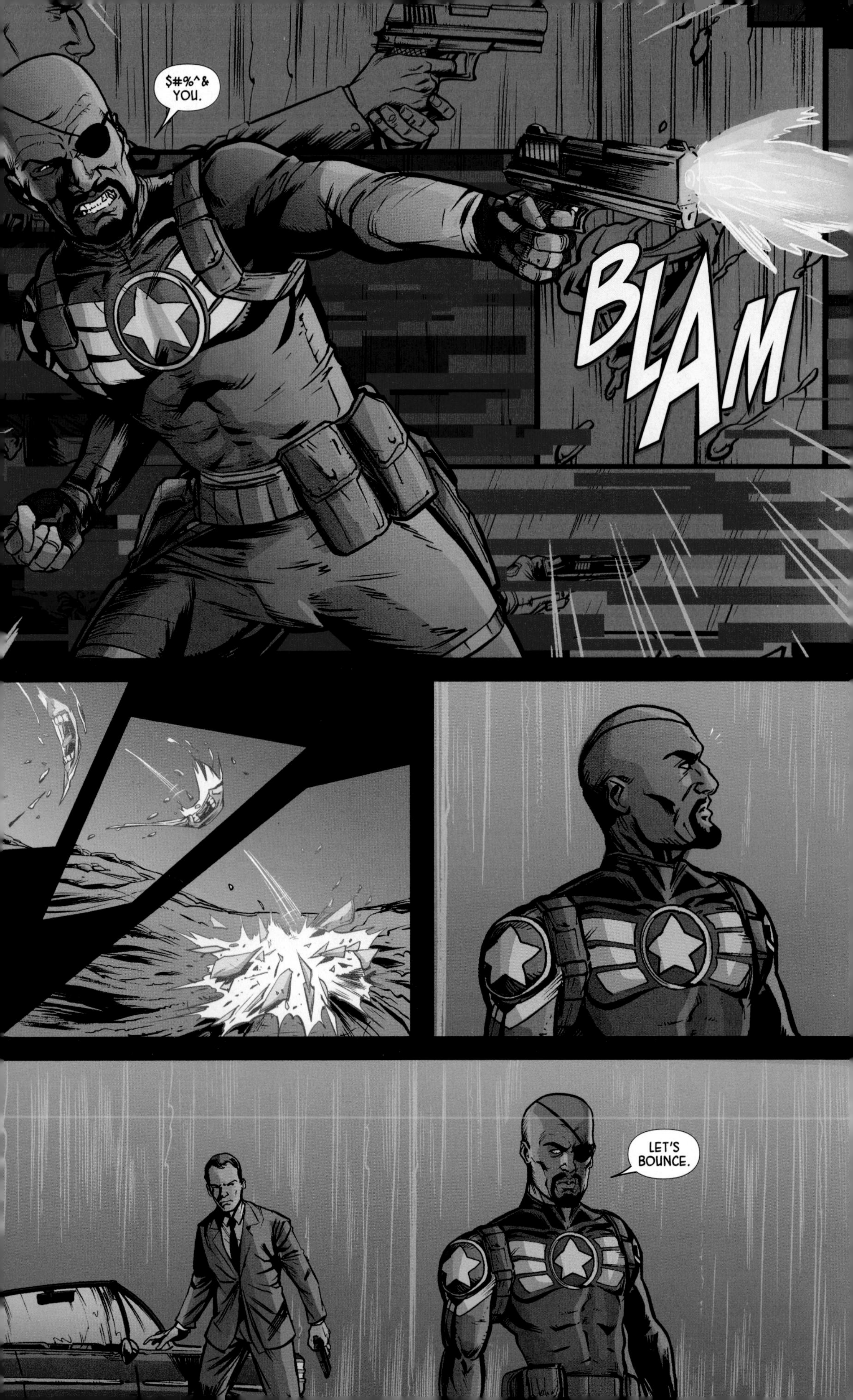
$#%^&
YOU.
BLAM
LET'S
BOUNCE.

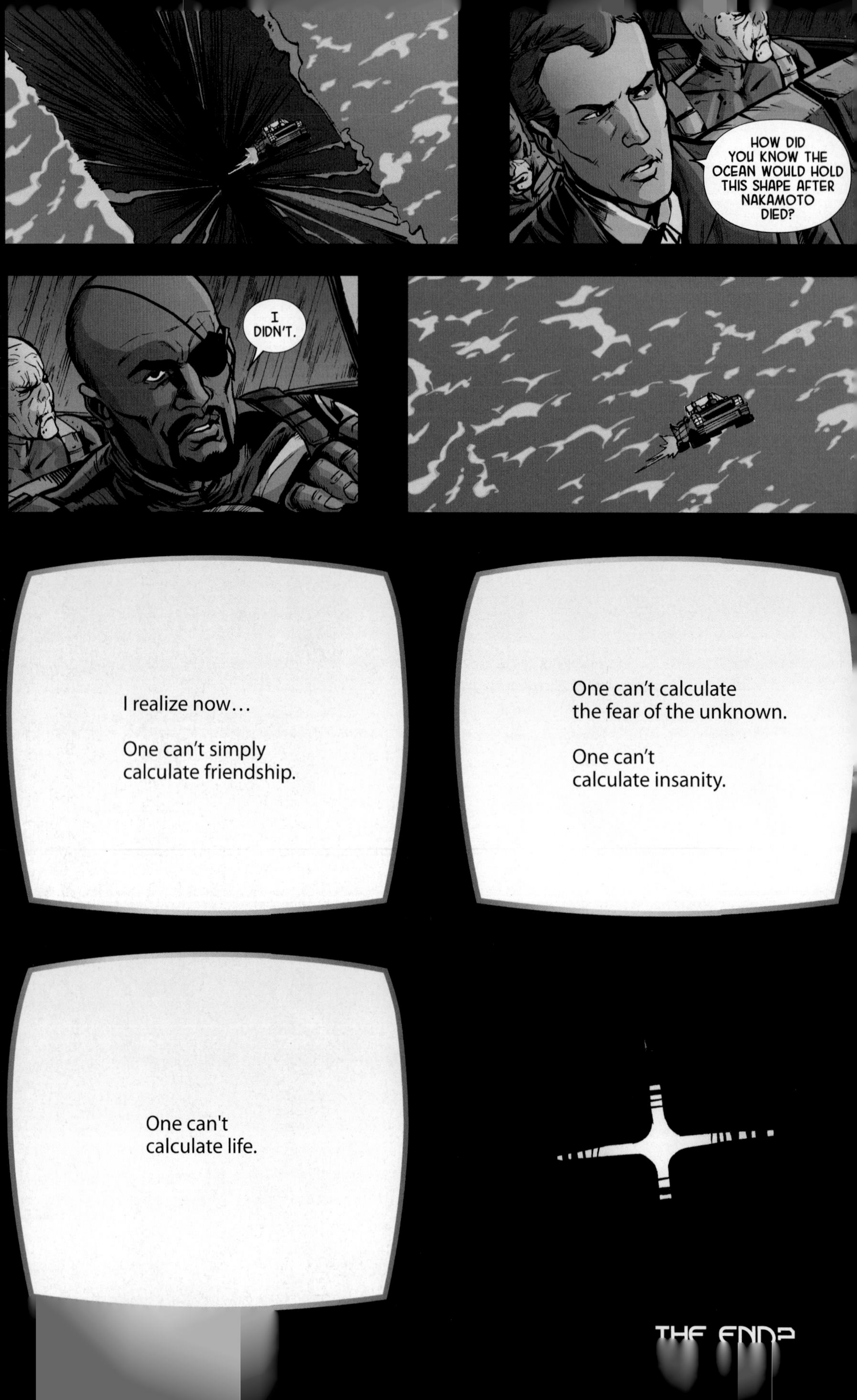
HOW DID YOU KNOW THE OCEAN WOULD HOLD THIS SHAPE AFTER NAKAMOTO DIED?
I DIDN'T.
I realize now…
One can't simply calculate friendship.
One can't calculate the fear of the unknown.
One can't calculate insanity.
One can't calculate life.
THE END?

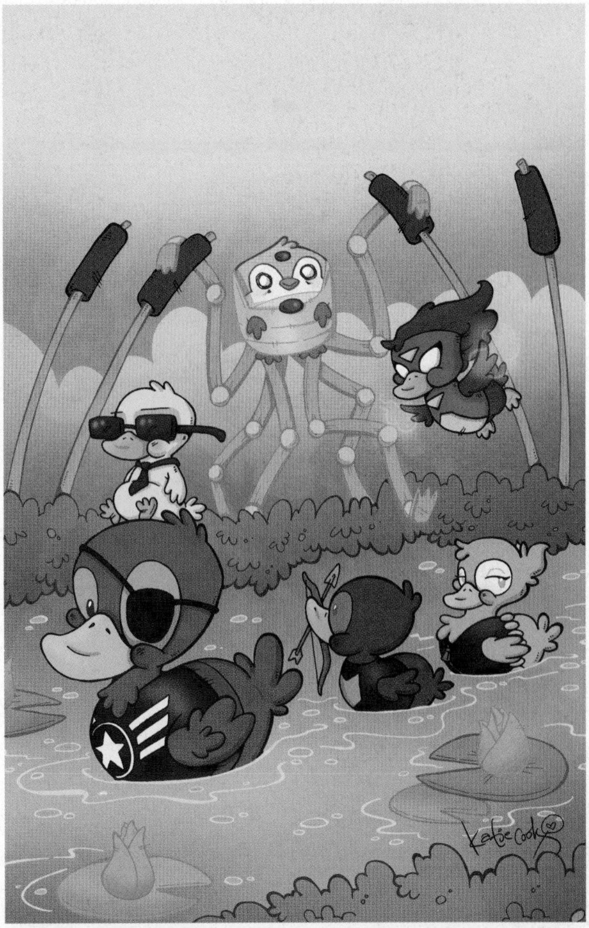
Katie Cook

#1 VARIANT
BY KATIE COOK

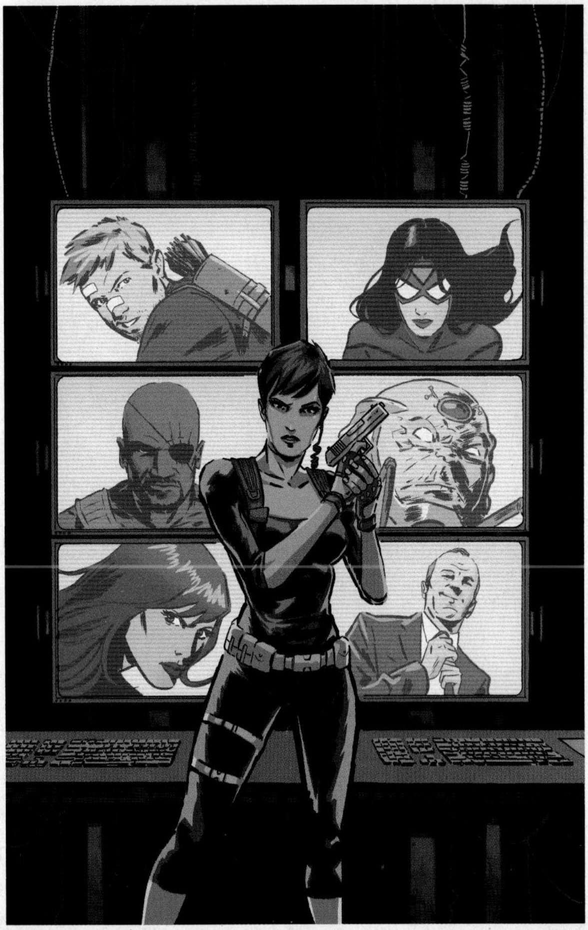

#2 VARIANT
BY MICHAEL WALSH
& MATTHEW WILSON

#3 VARIANT
BY RAGS MORALES
& MATTHEW WILSON

#4 VARIANT
BY DECLAN SHALVEY
& JORDIE BELLAIRE